# ARTHURIAN LITERATURE

# XXXI

# ARTHURIAN LITERATURE

Incorporating *Arthurian Yearbook*

ISSN 0261-9946

*Arthurian Literature* is an interdisciplinary publication devoted to the scholarly and critical study of all aspects of Arthurian legend in Europe in the medieval and early modern periods. Articles on writings from later periods are included if they relate very directly to medieval and early modern sources, although the editors welcome bibliographical studies of all periods. Articles may be up to 20,000 words in length; short items, of under 5,000 words, are published as Notes. Updates on earlier articles are also welcomed.

Material for consideration should be sent to Boydell & Brewer: contributors should follow the style sheet printed at the end of XII of the series. The contents of previous volumes are listed at the back of this book.

# Arthurian Literature XXXI

Edited by
ELIZABETH ARCHIBALD AND DAVID F. JOHNSON

D. S. BREWER

First published 2014
D. S. Brewer, Cambridge


ISBN  978-1-84384-386-3


D. S. Brewer is an imprint of Boydell & Brewer Ltd
PO Box 9, Woodbridge, Suffolk IP12 3DF, UK
and of Boydell & Brewer Inc,
668 Mt Hope Avenue, Rochester, NY 14620-2731, USA
website: www.boydellandbrewer.com


A catalogue record for this book is available
from the British Library


The publisher has no responsibility for the continued existence or accuracy of
URLs for external or third-party internet websites referred to in this book, and
does not guarantee that any content on such websites is, or will remain, accurate
or appropriate.


This publication is printed on acid-free paper

# CONTENTS

# ILLUSTRATIONS

## Tristan and Iseult at the Cathedral of Santiago de Compostela
### *Joan Tasker Grimbert*

## Trevelyan Triptych: A Family and the Arthurian Legend
### *Roger Simpson*

The editors, contributors and publishers are grateful to all the institutions and persons listed for permission to reproduce the materials in which they hold copyright. Every effort has been made to trace the copyright holders; apologies are offered for any omission, and the publishers will be pleased to add any necessary acknowledgement in subsequent editions.

# GENERAL EDITORS' FOREWORD

This volume of *Arthurian Literature* ranges from Chrétien's Camelot to the French televison series *Kaamelott*. Irit Kleiman describes Chrétien's *Conte du Graal* as 'an elaborate architecture of imperfect doublings'. Using both psychological and mythological approaches, she discusses the impact of Lévi-Strauss's description of Perceval as an 'inverted Oedipus', and the links between Chrétien's poem and its Anglo-Norman context (especially the legal context). A key term for her arguments is *mahaign*, a wound or mutilation. Wounds are central to two essays on Malory which originated as papers for a session at Kalamazoo in 2013 sponsored by *Arthurian Literature*, 'Wounds and Emotions in Arthurian Literature'. Karen Cherewatuk notes that Malory is not much interested in the metaphorical wound of love so popular with medieval authors; she focuses on physical wounds, not those which bring honour but those which mark dishonour, such as the arrow in Lancelot's buttock. Depending on the context, she argues, readers may interpret such wounds as indications of moral transgression. Kevin Whetter resists the mainstream of Malory criticism to argue that wounds are to be accepted as inevitable concomitants of knightly activity and the winning of *worshyp*; it is 'communal damage', rather than individual wounding, that gives cause for concern. Whetter also discusses weeping, of which there is much in Malory. Megan Leitch, who spoke in the same session, focuses on sleeping and swooning, and concludes that while swooning can convey appropriately positive moral stances (even if remorseful), sleeping is more problematic: 'For those who wish to "doo after the good and leve the evyl", it does not do to be a "slepynge knyght"'. Wounds also feature in Erin Kissick's discussion of 'transformative female corpses' in the form of Sir Pedivere's wife and Percival's sister; she sees these corpses as critical comments on the chivalric community 'that depends on defining itself against the female body'.

This volume includes a welcome group of essays on art and material culture, an important source of information about the reception of the Arthurian legend. Joan Tasker Grimbert considers the surprisingly early twelfth-century images on a marble column from the cathedral at Santiago de Compostela which have been identified as Tristan and Iseult, and an account of the burial of the lovers in the same cathedral in the Icelandic version of their story from 1400. Why this connection with Santiago? She discusses the arrival of the Tristan story in Spain, the christianization of the legend in Scandinavia and the importance of the pilgrimage route to north-west Spain. A twentieth-century tapestry is Roger Simpson's subject, created by Lady Trevelyan for the family home at Wallington Hall: it portrays their legendary ancestor Sir Trevelyan, supposedly an Arthurian knight. Simpson links this to the Arthurian interests of several family members. Finally, Tara Foster brings us into the twenty-first century with her discussion of *Kaamelott*, an irreverent French Pythonesque television series which departs so far from the traditional tone as to have Lancelot shouting 'Le Roi, je l'emmerde!' (Screw the king!).

The Editors wish to acknowledge the support and extreme patience of Boydell & Brewer's Editorial Director, Caroline Palmer. We are also very grateful to our Editorial Board referees for their hard work and diligence, and to Anna Dow, our very efficient assistant editor, for her excellent work in preparing this volume for publication.

Elizabeth Archibald
Durham UK

David F. Johnson
Tallahassee, Florida

# CONTRIBUTORS

**Karen Cherewatuk** is a Professor in English at St Olaf College in Northfield, MN. She is the author of *Marriage, Adultery and Inheritance in Malory Morte Darthur* and co-editor with K. S. Whetter of *The Arthurian Way of Death* (Cambridge, 2006 and 2009). She is currently working on two essays on the visual arts and medievalism in the American mid-west.

**Tara Foster** is an Associate Professor of French at Northern Michigan University. Her research interests range from Old French narrative and hagiography to medievalism and popular culture. Her publications include articles on Clemence of Barking, Juana of Castile and literary representations of the Third Crusade. She is currently working on two projects on Arthurian television and on two translations of medieval French texts.

**Joan Tasker Grimbert** is Emerita Professor of French and Medieval Studies at the Catholic University of America in Washington, DC. She is president of the North American Branch of the International Arthurian Society, and was for nine years the international treasurer of the IAS. She has published six books: *'Yvain' dans le miroir: Une Poétique de la réflexion dans le «Chevalier au lion» de Chrétien de Troyes* (Amsterdam, 1988); *Tristan and Isolde: A Casebook* (New York, 1995; London, 2002); *Songs of the Women Trouvères* (New Haven, CT, 2001), with Eglal Doss-Quinby, Wendy Pfeffer and Elizabeth Aubrey; *Philologies Old and New: Essays in Honor of Peter Florian Dembowski* (Edward C. Armstrong Monographs, 2001), with Carol J. Chase; *A Companion to Chrétien de Troyes* (Cambridge, 2005, 2008), with Norris J. Lacy; and *Chrétien de Troyes in Prose*: *The Burgundian* Erec *and* Cligés (Cambridge, 2011), with Carol J. Chase.

**Erin Kissick** is a PhD candidate in English medieval literature at Purdue University, where she also completed her BA in English and Creative Writing and MA in Literary Studies. Her dissertation is on the topic of 'Constructing Community from Corpses in Medieval English and Icelandic Literature', under the supervision of Professor Shaun Hughes. Her research interests include the medieval undead, the Arthurian tradition, Old Norse sagas, medieval theology of the body, sand English and Icelandic textual landscapes.

**Irit Ruth Kleiman** is Associate Professor of Romance Studies at Boston University. Her research interests include historiography, written cultures, psychoanalysis and literature, archetypes of betrayal, the cultures of memory, questions of law and political authority, and the tropes of embodiment. She has published book chapters and essays on topics including Chrétien de Troyes, the medieval Judas Iscariot and the poetics of political rhetoric. Her book *Philippe de Commynes: Memory, Betrayal, Text* (Toronto, 2013) received the Newberry Library's Weiss/Brown Award.

**Megan Leitch** is Lecturer in English Literature at Cardiff University. Her research interests include Middle English romance, Arthurian literature and the fifteenth century. She is the author of *Romancing Treason: The Literature of the Wars of the Roses* (Oxford, forthcoming 2015). She is currently working on a monograph on sleep and its spaces in medieval and early modern literature.

**Roger Simpson** was, until his retirement, at the University of East Anglia. He is the author of *Camelot Regained* (1990), *Radio Camelot* (2008) and many articles on the post-1800 Arthurian Revival.

**K. S. Whetter** studied Malory with Professor P. J. C. Field and is himself now Full Professor of English at Acadia University. His principal research interests are heroic literature, genre theory and Arthurian literature, especially Malory's *Morte Darthur*. His recent publications include *The Arthurian Way of Death*, co-edited with Karen Cherewatuk (Cambridge, 2009), and 'Malory's Secular Arthuriad', in *Malory and Christianity: Essays on Sir Thomas Malory's Morte Darthur*, ed. D. Thomas Hanks Jr and Janet Jesmok (Kalmazoo, MI, 2013).

# I

# CHRÉTIEN'S *CONTE DU GRAAL* BETWEEN MYTH AND HISTORY

## Irit Ruth Kleiman

*Mahing* si est poing copé, doi copé, pié copé, manbre brisié qui ne pot renoier, ouil crievé, oreille copee, nes copé et totes bleceures dont l'en pert la force de son cors et de ses membres, et de totes ces choses devant dites, donc sanc ist.[1]

## Mahaign

This essay examines the *Conte du Graal*, Chrétien de Troyes's final, incomplete romance and the earliest known text in the Grail tradition. Chrétien's narrative takes its structure from an elaborate architecture of imperfect doublings. Like Chrétien's bifurcated romance, my argument on these pages also has two strands. The first considers the legacy of Claude Lévi-Strauss's description of Perceval as an 'inverted Oedipus' in relation to the intellectual history of the twentieth century.[2] The second examines the imprint of Anglo-Norman legal history and the intertextual allusions

[1] '*Mahing* means a cut-off hand, a cut-off finger, a cut-off foot, a broken limb which cannot heal, an eye put out, an ear cut off, a nose cut off, and all wounds from which a man loses the force of his body and his limbs, and all these things above stated, when blood flows.' *Livre de jostice et de plet*. Translation mine. I wish to thank Matilda Tomaryn Bruckner, Virginie Greene and Arthur Groos for their comments on an earlier draft of this essay, and Stephen D. White for his generous response to my queries.

[2] The implications of the argument which follows for the Gauvain portions of the *Conte du Graal* require separate treatment. On the romance's bipartite structure, see especially E. Baumgartner, *Chrétien de Troyes, Le Conte du Graal* (Paris, 1999); and A. Saly, 'La Récurrence des motifs en symétrie inverse et la structure du *Perceval* de Chrétien de Troyes', *Travaux de linguistique et de littérature* 21.2 (1983), 20–41.

that tie Chrétien's historical romance to Wace's *Brut* as romanced history. The necessity of the relation between the two lies in the lexicon that surrounds the Old French root *mahaign*. In this essay I will show how the shadow of a juridical violence of a sexual nature has the potential to bring greater harmony between distinct approaches to the Grail romance by reconciling psychoanalytical or myth-inflected readings of the text with a social logic characterized by Wace's Arthurian history and a vision of transcendent chivalry.

## The Isles of the Sea

*Le Conte du Graal* opens with an image of lush but treacherous innocence. A teenage boy cavorts in a green forest, serenaded by birdsong. Chrétien's description abounds in the tropes of the lyric, but the romance begins with a fall into History. A group of five knights arrive, the clang of their armour shattering the morning's calm. The conversation the boy has with them leads to further discoveries. It turns out that the boy has not always lived in this Welsh forest. The paradise where he hunts deer and kisses the servant girls turns out to be a kind of hinterland. He and his mother are refugees from a war that destroyed their lands on the far-off Isles of the Sea and all of their lineage. It turns out the boy once had two older brothers, and a crippled father now dead from grief. The boy, like the reader, learns of their existence through the story of exile and mutilation his mother tells.

It all happened during the unrest that followed Utherpendragon's death. The family, having lost lands, health and reputation on the Isles of the Sea, escaped to the Waste Forest.[3]

> Vostre peres, si nel savez,
> Fu par mi les hanches navrez
> si que il mahaigna del cors. (vv. 417–19)[4]
> [...]
> Vostre peres cest manoir ot
> Ici an ceste foreste gaste;

---

[3] They have lost even their names. Perceval guesses at his own several thousand verses later, while the reader knows his mother only as the 'Widow Lady of the Waste Forest'.

[4] Chrétien de Troyes, *The Story of the Grail (Li Contes del Graal), or Perceval*, ed. R.T. Pickens, trans. W. W. Kibler (New York, 1990). Capitalization and punctuation have occasionally been adapted to fit the context, especially in run-in citations. Translations are my own, adapted from Pickens's rendering. For discussion of *par mi*, *mahaigner* and *hanches*, see below.

2

> Ne pot foïr, mes a grant haste
> An litiere aporter se fist,
> Qu'aillors ne sot ou il foïst. (vv. 432–6)

(Your father, though you do not know it, was wounded between his haunches so that he was mutilated in body. [...] Your father had this manor here in this wild forest; he couldn't flee, but he had himself carried here in a litter in great haste, since he didn't know where else to go.)

The wound on the father's body serves as both anchor and origin to the story the Widow Lady of the Waste Forest now tells. Her words bring an extradiegetic past into the narrative's diegetic present. Simultaneously revealing and obscuring events she has long kept secret from her son, she points to her dead husband's body as the site of untold stories. History has written the origins of the family's downfall, exile and dispossession in enigmatic signs on the father's scarred limbs.

Chrétien lets the Widow Lady's voice carry this tale, confident that his listener – the reader, not the boy – will hear behind her words the history that Wace recounts, of Uther carried to battle on a litter, of the Saxon revolts that followed his death and of the vigour with which a fifteen-year-old Arthur conquered the lawless wilds of Scotland and brought justice to reign.[5] The mother's words are potent ones, steeped in nostalgia for a homeland and a way of life now vanished. In terms borrowed directly from the *Roman de Brut*, she speaks of the ruin of her husband and everyone she once knew, painting a sweeping panorama of dishonour, calamity and disfigurement.[6]

> Sa granz terre, ses granz tresors,
> Que il avoit come prodom,
> Ala tot a perdecïon,
> Si cheï an grant povreté.
> Apoveri et deserité
> Et essillié furent a tort
> Li gentil home aprés la mort
> Utherpandragon, qui rois fu
> Et peres le bon roi Artu.
> Les terres furent essilliees

---

[5]   See *Wace's Roman de Brut, A History of the British*, ed. and trans. J. Weiss (Exeter, 1999), vv. 8879 sqq.

[6]   See M. Delbouille, 'Les Hanches du Roi-Pêcheur et la genèse du *Conte del Graal*', in *Festschrift Walter von Wartburg zum 80. Geburtstag*, ed. K. Baldinger (Tübingen, 1968), pp. 359–79 (p. 376).

Et les povres genz avilliees,
Si s'an foï qui foïr pot. (vv. 420–31)

(The extensive lands and great treasures that he held as a nobleman all went to ruin, and he fell into great poverty. After the death
of Utherpendragon, who was king and father of good King Arthur,
the nobles were wrongfully impoverished, disinherited and cast
into exile. Their lands were devastated, and the poor people made
wretched; those who could flee, fled.)

Strong emotion propels her story forward, and the Widow Lady reveals
all at once the many injuries she has nursed since that time.

Et vos, qui petiz esteiez,
Deus mout biax freres aveiez.
Petiz esteiez, aleitanz,
Po aveiez plus de deux ans. (vv. 437–40)

(And you, who were so little, had two very handsome brothers.
You were so little, still nursing, you were barely more than two
years old.)

The Widow Lady insists on her son's childish oblivion. You don't know
that your father was wounded ('nel savez'), she says. In this way the father's
mutilation is directly tied to knowledge and ignorance, and to enigmas great
and small. Twice she repeats 'petiz esteiez', and again 'alleitanz'. But the
child the Widow Lady describes was two already, old enough to be capable
of remembering events as disruptive as those she describes. At two, the boy
would have been walking – unlike his father – and talking, too, although he
seems ill-prepared for language now that he is fully grown.
   The mother's tale has not reached its terrible end.

Quant grant furent vostre dui frere,
Au los et au consoil lor pere
Alerent a deus corz reax
Por avoir armes et chevax.
Au roi d'Escavalon ala
Li ainz nez, et tant servi l'a
Que chevaliers fu adobez.
Et li autres, qui puis fu nez,
Fu au roi Ban de Gomeret. (vv. 441–9)

(When your two brothers were grown, at their father's urging and
advice they went to two royal courts to receive their armour and
horses. The first born went to the king of Escavalon and served
him until he was knighted. And the other, the younger son, went
to King Ban of Gomeret.)

4

This news gives the reader pause. Why don't the brothers go to Arthur's court? Before we have had time wonder about this surprising detail, the Widow Lady's story has already taken a further turn.

> An un jor andui li vaslet
> Adobé et chevalier furent;
> Et an un jor meïsmes murent
> Por revenir a lor repeire,
> [...]
> Qu'as armes furent desconfit.
> As armes furent mort andui,
> Don j'ai grant duel et grant enui.
> De l'ainz né avindrent mervoiles,
> Que li corbel et les cornoilles
> Anbedeus les ialz li creverent.
> Ensi la gent morz les troverent. (vv. 450–62)

> (On the same day both lads were dubbed and knighted, and on the same day set forth to return to their home. [...] They were defeated at arms. Both were killed violently, which brings me great grief and sadness. A strange thing happened to the older one, the crows and rooks plucked out both his eyes. This was how the people found them dead.)

First born and second are crossed off in a single gesture: they will never take the place of the father, nor produce any offspring to continue their line.

When he hears his mother's words, the boy is so completely alienated from the world they describe that he understands 'mout petit / a ce que sa mere li dit' (scarce little of what his mother is saying to him [vv. 471–2]). He is not even interested. 'Be quiet!' he barks at the distraught widow ('Teisiez, mere!' [v. 372]). The child does not want to know what his parents lost. It is not *his* loss: he has grown up happy in the forest and seems to know nothing of the history from which his family is hiding, and to remember nothing of events that his mother – poignantly, obviously – cannot forget. The ethics of remembrance, both familial and cultural, are powerfully present at the vital heart of Chrétien's narrative from these first verses.[7] The *Conte du Graal* is deeply preoccupied by the obligation and ambivalence of remembrance, especially of remembering the father, but the romance begins with the troubling revelation of things forgotten.

---

[7]  On ethics and the father, see I. R. Kleiman, 'X Marks the Spot: The Place of the Father in Chrétien de Troyes's *Conte du Graal*', *Modern Language Review* 103.4 (2008), 970–84.

IRIT RUTH KLEIMAN

The boy leaves home. He becomes a knight, and he finds himself watching as a bleeding lance and a glowing platter pass in procession before him. He watches a king 'navrez et mahaigniez [...] par mi les hanches ambedos' (wounded and mutilated [...] between both his haunches [vv. 3476–89]) being carried away on a litter. Through it all he remains absolutely silent, 'qu'ausi bien se puet an trop taire / con trop parler' (for one can keep too silent just like one can talk too much [vv. 3216–17]). The boy does not have the gumption to ask his lame and white-haired host whom the luminous dish serves. His inability to speak is both a punishment exacted upon him and the cause of a whole people's promised suffering.

## Enigma, Incest, Episteme: The Inverted Oedipus

### Locating and Dislocating the Origin

In 1960, during his inaugural address to the Collège de France, Claude Lévi-Strauss described the Grail hero Perceval as an inverted Oedipus.[8] His formulation posited the Wasteland to be healed by Perceval as a variation of the Theban plague that Oedipus must lift. Lévi-Strauss explained that the structure of the Oedipus myth concerns a question for which there is no postulated answer. Its inverse, exemplified by the myth of the Grail, concerns an answer for which there is no question. The enigma provides a socket between the two, the point at which their inverted but symmetrical structures meet: Oedipus replies unafraid to the Sphinx's riddle. Others must answer for Perceval the question he did not dare to ask.[9]

---

[8] C. Lévi-Strauss, *Leçon inaugurale faite le mardi 5 janvier 1960* (Paris, 1960), p. 34. Lévi-Strauss returned to the Grail repeatedly over the next decades, but the 1960 inaugural lecture appears to mark his first, most lapidary articulation of this idea. Cf. Lévi-Strauss, *Le Regard éloigné* (Paris, 1983), chapter 17: 'De Chrétien de Troyes à Richard Wagner', pp. 301–18; and Lévi-Strauss, *Paroles données* (Paris, 1984), chapter 6: 'Le Graal en Amérique (année 1973–1974)', pp. 129–37.

[9] After Perceval's failure, first his mysterious cousin, then the Hideous Damsel, tell him what would have happened had he asked the fateful question and what will happen since he did not (vv. 3550–6 and 4636–49). Perceval at last learns whom the Grail serves from his hermit uncle. 'Cil cui l'an sert est mes frere: / ma suer et soe fu ta mere, / et del Riche Pescheor croi / que il est filz a celui roi / Qui del graal servir se fait' (He who is served from it is my brother. My sister and his was your mother, and the rich Fisher King, I think, is the son of that king who is served by the Grail [vv. 6381–5]). In fact, Perceval is supposed to ask *two* questions, 'whom does the Grail serve?' and 'why does the lance bleed?' See P. Ménard, 'Graal ou lance qui saigne? Réflexion sur l'élément de structure essentiel dans *Le Conte du Graal* de Chrétien de Troyes', in *Furent les merveilles pruvées [...] Hommage à Francis Dubost*, ed. F. Gingras et al. (Paris, 2005), pp. 423–35.

6

The crux – and the controversy – of Lévi-Strauss's idea lies in the symbiosis between language, kinship and fertility.[10]

> Entre la solution de l'énigme et l'inceste, il existe une relation, non pas externe et de fait, mais interne et de raison [...]. Comme l'énigme résolue, l'inceste rapproche des termes voués à demeurer séparés : le fils s'unit à la mère, le frère à la soeur, *ainsi que fait la réponse en réussissant, contre toute attente, à rejoindre sa question.* [...] L'union audacieuse de paroles masquées, ou de consanguins dissimulés à eux-mêmes, engendre le pourrissement et la fermentation, déchaînement des forces naturelles [...] comme l'impuissance, en matière sexuelle (aussi bien qzu'à nouer un dialogue proposé), tarit la fécondité animale et végétale.[11]

> (Between the solution to the enigma and incest there is a relation not external or factual but internal and logical [...]. Like the solved enigma, incest brings together terms which are supposed to remain separate: the son joins himself to the mother, the brother to his sister, *as does the answer when it succeeds, against every expectation, in joining itself to the question.* [...] The audacious union of masked words, or of family members concealed from one another, engenders rot and fermentation, the unleashing of natural forces [...] as impotence, in sexual matters (as well as to renew a dialogue), diminishes animal and plant fecundity.)

It is important to my arguments regarding the legacy of this hypothesis that we begin by considering the context in which it was first advanced. Lévi-Strauss's discussion of the Grail enigma comes in the midst of what is essentially a *discours de la méthode*. His inaugural address confronts the rivalry between *sciences humaines* and *sciences naturelles*.[12] Like the natural sciences, argues Lévi-Strauss, structural anthropology transcends the contingencies and contaminations of history and realizes a mode of access to universal truth.[13] To state things baldly, Lévi-Strauss makes

[10] Lévi-Strauss's words have sparked numerous interpretations of Chrétien's romance, many mutually incompatible. See, for example, J.-G. Gouttebroze, *Qui perd gagne: Le 'Perceval' de Chrétien de Troyes comme représentation de l'Oedipe inversé* (Nice, 1983); J.Rider, 'The Perpetual Enigma of Chrétien's Grail Episode', *Arthuriana* 8.1 (1998), 6–21; J.-J. Vincensini, 'Impatience et impotence, l'étrangeté des rois du château du graal dans *Le Conte du Graal*', *Romania* 116 (1998), 112–30. See below for my discussion of responses by Daniel Poirion and Sara Sturm-Maddox. On Lévi-Strauss and medieval literature, see R. H. Bloch, *Etymologies and Genealogies: A Literary Anthropology of the French Middle Ages* (Chicago and London, 1983), especially, as regards this essay, the Introduction and chapter 6, 'Grail Family and Round Table'. On Lévi-Strauss and the Grail continuations, consider T. Hinton, 'The Aesthetics of Communication: Sterility and Fertility in the *Conte del Graal* Cycle', *Arthurian Literature* 26 (2009), 97–108.

[11] Lévi-Strauss, *Leçon inaugurale*, pp. 34–5. Italics in the original; translations mine.

[12] Lévi-Strauss, *Leçon inaugurale*, p. 27.

[13] Lévi-Strauss, *Leçon inaugurale*, p. 26.

7

the Grail into an argument against history. The Grail romance and its continuations (Lévi-Strauss marks no distinction between them) furnish an example through which to demonstrate the formal coherence between narratives from contexts so disparate as to render impossible any question of mutual influence.[14] His analysis militates against traditional views that a literary text is the product of a specific historical moment, and against the capacity of historicist modes of reading to locate meaning. Lévi-Strauss's comments on Perceval are less an interpretative statement than a statement about interpretation itself.

Lévi-Strauss's words concerned the specific interpretation of Chrétien's *Conte du Graal*, but he also struck at larger methodological debates about the status of medieval literary texts, and the relations between history, philology, myth and the bubbling cauldron of literary theory – including, especially, the rivalries between structuralist, historicist and psychoanalytic approaches to literature. Until Lévi-Strauss put forth his hypothesis, scholarship's great, frustrated quest had been for the origins of the Grail as both object and ceremony.[15] The model suggested by Levi-Strauss's theorization broke radically with these traditions. Instead, Lévi-Strauss's hypothesis itself came to occupy a central position in scholarly debate, arguably displacing the quest for sources as the primary engine of Grail studies.[16] Lévi-Strauss's theory set in motion the transformation of a critical landscape where everybody was looking for an origin *for* the Grail text into one where the question of origin became recognized as a preoccupation *within the text itself.*

## The Tangle of Lineage and the Enigma of the Father

The most problematic potential consequence of Lévi-Strauss's hypothesis lies in the implication that the Grail text conceals its most fundamental enunciation – in this case, incest or its narrow avoidance. Lévi-Strauss

---

[14] The corpus Lévi-Strauss identifies includes the ancient Greek Oedipus, the medieval Perceval and a family of myths indigenous to North America.

[15] For overviews of the most influential theories, see especially J. Frappier, 'Le Graal et ses feux divergents', *Romance Philology* 24.3 (1971), 373–440, reprinted in *Autour du Graal* (Geneva, 1977); G. W. Goetinck, 'The Quest for Origins', chapter 1 of *The Grail, A Casebook*, ed. D. B. Mahoney (New York and London, 2000), pp. 117–47; and R. O'Gorman, 'Deux siècles de recherches sur le Graal', in *Polyphonie du Graal*, ed. D. Hüe (Orleans, 1998), pp. 181–8, translated and adapted from *The New Arthurian Encyclopedia*, ed. N. J. Lacy (New York, 1991), pp. 406–9.

[16] Lévi-Strauss's words had the greatest impact on scholars working in the French tradition, where at least one critic explicitly described Lévi-Strauss's hypothesis as furnishing the romance's 'principe organisateur' (J.-G. Gouttebroze, 'Cousin, cousine: dévolution du pouvoir et sexualité dans *Le Conte du Graal*', in *Chrétien de Troyes et le Graal*, ed. J. Steinnon et al. [Paris, 1984], pp. 77–87 [p. 77]).

never says where or how the notion of incest fits into the *Conte du Graal*, and as a result a number of different critics have sought to 'locate' the incest (or incest avoided) within the narrative. Daniel Poirion's 'L'Ombre mythique de Perceval dans le *Conte du Graal*' was one of the earliest and most influential of these responses to Lévi-Strauss's hypothesis.[17] Poirion's essay preached caution: 'La littérature n'obéit pas au mythe: c'est elle qui le crée.'[18] Literature does not obey myth: literature creates myth. Caution, however, is not what scholars largely took from Poirion's article. Far more influential than Poirion's call for moderation was his imaginative hypothesis of a brother–sister incest in Perceval's family's pre-diegetic past, an incest of the kind so frequently found in medieval literature, and associated in legend with both Arthur and Charlemagne.

The contrasting position, and the intellectual tradition it represents, come into view in Sara Sturm-Maddox's 'Lévi-Strauss in the Waste Forest'.[19] Sturm-Maddox flatly rejected Poirion's suggestion of occulted incest, arguing that Chrétien's romance 'is fundamentally concerned, not with the psychology or the fate of the individual hero, but with the reconciliation of tensions necessary for the maintenance of a viable social order'.[20] The *Conte du Graal* identifies a 'larger pattern of dislocation' marked by a 'general disruption of social justice and order' whose point of origin lies in the death of Utherpendragon.[21] In the *Conte du Graal*, concludes Sturm-Maddox, Chrétien 'establishes a past tense for his Arthurian narrative'.[22] The divide between Poirion and Sturm-Maddox's arguments crystallizes in their contrasting ideas about Perceval's father. Whereas for Sturm-Maddox, Perceval's father stands as the emblem of a lost and better past, Poirion conjures a father shrouded in controversy, sinful, incestuous and already fallen. The incommensurability of their

---

[17]  D. Poirion, 'L'Ombre mythique de Perceval dans *Le Conte du Graal*', *Cahiers de civilisation médiévale Xe-XIIe siècles* 16.2 (1973), 191–8.

[18]  Poirion, 'Ombre mythique', p. 195.

[19]  S. Sturm-Maddox, 'Lévi-Strauss in the Waste Forest', *L'Esprit Créateur* 18.3 (1978), 82–94 (p. 92). Work that builds on Sturm-Maddox's arguments includes D. Maddox, *The Arthurian Romances of Chrétien de Troyes: Once and Future Fictions* (Cambridge, 1991), especially chapter 4: '*Rexque Futurus*: The Anterior Order in *Le Conte du graal*'; R. T. Pickens, 'Arthurian Time and Space: Chrétien's *Conte del Graal* and Wace's *Brut*', *Medium Aevum* 75.2 (2006), 219–46; and S. Sturm-Maddox, '"Tenir sa terre en pais": Social Order in the *Brut* and in the *Conte du Graal*', *Studies in Philology* 81.1 (1984), 28–41.

[20]  Sturm-Maddox, 'Lévi-Strauss in the Waste Forest', p. 94.

[21]  Sturm-Maddox, 'Lévi-Strauss in the Waste Forest', p. 93; see also 'Tenir sa terre', pp. 38–9.

[22]  Sturm-Maddox, 'Lévi-Strauss in the Waste Forest', p. 93; see also 'Tenir sa terre', pp. 38–9.

arguments heralds a methodological estrangement that has never been bridged.

Although 1960 marks the first appearance of Perceval in Levi-Strauss's public thought, the Oedipus myth had already served as an exemplary point of demonstration in his fundamental 1955 article, 'The Structural Study of Myth'.[23] In that landmark essay, Lévi-Strauss asserted that all the developments in the myths surrounding Oedipus's family concern the excessive character of a family bond, that all the male characters in the myth are maimed in some way, and that all these male characters are named for their inability to stand or walk upright. Lévi-Strauss concludes that the Oedipus myth responds to the problem of the origins of *humanity* (i.e., in contrast to the origin of a single individual), and that it confronts the structural problem of whether man is born of the earth (autochthonous) or born of the sexual union between man and woman. He locates the structural problem the Oedipus myth resolves in the contrast between these two kinds of fertility, one sexual and the other plant-like.

Taking seriously the problem of autochthonous or sexual generation raised by Lévi-Strauss enables us to consider a new solution to an old and insistent problem in Chrétien's Grail romance, namely the imbalance between patrilineal and matrilineal kinship structures. The Widow Lady's explanation of the family's lost reputation mixes together her husband's line and her own. Speaking to her son about his father's former prowess, she abruptly says,

> Vous ne decheez de rien
> De son linage ne del mien,
> Que je sui de chevaliers nee,
> [...]
> Es isles de mer n'ot linage
> Meillor del mien an mon aage. (vv. 403–8)

> (Neither his lineage nor mine is any disgrace to you, for I am born from knights [...]. In the Isles of the Sea there was no finer lineage than mine in my day.)

Her statement conflates the two (mother and father have separate lines) and the one (a single history) in a way that meshes, subtly but perfectly, with the question of *one from one* (autochthonous) or *one from two* (sexual). Thus viewed in extenso, the Widow Lady's explanation of her son's lineage joins the incest between Oedipus and Jocasta as a variable

---

[23]  First published in English as 'The Structural Study of Myth', *Journal of American Folklore* 68 (1955), 428–44; and in French as 'La Structure des mythes', in *Anthropologie structurale* (Paris, 1958).

representation of the problem of origins. Incest takes a secondary position to the relation between fertility and the wound. By extension, in theory and in fact, the enigmatic wound which makes the Fisher King suffer provides the constant structuring element amongst the family of Grail texts.[24]

## A Very Brief History of the Theban Plague

At the time of Lévi-Strauss's inaugural lecture in January 1960, only a handful of studies had touched on the theme of incest in medieval literature. Since then, an abundant literature, including Elizabeth Archibald's *Incest and the Medieval Imagination* and Zrinka Stahuljak's *Bloodless Genealogies*, has radically shifted scholars' appreciation of the ubiquity of incest as a theme in medieval literature and, just as importantly, of its versatility.[25] For the legacy of Lévi-Strauss's judgement to be fully apprehended, it must further be contextualized in relation to the cultural dominance of Freud's Oedipus complex.[26] Freud's analysis of the Oedipus myth is not simply a canonical text; it is the manifesto of an epistemology which privileges the libidinal and its conflicts as the fateful origin of identity. Scholars of medieval literature authorized themselves in the anthropologist's words, but many tended to focus on the psychodynamics of incest, its prohibition or its repression – especially surrounding the Widow Lady and her 'biax filz' (handsome son).[27] However, Freud's reading of Sophocles' play concentrates on only one detail in a much larger tapestry of family and politics. The Oedipus known to twelfth-century readers from the works of Statius and Seneca was a far different character from the Oedipus generally familiar to twenty-first-century readers of either Freud or Sophocles. Elizabeth Archibald points out that,

[24] This mythic, archetypal association between the earth's fertility and its wounding might lead us to view the *Conte du Graal*'s early scenes of the Widow Lady's servants tilling the land differently as well.

[25] E. Archibald, *Incest and the Medieval Imagination* (Oxford, 2001); Z. Stahuljak, *Bloodless Genealogies of the French Middle Ages: Translatio, Kinship, and Metaphor* (Gainesville, FL, 2005).

[26] See S. Freud, *The Interpretation of Dreams*, trans. J. Strachey (London, 1954), pp. 261–4. On Freud and Oedipus, see the Introduction to B. W. Buchanan, *Oedipus against Freud: Myth and the End(s) of Humanism in Twentieth-Century British Literature* (Toronto, 2010).

[27] I am not the first to observe this slippage from myth to psychoanalysis; see also F. Olef-Krafft, 'Oedipe au château du Graal', *Le Moyen Age* 101.2 (1995), 227–57 (p. 240). My concern with psychoanalysis in the present essay is necessarily limited to signalling how the cultural currency of Freud's Oedipus complex has sometimes led to a narrowing or misprision of Lévi-Strauss's theory. My arguments on these pages should be received as sympathetic to but entirely distinct from any discussion of psychoanalytic, and especially Lacanian, readings of the *Conte du Graal*.

11

'for Seneca, though the incest is certainly horrifying, this is very much a story about power and kingship'.[28] Similarly, says Archibald, although 'Statius retells the story of Oedipus very briefly at the beginning of his epic *Thebaid*', his narrative 'is mainly concerned with the story of the internecine war between Oedipus' sons'.[29] For a medieval public, the values attached to the myth of Oedipus and his line were above all political ones.[30]

It was the war between the brothers Eteocles and Polynices that provided the material for the twelfth-century's own rewriting of Oedipus, the *Roman de Thèbes* (*c.* 1150).[31] *Yvain*, the romance Chrétien penned just prior to the *Conte du Graal*, contains clear allusions to the *Roman de Thèbes*, so there is no question over whether or not Chrétien knew it.[32] Could he have been reading the work while writing *Yvain*, just prior to beginning the *Conte du Graal*? The hint of such proximate influence is provocative. What is certain is that Chrétien would have known the Oedipus myth as a story about political rivalry, hostility between generations, fratricide and the consequences of treason.[33]

## The Virile Body and the Fertile Kingdom

### The Father and his Double

The next stage of my argument examines the wounded male bodies at the heart of Chrétien's tale. Lévi-Strauss's articulation of the Oedipus–Perceval family of myths places great emphasis on the importance of the double. The *coup de théâtre* of the Greek myth is that people who seemed to be distinct turn out to be the same.[34] The king of Thebes, Oedipus's father and the stranger he meets on the road and kills are all finally revealed as one. Lévi-Strauss raises this feature to a structural principle, asserting that the corresponding element in Percevalian myth is that people who seem to be identical are in fact distinct. This Percevalian inverse

---

[28] Archibald, *Incest and the Medieval Imagination*, p. 72.

[29] Archibald, *Incest and the Medieval Imagination*, p. 72.

[30] On medieval Oedipuses, see Archibald, *Incest and the Medieval Imagination*, pp. 71–8, and the dated but still important L. Constans, *La légende d'Oedipe* (Paris, 1881; reprint Geneva, 1974).

[31] *Le Roman de Thèbes*, ed. and trans. F. Mora-Lebrun (Paris, 1995).

[32] T. Hunt, 'Le Chevalier au Lion: Yvain Lionheart', in *A Companion to Chrétien de Troyes*, ed. N. J. Lacy and J. T. Grimbert (Cambridge, 2005), pp. 156-68 (p. 164).

[33] See also Zrinka Stahuljak's highly pertinent discussion of the overlap between treason and incest in *Bloodless Genealogies*, chapter 2, 'Unnatural Speech Acts: Ramifications of Incest in the *Roman de Thèbes*', pp. 50–79.

[34] Lévi-Strauss, *Leçon inaugurale*, p. 31.

presents itself most viscerally to the reader in the uncanny resemblance between Perceval's father and the Fisher King of the Grail kingdom, who is the hero's maternal uncle, and thus *already* marked as a paternal figure according to the codes of medieval romance. Both men are described in identical terms as *mahaigné* in conjunction with the description 'parmi les hanches'.[35] These twinned, mutilated male bodies form the keystone of both Lévi-Strauss's anthropological manifesto and Chrétien's romance, and they are the keystones of my reading as well.

The Widow Lady explains that after her husband,

> Fu par mi les hanches navrez
> Si que il mahaigna del cors
> Sa granz terre, ses granz tresors,
> Que il avoit come prodom,
> Ala tot a perdiciön,
> Si cheï an grant povreté. (vv. 418–23)

> (was wounded between his haunches so that he was mutilated in body, the extensive lands and great treasures he held as a nobleman all went to ruin, and he fell into great poverty.)

The word *perdition* that she uses to describe the ruin of her husband's lands can describe the destruction of a place, the soul's damnation or, importantly, the loss of use of a part of the body.[36] The wasting of the father's lands comes as an extension of his body's wasting. *Cheoir* and *être mahaigné* – to fall and to be mutilated – are more than simultaneous, they are fused in a way which exceeds rational cause and effect.[37] The

---

[35] *Hanches, jambes* or *cuisses*? Haunches, legs or thighs? In the Widow Lady's tale, the majority of manuscripts (eight) give the lesson 'hanches' or 'la anche'. The cousin's account of the Fisher King's wound leans still more pronouncedly towards *hanches*; only three manuscripts contain the variant 'jambes'. See Chrétien de Troyes, *Le Roman de Perceval ou Le Conte du Graal, édition critique d'après tous les manuscrits,* ed. K. Busby (Tübingen, 1993), pp. 18 and 150.

[36] Godefroy's dictionary, s.v. *perdition*, pays scant attention to the word *perdition*, defining it initially as loss or calamity, and in the *complément* adding 'the state of a person who has lost his soul' (F. Godefroy, *Dictionnaire de l'ancienne langue française et de tous ses dialectes du IXe au XVe siècle* [Paris, 1891–1902; repr. Geneva and Paris, 1982], 6: 96 and 10: 316; re-edited for the Web at http://www.classiques-garnier.com/numerique; my translation). In contrast, the *Dictionnaire du Moyen Français* answers: 'Au propre "fait de perdre quelque chose"'; these literal losses include 'l'usage d'un membre, d'un sens' and 'perdition d'un office'. In figurative usage, *perdition* denotes 'destruction, ruine', 'être tué (au combat)' and 'perte spirituelle, damnation' (*Dictionnaire du Moyen Français* [*DMF*], ATILF, http://www.atilf.fr/dmf; s.v. *perdition*, accessed 26 December 2011).

[37] Sturm-Maddox emphasizes the historical frame which surrounds the two, and downplays the mythic value of their common invalidity. 'Uther, obliged to have himself

information the Widow Lady provides about her husband early in the romance's exposition foreshadows the Fisher King's withered body and establishes a symbiotic relation between the health of Perceval's father's body and the health of his lands akin to the relation that will later govern the Grail kingdom.

## Mutilation and Mayhem

A vigorous, long-standing quarrel surrounds the intended meaning of the phrase *mahaigné parmi les hanches*. The debate has concerned, in nearly equal parts, the anatomical interpretation of the Fisher King's wound and its relation to the health of his kingdom. Some scholars have categorically refused to consider the insinuation of sexual dysfunction; for others, such allusions are self-evident. In recent decades, interpretations favouring some form of implied sexual content have gained currency; however, this has not eliminated disagreement over precisely what is meant in bodily terms. My own analysis begins with two assertions. First, the description given of the wound which cripples both men can only be made to signify logically and without recourse to convoluted imaginings if the phrase 'parmi les hanches' is understood to refer to the characters' genital area.[38] Next, after careful examination, it has become clear that the word *mahaigné* describes castration in its most literal sense, and is not simply an allusion to paralysis, wasting or impotence, as has sometimes been suggested. The word's lexical nuances for a twelfth-century francophone provide the necessary link between Lévi-Strauss's 'inverted Oedipus' hypothesis, with its incontrovertible revelations of ahistoric, mythic structures within the Grail cycle, and a politically conscious, historically specific understanding of Chrétien's romance. The mutilations that afflict the two men function simultaneously in two distinct narrative economies; understanding how this is so enables us to move beyond a critical impasse first

transported *en litière* [...] serves as model for the depiction of both' ('Tenir sa terre', p. 37). However, one of the lexical specificities of the word *mahaigné* (see below) is that it denotes an injury which renders one unfit for battle and which cannot heal. Therefore Uther, even lame, cannot be *mahaigné*, since he rises from his litter and fights.

38  The English 'haunches', which I have used throughout this essay, shares a certain ambiguity with the French *hanches*. For the use of *hanches* to mean testicles, see C. Brunel, 'Les Hanches du Roi Pêcheur', *Romania* 81.321 (1960), 37–43. In my view, the precise anatomical translation of this word, like the presence of *jambes* or *cuisses* as variants, does not alter the phrases' significance, only the degree of euphemism perceived. Of greater importance is the understanding of *parmi* in the sense of 'between'. See J. Frappier, 'La Blessure du Roi Pêcheur dans *Le Conte du Graal*', in *Jean Misrahi Memorial Volume, Studies in Medieval Literature*, ed. H. R. Runte, H. Niedzielski and W. L. Hendrickson (Columbia, SC, 1977), pp. 181–96.

inscribed more than fifty years ago. My reading explains the coordination of formal and contingent elements in Chrétien's narrative, but it also highlights the possibilities and broader necessity of working through and across theoretical divides.

The Anglo-Norman lexeme *mahaign* appeared around 1160, and entered Latin as *mahemiare* shortly afterwards.[39] The root has entirely disappeared from Modern French, but persists doubly in the English words *maim* and *mayhem*. The complexity of establishing an etymology for *mahaigner* is a fact, but the received best hypothesis favours an original Old Low Franconian root that 'denotes the castration of stallions and, ultimately, any sort of mutilation'.[40] Godefroy's *Dictionnaire de l'ancienne langue française* devotes three pages to the lexeme and its forms.[41] The *Oxford English Dictionary* and du Cange's *Glossarium mediae et infimae latinitatis* award it comparable attention.[42]

Godefroy's initial definitions for s.v. *meshaignier* include the literal meanings, 'mutiler, estropier, blesser, meurtrir, rendre impotent de quelque membre' (mutilate, maim, wound, crush, make impotent of some limb), and the figurative meanings, 'maltraiter, tourmenter, offenser, violer' (mistreat, torment, attack, violate [rape]).[43] As a verb, *mahaigner* describes a particular quality of violence, often transgressive; these semantics are preserved in the English 'mayhem'. In its noun forms, the word *mahaing* serves to classify a variety of crimes, their perpetrators and the resulting injuries. The *Coutumes de Normandie* speak of 'les *mehaingneurs* et les autres malfaicteurs' (the *méhaigneurs* and other wrongdoers),[44] while the *Anciennes Coutumes de Normandie* refer to 'ceulx qui despucellent les vierges a force, les haigneurs et les autres malfaicteurs' (those who rape

---

[39]   *Oxford English Dictionary*, s.v. *maim* (n.), http://www.oed.com/view/Entry/112503; s.v. *maim* (v.), http://www.oed.com/view/Entry/112505; and s.v. *mayhem* (n.), http://www.oed.com/view/Entry/115310; B. Diensberg, 'Old French Loanwords of Germanic Origin Borrowed into English', in *Symposium on Lexicography X*, ed. H. Gottlieb, J. E. Mogensen and A. Zettersten, *Lexicographica* (Tübingen, 2002), pp. 91–106.

[40]   Diensberg, 'Old French Loanwords', p. 101.

[41]   Godefroy, *Dictionnaire*, 5: 283–6.

[42]   See s.v. *mahamium* in du Cange et al., *Glossarium mediae et infimae latinitatis*, expanded edition (Niort, 1883–87), 5, column 177a, http://ducange.enc.sorbonne.fr/mahamium. Note that s.v. *mahamium* serves as the organizing entry point for no fewer than twenty-one forms of the word. The majority of the examples given derive from juridical sources.

[43]   Godefroy, *Dictionnaire*, 5: 284, column 3. On the assimilation of *mahaignier* into *meshaignier*, *méhaigner*, etc., see Diensberg, 'Old French Loanwords', p. 100.

[44]   Godefroy, *Dictionnaire*, 5: 284, column 1, Coust. de Norm., f°37 r°, éd. 1483. Godefroy's abbreviations have sometimes remained obscure; my citations refer to the source as presented by Godefroy. An effort to provide systematic identification is under way; see the *Bibliographie Godefroy*, ATILF, http://www.atilf.fr/BbgGdf.

virgins by force, the *haigneurs* and other wrongdoers).[45] A document from 1232 grants jurisdiction, 'excepté le justiche de homicide, de mehengnure de membréz' (excepting justice for homicide and amputation of limbs).[46] The word can similarly be found in a Latin text from the reign of Henry II Plantagenet: 'Haec omnia concessi cum murdro et morte hominis et plaga et *mahaim* et sanguine' (All these things I have conceded with the murder and killing of a man and wounding and *mahaim* and blood).[47] The examples Godefroy cites are not limited to the legal context, but these legal texts do provide substantial, telling examples of the word's connotations. The thirteenth-century *Livre de jostice et de plet* states clearly: '*Mahing* si est poing copé, doi copé, pié copé, manbre brisié qui ne pot renoier, ouil crievé, oreille copee, nes copé et totes bleceures dont l'en pert la force de son cors et de ses membres, et de totes ces choses devant dites, donc sanc ist et *mahen*' (*Mahing* means a cut-off hand, a cut-off finger, a cut-off foot, a broken limb which cannot heal, an eye put out, an ear cut off, a nose cut off, and all wounds from which a man loses the force of his body and his limbs, and of all these things above stated, when blood flows and *mahen*).[48] Wounds that are *mahaing* share two further traits: they cannot be repaired and they leave their victims unfit for combat.[49] It bears acknowledgement that Chrétien's description of the wounds suffered by Perceval's father and the Fisher King correspond to these normative definitions with exacting precision.[50]

## Crows Ate his Eyes

The narrative the Widow Lady offers to explain her family's origins, downfall and exile occupies a somewhat paradoxical position in schol-

---

[45] Godefroy, *Dictionnaire*, 5: 284, column 1, *Anc. Cout. de Norm.*, Nouv. Cout. gén., IV, 7b.

[46] Godefroy, *Dictionnaire*, 5: 285, column 2, Ch. de 1232, Clermont, Richel. 4663, f° 101 v°.

[47] Godefroy, *Dictionnaire*, 5: 285, column 2, Charte de Henri II d'Anglet; see also du Cange, *Glossarium*, s.v. *mahamium*.

[48] Godefroy, *Dictionnaire*, 5: 285, column 2, *Liv. de jost. et de plet*, XIX, 9, §2 et 3.

[49] 'membri mutilatio, vel enormis læsio, qua quis ad serviendum Principi in bello redditur imbecillior' (du Cange, *Glossarium*, s.v. *mahamium*).

[50] The online *Dictionnaire Electronique Chrétien de Troyes* makes it possible to review every occurrence of each form of *mahaigner* in Chrétien's romances (*Dictionnaire Électronique de Chrétien de Troyes* [*DECT*], ATILF, http://www.atilf.fr/dect). In Chrétien's usage, *mahaigner* and its forms always mean either 'to hack away at' or 'to dismember'. In *Yvain* the word is paired with 'blesser' and with 'ferir'. The Widow Lady uses the doublet 'navré et méhaigné' to describe her husband. When the Hideous Damsel curses Perceval, the words she uses to describe the Fisher King are equally precise; twice she speaks of his 'plaies', that is, open wounds (vv. 4638 and 4643).

arship. Frequently cited as a backdrop to discussion of other strands in the romance, her story remains both under-read and overdetermined.[51] The excess of meaning that surrounds the word *mahaigné* implicates Chrétien's romance narrative within the 'real' political framework of Arthurian geopolitics.

The wounds that afflict Perceval's father and his avatar are tightly related to the romance's historical character. I begin with Perceval's brothers, 'killed on the same day'. Did they, like Eteocles and Polynices, fight one another to the death over a birthright that only one could possess? Perhaps. Chrétien insists on the Welsh setting of his tale. In twelfth-century England, Welshness could be synonymous with clichés of wild savagery; scandalous tales of brothers killing each other in brawls over inheritance were a stock-in-trade, a point immortalized by Gerald of Wales.[52] Rivalry between the two elder brothers, combined with their convenient effacement from the path of the third, youngest brother, meshes nicely with both the themes of folklore and the laws of primogeniture – laws closely entwined with ecclesiastical rulings about endogamy and incest. These interpretations, however, leave aside what I see as the crucial signifying detail in the mother's narrative. The sons' fate transforms and retells the wounding of the father's own body. Of the older brother, the Widow Lady says that crows ate his eyes, 'De l'ainz né avindrent mervoiles, / Que li corbel et les cornoilles / Anbedeus les ialz li creverent' (vv. 459–61). But, as Ewa Slojka points out, the verb she chooses implies violence rather than a bird's pecking – she says *crever* instead of *bechier*.[53] How do the brothers die or why are they killed? Is this the random violence of a lawless countryside, an act of vengeance or something else? In coming to the Waste Forest, the father fled history. His sons have been forcibly excluded from it. Before the crows can eat a dead man's eyes, the body must be left to rot on a gibbet or battlefield where all can see and smell it. Is this the insignia of an exemplary punishment or the tell-tale sign that the historical world from which the family is hiding is one in which cadavers are strewn along the roadside?[54]

In recalling this past for her youngest and now only son, the Widow Lady confesses to a radical, annihilating failure of the threads that tie

---

[51] On the ways medieval authors responded to this aporia, see L. Wolfgang, 'Perceval's Father: Problems in Medieval Narrative Art', *Romance Philology* 34.1 (1980), 28–47. For the diversity of approaches in contemporary discussions, see E. Slojka, 'Escape from Paradox: Perceval's Upbringing in the *Conte du Graal*', *Arthuriana* 18.4 (2008), 66–87.

[52] Gerald of Wales, *The Description of Wales*, book 2, chapter 4.

[53] Slojka, 'Escape from Paradox', pp. 68 and 84, n. 7.

[54] Note that both of these desecrations are also visited on Oedipus and his sons. Oedipus blinds himself; the body of Polynices is left to rot unburied.

one generation to the next. A pernicious confusion infests Perceval's family structure. There is no transmission of knowledge from one generation to the next and no remembrance of past generations. Fathers have no sons and sons have no fathers. Patriarchs must be carried like babies. Adolescents cannot cross the threshold into manhood. Mother and son have been cast aside to form an infertile couple, where there can be (to play with Chrétien's own rhetoric in the romance's prologue) neither *semence* nor *récolte*. In all these ways, the Widow Lady of the Waste Forest portrays a landscape as barren as the one promised by Lévi-Strauss's inverted-Oedipus theorem.[55] However, there is also a legal problem hidden in the mother's story, one centred on the breakdown of patrilineal succession, that point at which genealogy and kingdom coincide. Both kinds of *patrimoine* are at stake in her tale, both heritage and inheritance. There are, in medieval lawbooks, few crimes which require the succeeding generation to pay for the father's sins, but the laws of treason call for the extinction of a whole line. The traitor's lands are pillaged or confiscated, and if he is left alive, he must leave them and go into exile.

### 'Let His Eyes Be Put Out and Let Him Be Castrated'

The use of castration, sometimes accompanied by blinding, as a sanction against sexual transgressions including rape, adultery or sodomy is well known and requires little comment. However, castration and blinding also had broad currency as punishment for other forms of felony. Discussion of this facet of Norman justice usually begins with mention of the *Consuetudine et Iusticie* of William the Conqueror, which date from *c.* 1091/1096.[56] Their final clause abolishes the death penalty and replaces it with blinding and castration. 'Interdico etiam ne quis occidatur aut suspendatur pro aliqua culpa, sed eruantur oculi, et testiculi abscidantur'.[57]

---

[55] Different meanings of the word *gaste* seem to be in play at different moments of Chrétien's romance. Unlike other landscapes the heroes encounter, the land of the Waste Forest where Perceval grows up is green and arable. It is *gaste* by virtue of being remote, isolated and wild. In my reading it is also figuratively *gaste* by virtue of the sterility inherent to the Widow Lady's project of withdrawing from history and because her Welsh homestead is bounded by imperatives born of the trauma of war and exile.

[56] On the context in which this document was prepared, see W. M. Aird, *Robert Curthose, Duke of Normandy (c. 1050–1134)* (Woodbridge, 2008), pp. 163–4. Aird argues for the date of 1096; the year 1091, first established by Charles Homer Haskins, is more traditional. See also T. Bisson, *The Crisis of the Twelfth Century* (Princeton, NJ, 2009), pp. 191–6.

[57] *Select Charters and Other Illustrations of English Constitutional History [...]*, ed. W. Stubbs, 9th edn, rev. H. W. C. Davis (Oxford, 1921), p. 99.

('I also forbid that anyone shall be slain or hanged for any fault, but let his eyes be put out and let him be castrated'.)[58] Treason was one of the crimes affected. Although the use of blinding and castration as punishment for treason also appears in Angevin lands on the Continent, their primary association is with Anglo-Norman justice.[59]

It is not necessary to reach all the way back to the eleventh century or the notorious case of William of Eu to find powerful examples of blinding and castration as punishments. As Robert Bartlett summarizes with regard to the 1166 Assize of Clarendon, 'harsh mutilatory justice was a feature of the criminal law of the time'.[60] Henry II's 1165 campaign against persistent Welsh rebellions culminated in the blinding and castration of numerous hostages, including several princely sons.[61] The incident is reported in many contemporary sources and it seems certain that Chrétien would have known of it. If hypotheses about Chrétien's relations with the Plantagenet courts are just, Chrétien could well have been in England at the time. Even without that specific connection, predation, exile and mutilation would all have been familiar features of the political landscape. As Bartlett notes,

> The Law-book attributed to Glanville, written in 1188, lists crimes punishable by execution or mutilation. These include treason, homicide, arson, robbery, and rape. The chronicler Ralph of Diceto distinguished the penal policy of Henry II's judges: fines or imprisonment for breach of the Forest Law, hanging for homicide, exile for treason, mutilation for lesser crimes. [§] Execution, mutilation, confiscation of property, exile, and imprisonment were all, at various times, visited by the Norman and Angevin kings on rebels and traitors.[62]

---

[58]   Cited in the Internet Medieval Source Book, http://www.fordham.edu/Halsall/source/will1-lawsb.asp, accessed 5 January 2012.

[59]   Castration and blinding, alone or in combination, functioned as a 'merciful' alternative to death. When castration and blinding were used as punishments for sexual crimes, leaving the victim alive enabled him to repent and find salvation. In a political context, singular interpretation is more difficult. Institutionalized castration in the context of political conquest reinforces a sexualized process of submission and domination. Mutilation also sidestepped the risk of blood feuds and vengeance cycles, although reconciliation seems significantly less likely to have occurred than in cases where exile alone was used as a punishment. One imagines, finally, that the punishment's value as an exemplary deterrent was also quite vivid.

[60]   R. Bartlett, ed., *England under the Norman and Angevin Kings 1075–1225* (Oxford, 2000), p. 184.

[61]   P. Latimer, 'Henry II's Campaign against the Welsh in 1165', *The Welsh Historical Review* 14 (1989), 523–52; see note 67 for a list of sources. Consulted at http://www.deremilitari.org/resources/sources/latimer.htm, accessed 5 January 2012.

[62]   Bartlett, *England under the Norman and Angevin Kings*, pp. 184–5.

The abolition of the death penalty promised by the *Consuetudine* did not remain a consistent feature of Norman law. Mutilation, castration and exile, however, did.[63]

Klaus van Eickels has recently examined this legal history in relation to Norman constructions of gender and authority. His study analyses the specifically political uses and significations of castration and blinding. Van Eickels demonstrates that events which may otherwise appear to be isolated instances in fact form part of a widespread and coherent phenomenon of clear import and symbolism. The Norman aristocracy, concludes van Eickels, 'construed physical and political impotence as two sides of the same coin. In the Norman world, sex and gender were closely intertwined in a way that defies any attempt to analyze the social construction of masculinity without referring to its physical embodiment.'[64] He continues,

> Royal ducal and noble honour were [not] only gendered male, but construed as masculine in a way that the boundaries between the physical and the social aspects of manhood collapsed. [...] As a prerequisite of power, masculinity was politically relevant. Punishing a political enemy by emasculating his body was therefore not perceived as unrelated violence, but as an appropriate form of royal revenge.[65]

Castrating rivals or rebels 'unmanned' them and thus severed them from political virility. These corporal punishments were used in combination with the confiscation of lands and/or exile of the offender.[66] It is worthwhile to recall at this point the coordination between regime change, exile

---

[63] For recent discussions of Norman treason law and mutilation, see K. Bosnos, 'Treason and Traitors in Norman and Anglo-Norman History, c. 1066–1135: Representation, Discourse, Practice' (unpublished PhD dissertation, Emory University, 2007), especially chapter 3: 'Prescription and Practice: Penalties for Treason'; J. Gillingham, 'Killing and Mutilating Political Enemies in the British Isles [...]', in *Britain and Ireland, 900–1300: Insular Responses to Medieval European Change*, ed. B. Smith (Cambridge, 1999), pp. 114–34; C. W. Hollister, 'Royal Acts of Mutilation: The Case against Henry I', *Albion* 10.4 (1978), 330–40; K. van Eickels, 'Gendered Violence: Castration and Blinding as Punishment for Treason in Normandy and Anglo-Norman England', *Gender and History* 16.3 (2004), 588–602. See also S. D. White, 'The Ambiguity of Treason in Anglo-Norman-French Law, c.1150–c.1250', in *Law and the Illicit in Medieval Europe*, ed. R. M. Karras, J. Kaye and E. A. Matter (Philadelphia, 2008), pp. 89–102.

[64] van Eickels, 'Gendered Violence', p. 591.

[65] van Eickels, 'Gendered Violence', p. 591.

[66] On political exile, see E. van Houts, 'L'Exil dans l'espace Anglo-Normand', in *La Normandie et l'Angleterre au Moyen Age*, ed. P. Bouet and V. Gazeau (Caen, 2003), pp. 117–27.

and the father's *corps mahaigné* within the Widow Lady's account of her family's past.

The question may pointedly be asked, 'How did twelfth-century authors refer to amputation, castration or blinding as legal punishments?' In French, we are confronted by an immediate, two-fold problem of language and sources. Whether in the *chansons de geste*, histories or legal texts, death and dismemberment are above all denoted by formulae such as *démembrer* or *perdre vie et membres*. Latin offers richer fare.[67] In 1124 Henry I sentenced those guilty of treasonously counterfeiting money to the amputation of their right hands and their testicles: 'truncatis dextris manibus et abscisis inferioribus corporis partibus', in the words of John of Worcester.[68] Orderic Vitalis imagines a scene in which Henry I defends the blinding of two of his own men in relation to the same affair, using the phrase 'priuatione membrorum puniri'.[69] William of Malmesbury recounts the 1096 punishment of William of Eu, who 'caecatus et extesticulatus est'.[70] By far the most common phrases, however, are *oculos eruere* and *testiculos abscidere*, the same ones used in the laws of William the Conqueror. An exhaustive lexical, semantic and socio-historic examination of the coordination and competition between Norman French *mahaigner* and Latin *abscidere* does not appear possible.[71] Yet there is thirteenth-century evidence that the two lexemes overlapped enough to have been perceived as contiguous and even synonymous.[72]

In the family history the Widow Lady kept secret from her son, castration and gouged-out eyes are inseparable from political downfall, forced exile and the failure of masculine prowess. The Widow Lady's descriptions of genital mutilation and torn-out eyes would have sustained certain very specific interpretations amongst Chrétien's readers. It was the fate of perjurers to be blinded, of sexual predators to be castrated, and of traitors

---

[67] Preparation of this rhetorical comparison was greatly facilitated by Bosnos, 'Treason and Traitors', pp. 153–7.

[68] *The Chronicle of John of Worcester*, ed. and trans. P. McGurk (Oxford, 1998), 3: 156 [for the year 1125], cited in Bosnos, 'Treason and Traitors', p. 153, n. 101.

[69] Orderic Vitalis, *The Ecclesiastical History*, book XII, chapter 39, ed. M. Chibnall (Oxford, 1978, 1986), 6: 352, cited in Bosnos, 'Treason and Traitors', p. 157, n. 114.

[70] William of Malmesbury, *Gesta Regum Anglorum*, book IV, §319, cited in Bosnos, 'Treason and Traitors', p. 155, n. 108.

[71] The essays in J. Beer, ed., *Translation Theory and Practice in the Middle Ages* (Kalamazoo, MI, 1997) provide several useful considerations of the relations between Latin and the French vernaculars. See also, more broadly, the work of Brian Merrilees and William Rothwell on medieval glosses and bilingual dictionaries.

[72] Lexical forms of *abscidere* are used as synonyms for the forms of *mahamium* in two supporting citations gathered by du Cange.

to forfeit both eyes and testicles.[73] The mutilations inflicted on the Widow Lady's husband and sons inscribe their bodies with the marks of justice.

The mutilated male body is the enigmatic sign of the *Conte du Graal*, the sign that brings together social and psychoanalytic readings, mythic and Christian ones. The central word *mahaigné* confounds the opposition between formal and historical modes of interpretation. The word alludes to a punishment associated with sexual crimes and also with treason – castration and blinding. Treason and incest share an overlapping set of symbolic markers and associations. Each results in a mutilation of the male body which is the conduit and embodiment of power and authority, of the *forces of life and order*. This is precisely what Lévi-Strauss is saying: the fertility and health of the ruler are in a symbiotic relation with his lands which is totemic, not rational. We now have a historically coloured, as well as a totemistic or mythic, way to conceive of the 'wasted' kingdom. Sexual virility and the ability to 'tenir sa terre' go together. Myth and history share a common armature and function together. The castrated male body (the *corps mahaigné*) presents itself as the scar of a polyvalent *conjointure* between an archetypal vocabulary of fertility on the one hand, and the indexed value of a historically determined corporal punishment meted out by the law in a specific time and place on the other.

## History and Romance

### Before and After

The implications of this echo of Norman legal history in Chrétien's romance spill over the edges of this essay, but that does not mean they can be set completely aside. There is a profound thematic coherence between the *Conte du Graal* and the history of the first century following the Conquest. Each confronts, over and over again, the difficult and sometimes violent encounter between old and new orders. This is the context from which both the *Consuetudine* and the 1116 Laws of Henry I emerge.[74] It is the background against which Arthurian tradition flowered

---

[73]  The frequency with which these punishments were enforced has become a matter of debate; their status as law (and widespread rhetoric) is assured. See the above-cited discussions of treason in Norman and Angevin law.

[74]  Bisson, *The Crisis of the Twelfth Century*, p. 192. Bisson notes that during the century which led up to *Chrétien*'s oeuvre, 'practically all extant princely genealogies' were 'witness to disputed or violent successions' (Bisson, *Crisis*, p. 188). His study includes a long list of succession crises, on whose rolls feature rivalries, fratricide and stymied lines with no direct heir (Bisson, *Crisis*, pp. 188–90). All three of the lineages in the *Conte du Graal* face a precipice. Arthur's only son is absent from this tale, but will

and from which the genre of romance was born. At least one scholar of Chrétien's oeuvre has argued that the encounter between the old law and the new endows the *Conte du Graal* with a structure of such potency that it 'retrospectively establishes the transtextual coherence of [Chrétien's] *oeuvre* as a whole'.[75]

The relation to history which gives the *Conte du Graal* such a unique character pivots on the problem of historical consciousness. At the moral heart of Chrétien's tale lies a son's quest to find his own place in the history of his family and his people, and to live within the present without forgetting the past. The memory and traumas of Arthur's conquest are still vividly *present* in the fictional time and space carved out by Chrétien's narration.[76] The words the Widow Lady chooses, and the words she does not teach her son, bear witness to what it means to live in the 'afterwards' of Arthur's ascent to the throne.[77] Her account of war, famine and exile allows the reader to align the memory of conquest modelled in Wace's *Roman de Brut* with the murky alliances and smouldering rebellions that linger in Chrétien's romance. What emerges is a situation in which both Perceval's father and the Grail King bear corporeal scars which mark them as members of an aristocracy for whom acceptance of Arthur's reign has not come easily. My point is emphatically not to identify anything so literal as the direct transposition of specific events, groups or personalities. Instead, I wish to highlight what I think of as a historical 'watermark' that emerges from this and other echoes of post-Conquest history and geography within the *Conte du Graal*.[78] All are speculative,

---

one day kill him; Gauvain, his nephew, quests after a lance prophesied to destroy Logres. The Grail kings have no heir except perhaps Perceval, who does not comprehend their kingdom or their reign. Perceval's own line has been shattered; he is the last of its scions. The fractured, incomplete or crippled passage between generations unites all three dynasties. See also P. Menard, 'Problèmes et mystères du *Conte du Graal*', in *Chrétien de Troyes et le Graal* (Paris, 1984), pp. 61–76 (p. 63); reprinted in *Polyphonie du Graal*, ed. D. Hüe (Orleans, 1998), pp. 59–75.

[75] Maddox, *Once and Future Fictions*, p. 6.

[76] The inexplicable disjunction caused by Perceval's five years of Godless forgetting, or Gauvain's bizarre reunion with his mother at a castle seemingly forgotten by time, are habitually noted. The king's age, also, oscillates between thirty and one hundred! Yet even without these flaws, the romance exists in a troubled relation to its own diegetic history. Children born at the time of the transition between Uther and Arthur have grown to maturity, but Arthur's grip on power seems more uncertain than in any of Chrétien's other romances.

[77] On the historical consciousness of 'afterwards', see M. Otter, '1066: The Moment of Transition in Two Narratives of the Norman Conquest', *Speculum* 74.3 (1999), 565–86.

[78] For a related study of English geography, see R. Morris, 'Aspects of Time and Place in Arthurian Verse Romance', *French Studies* 42.3 (1988), 257–77.

but compelling enough to influence the way we think about the uses of history in Chrétien's fiction(s).

Elisabeth van Houts's study of European reactions to the Norman Conquest, for instance, inspires serious reflection on the imprint made by collective historical memory on the Grail romance.[79] The Conquest and its long-running political aftermath provoked a general collapse within the Saxon nobility. A whole social class lost their lands and titles, and a great many went into exile; van Houts notes that Byzantine sources were already speaking of an 'exodus' by the 1080s.[80] This is the kind of dramatic, sweeping material that continues to inspire writers of fiction today. This is also exactly the theme of the story the Widow Lady tells her son at the beginning of the *Conte du Graal*. 'The nobles were wrongfully impoverished, disinherited and cast into exile ... Those who could flee, fled' (vv. 426–31). Her husband's ruin was part of a broader pattern amongst men of his social class; her own father was also affected.[81] Of the men who once ruled the Isles of the Sea, nothing now remains. This is not to say Chrétien did not also have in mind the history of more recent decades. It is rather to suggest that the author's imagination may have nourished itself on a past just beyond the reach of living memory, a past whose consequences were still reverberating through political life during Chrétien's maturity, and about which Wace wrote distinctly in the *Roman de Brut* and the *Roman de Rou*, both of which Chrétien's own work acknowledges.[82] In *Yvain*, Chrétien coyly answers Wace's discourse about historical truth with his own affirmation of the truth of fiction.[83] In the *Conte du Graal* the past and its endurance become the material of fiction, and a means of access to historical truth.

---

[79] E. van Houts, 'The Norman Conquest through European Eyes', *The English Historical Review* 110.438 (1995), 832–53. Van Houts's essay takes its survey up to 1150, only a few years before Wace wrote his *Roman de Brut* and as little as ten years before his *Roman de Rou*.

[80] van Houts, 'Norman Conquest through European Eyes', p. 842.

[81] Elsewhere van Houts reports that political exile from Norman England was predominantly temporary and was often followed by reconciliation and the recovery of property. Comparison of the situation faced by Perceval's family with her findings reinforces the impression that the romance has in mind something more cataclysmic (see van Houts, 'L'Exil dans l'espace Anglo-Normand').

[82] Chrétien knew both these works, and cites Wace's *Roman de Rou* in *Yvain*. Scholarship once tended to dismiss Chrétien's concern for Wace as a historian, but it becomes increasingly evident that, on the contrary, we have only begun to plumb the depths of that intertextual relation. On the twelfth-century literary uses of the eleventh-century past, see P. Eley and P. E. Bennett, 'The Battle of Hastings according to Gaimar, Wace and Benoît: Rhetoric and Politics', *Nottingham Medieval Studies* 43 (1999), 47–78.

[83] D. Green, 'King Arthur: From History to Fiction', *Arthurian Studies* 64 (2005), 66–76 (p. 73).

*Intertextuality and Arthurian Geography*

Chrétien's *Conte du Graal* appears together with Wace's *Brut* in three manuscripts.[84] Each one is remarkable for a distinct reason. I will return to the first, Bibliothèque nationale de France, ms fr 1450, in a moment. In the second, Guiot's copy (Bibliothèque nationale de France, ms fr 794), the *Conte du Graal* has been separated from Chrétien's other four romances and placed with more 'historical' works in the manuscript's final section, where it fraternizes with Wace's *Brut*, the *Roman de Troie* and Calendre's verse history *Les Empereors de Rome*.[85] The third, London, College of Arms, Arundel ms XIV, which contains the only Anglo-Norman copy of the *Conte du Graal*, places Chrétien's narrative alongside the *Brut* and other works of Anglo-Norman history such as Gaimar's *L'Estoire des Engleis*.[86] The relationship between Chrétien's romance and Wace's history, or indeed the privilege that his *Conte du Graal* enjoys as a historical text within medieval manuscript compilations, is not the fruit of chance. It is an indication that medieval readers found something recognizably historical in Chrétien's text, something that spoke to the same 'receptors' as historical accounts in much more direct relation to the dynastic violence, ethnic hostilities, civil unrest and famine that marked twelfth-century Norman England. London, College of Arms, Arundel ms XIV rings this historical note most clearly, and its Anglo-Norman character is no trivial adornment to this coincidence.

The *Conte du Graal* leaves unresolved the relations between the Grail kingdom and Arthur's kingdom of Logres. It also leaves unanswered why Perceval's brothers go to the courts of Escavalon and Ban to be knighted (vv. 441–52). By every evidence of Chrétien's verses, the court of Escavalon seeks to destroy Arthur's kingdom: Gauvain is wanted there for murder, and is afterwards sent in pursuit of a lance fated to destroy Logres. In later Grail texts Ban is closely associated with Lancelot and thus with Guenevere's adultery, leading Madeleine Blaess to suggest that Ban's court might also 'avoir de lointaines raisons d'inimitié envers

---

[84] On the manuscript evidence of a 'special affinity' between *Perceval* and the *Brut* and its implications, see Pickens, 'Arthurian Time and Space', p. 221. For a comprehensive view of Chrétien's romances in the manuscript tradition, see *Les Manuscrits de Chrétien de Troyes / The Manuscripts of Chrétien de Troyes*, ed. K. Busby, T. Nixon, A. Stones and L. Walters, 2 vols. (Amsterdam, 1993).

[85] On the Guiot manuscript, see K. Busby, *Codex and Context: Reading Old French Verse Narrative in Manuscript*, 2 vols. (Amsterdam and New York, 2002), 1: 93–108.

[86] See K. Busby, 'The Text of Chrétien's *Perceval* in MS London, College of Arms, Arundel XIV', in *Anglo-Norman Anniversary Essays*, ed. I. Short (London, 1993), pp. 75–85. It is noteworthy that this manuscript does not contain any of the continuations.

Arthur' (have deep-seated reasons for enmity against Arthur).[87] Moreover, outlaw knights bearing the moniker 'of the Isles' continue to violate the would-be peace of Arthur's rule, further calling into question the hero's potential alliances.[88]

Intertextual allusions deepen this anti-Arthurian malaise. When the Hideous Damsel curses Perceval, she tells him that, because of his silence,

> Dames an perdront lor mariz,
> Terres an seront essilliees
> Et puceles desconseilliees
> Qui orfelines remandront,
> Et maint chevalier an morront. (vv. 4644–8)

> (ladies will lose their husbands, lands will be laid waste, and maidens, helpless, will remain orphans; many knights will die.)

Maurice Delbouille was the first to notice that these verses directly echo an appeal for mercy directed to Arthur as conqueror of Scotland in the *Roman de Brut*.[89] In Wace's history, bishops, abbots and monks bearing relics come out to plead for Arthur's mercy. A second delegation follows, made up of barefoot women weeping, carrying their infant children in their arms. The Scottish mothers' complaint, like the Hideous Damsel's curse, exactly describes the world where Perceval was raised.[90]

> Ez vus lé dames des cuntrees,
> Tutes nu piez, eschevelees,
> Lur vesteüres decirees
> E lur chieres esgratinees,
> En lur braz lur enfanz petiz;
> Od pluremant e od granz criz
> As piez Artur tuit s'umilient,
> Plurent e braient, merci crient:
> Sire, merci! ce dient tuit;
> Pur quei as cest païs destruit?

---

[87] M. Blaess, 'Perceval et les "Illes de mer"', in *Mélanges de littérature [...] offerts à Mademoiselle Jeanne Lods*, vol. 1 (Paris, 1978), pp. 69–77 (p. 72).

[88] On the idea that unresolved past conflict stands between Perceval's family and Arthur's rule, see Blaess, 'Perceval et les "Illes de mer"'; and B. Cazelles, *The Unholy Grail* (Stanford, CA, 1996), especially pp. 8–9 and 49–53. I am sceptical of several conclusions that Blaess and Cazelles develop as extensions of these observations.

[89] Delbouille, 'Les Hanches du Roi-Pêcheur', pp. 375–8; Wace, *Roman de Brut*, ed. and trans. Weiss, p. 238, vv. 9469–86.

[90] The coincidence raises unanswerable questions about the coordination of historical and fictional temporalities, and the recurrent moments of prophetic speech within the *Conte*.

Aies merci des entrepris
Que tu, sire, de faim ocis.
Se tu nen as merci des peres,
Veies ces enfanz et ces meres,
Veies lur fiz, veies lur filles,
Veies lur genz que tu eissilles!
Les peres rend as petiz fiz,
E as meres rend lur mariz [...][91]

(And on the other side appeared the women of the land, their feet and heads quite bare, their clothes torn and their faces scratched, their little children in their arms. With tears and loud cries they all fell at Arthur's feet, weeping and wailing and begging for mercy. 'Mercy, my lord!' they all said. 'Why have you destroyed this land? Have mercy on those wretches whom you, my lord, are starving to death. If you don't have mercy on the fathers, then look at these children and these mothers. Look at their sons, their daughters, their families, whom you are ruining! Give fathers back to their little sons, husbands back to the mothers' [...])

Their plea seeks a political middle ground in humility. The women admit that they aided Arthur's enemies, the Saxons, but argue that they were coerced into doing so. In Wace's history, Arthur decides that he will forbear from killing or mutilating them: 'Vie e membre lur parduna / Lur humages prist sis laissa' (He spared them life and limb, received their homage and left them alone).[92] The king's largesse enacts a politics of reconciliation and signals the possibility of new beginnings.

It is one of the more agreed-upon compass points of Arthurian geography that the phrase 'Isles of the Sea' refers to Scotland, especially the Hebrides and Western Isles.[93] On further reflection, we realize that in the Widow Lady's account of how she fled with her nursing infant from the Isles of the Sea to her husband's Welsh manor, she gestures towards a portrait of herself in precisely the same posture as the Scottish women in Wace's verses – that is, weeping with a child in her arms. Medieval custom granted Scotland and Wales a unique sympathy, and Matthew of Paris's maps show the two as being much closer together than they

---

[91] Wace, *Roman de Brut*, ed. and trans. Weiss, p. 238, vv. 9469–86; English text on p. 239. I have amended the syntax of Weiss's translation of v. 9484.

[92] Wace, *Roman de Brut*, ed. and trans. Weiss, p. 240, vv. 9525–6; English text on p. 241.

[93] See Blaess, 'Perceval et les "Illes de mer"'; and C. Luttrell, 'Arthurian Geography: The Islands of the Sea', *Neophilologus* 83 (1999), 187–96. On Scotland in the Arthurian kingdom, see Morris, 'Aspects of Time and Place'; and R. L. G. Ritchie, *Chrétien de Troyes and Scotland, The Zaharoff Lecture* (Oxford, 1952).

appear in maps drawn according to modern conventions.[94] Despite Wace's praise for Arthur's mercy, the more closely we look, the more we realize that the Widow Lady portrays her family in an ambiguous relation to Arthur's rule, confirming the anxiety that surrounds the description of her husband's mutilation.

It is of some notoriety that the manuscript mentioned first, BnF ms fr 1450, inserts Chrétien's romances immediately following Wace's claim that after Arthur had vanquished the last Island king, he reigned over twelve years of peace, during which time he founded the Round Table.[95]

> Duze anz puis cel repeiremant
> Regna Artur paisiblement,
> Ne nuls guerreier ne l'osa,
> Ne il altre ne guereia.[96]
> [...]
> Fist Artus la Runde Table,
> Dunt Bretun dient mainte fable.[97]
> [...]
> En cele grant pais ke jo di,
> Ne sai se vus l'avez oï,
> Furent les merveilles pruvees
> E les aventures truvees
> Ki d'Artur sunt tant recuntees
> Ke a fable sunt aturnees:
> Ne tut mençunge ne tut voir,
> Ne tut folie ne tut saveir.[98]

(For twelve years after his return, Arthur reigned in peace. No one dared to make war on him, nor did he go to war himself. [...] Arthur had the Round Table made, about which the British tell many a tale. [...] In this time of great peace I speak of – I do not know if you have heard of it – the wondrous events appeared and the adventures were sought out which are so often told about

94 See Morris, 'Aspects of Time and Place', p. 266; for Matthew of Paris's map, see British Library, Cotton MS Claudius D.vi, f.12v; consultable in digitized form on the website of the British Library, www.bl.uk, accessed 26 January 2012. Morris's essay offers a useful point of departure for thinking through the puzzle of Saxon, Scottish and Welsh identities.
95 See L.Walters, 'Le Rôle du scribe dans l'organisation des romans de Chrétien de Troyes', *Romania* 106 (1985), 303–25; and S. Huot, *From Song to Book [...]* (Ithaca, NY, 1987), pp. 27–32.
96 Wace, *Roman de Brut*, ed. and trans. Weiss, p. 244, vv. 9731–4.
97 Wace, *Roman de Brut*, ed. and trans. Weiss, p. 244, vv. 9751–2.
98 Wace, *Roman de Brut*, ed. and trans. Weiss, p. 246, vv. 9787–94.

Arthur that they have become the stuff of fiction: not all lies, not all truth, neither total folly nor total wisdom.)[99]

In the *Brut* the foundation of the Round Table signals a time of peace and prosperity.[100] The scribe's interpolation allows Chrétien's romances to burgeon from the splice in Wace's narrative as if the heroes' adventures were themselves the bounty of peace and plenty. The duration of reading coincides with the time of peace, so that the pleasurable rewards of Arthur's dominion are literally made to last longer, and seem to swell to an interlude of untroubled fictionality.[101]

My reading suggests the need for a different perspective. The *Conte du Graal* is tethered to a historical and political relationship of uncertain character, but of certain force. The five knights' violent eruption into the Waste Forest in the romance's opening scene puts the relations between the lyric, fiction and history into doubt. The five knights tear through Perceval's green forest, literally and metaphorically. As they ride away, they leave behind a rent in its veil, stripping away the Widow Lady's fictions and exposing the persistence of time and violence, that is, of Arthurian history itself. Just as the Widow Lady's manor in the Waste Forest cannot protect her son from the diegetic world of Arthurian chivalry, so Chrétien's fiction cannot hold at bay the temporality and violence of the history Wace recounts. This interpretation places the intrusion of historical violence over the lintel of the Grail's fictions.

## The Enigma of the Body and the Ethics of Remembrance

According to Lévi-Strauss, repetition serves to make the structure of a myth apparent. In Freudian psychoanalytic theory, repetition is traditionally associated with unmastered trauma. When Perceval dines with the Fisher King, he returns to the same position as he occupied in his mother's narration of the family's exile. He again becomes the silent and passive recipient of nourishment from a parent (figure) and an observer in

---

[99] Wace, *Roman de Brut*, ed. and trans. Weiss, pp. 245–7. This is Weiss's translation of all three extracted passages; the English translation has been slightly amended so as to remove a couplet not retained in the French extract.

[100] On Wace's Round Table, see B. Schmolke-Hasselmann, 'The Round Table: Ideal, Fiction, Reality', *Arthurian Literature* 2 (1982), 41–75.

[101] Cf. Green, 'King Arthur: From History to Fiction'; and A. Putter, 'Finding Time for Romance: Medieval Arthurian Literary History', *Medium Ævum* 63.1 (1994), 1–16. On Wace's use of 'truth' and 'fable', see also M. Bruckner, *Shaping Romance: Interpretation, Truth, and Closure in Twelfth-Century French Fictions* (Philadelphia, 1993).

a history that is both someone else's and his own.[102] The regression to a savage muteness (a 'mutisme brutal')[103] that seizes Perceval on this occasion catches him between two poles of ambivalence. Is the father absent or present? Omnipotent or abject?

It has been twelve years since the Grail King left the closed concealment of his room.[104]

> Et il est si esperitax
> Qu'a sa vie plus ne covient
> Que l'oiste qui el graal vient.
> Doze anz a ja esté ensi,
> Que hors de la chanbre n'issi. (vv. 6392–6)

> (And he is so holy that nothing more sustains his life than the Host that comes in the Grail. Twelve years has he lived thus, without ever leaving the room.)

Nor, in all this time, has he nourished himself on fare heavier than a communion wafer. Who could survive on such a diet? Only the dead don't need to eat. The nature of this sustenance that the father's semblance offers to his own father is entirely spiritual.[105] He who takes the Eucharist nourishes himself from the body of the Son who is really the Father. When the communicant receives the wafer into his mouth, the body of the absent Father becomes present in his own. The oneiric Grail service enacts a liturgical drama about thanksgiving and remembrance between fathers and sons, one that pivots on the paradoxes of bodily presence and the transcendent symbol. The male bodies in this ritual are both ciphers and what is concealed, both the signifiers and the signified. Whom does the Grail serve? It serves the Fisher King's father. It is the *father* and not the dish on which Chrétien insists, and it is this essential nuance which suffices to resolve – not externally and factually, but internally and logically – the resemblance between Perceval's father and his avatar, and the symmetry between an irredeemable past and an uncertain future. Yet what would it mean for the Fisher King to be healed – would his wounds literally close and his body regrow its manhood?[106] If the Fisher King

---

[102]  I refer to the Widow Lady's insistent description of her son as a nursing infant at the time of the family's escape to the Welsh Waste Forest.

[103]  Baumgartner, *Le Conte du Graal*, p. 54.

[104]  The reader never learns how long it has been since Perceval's father succumbed to his grief. Calculations based on the Widow Lady's story combined with Perceval's implied age lead to the conclusion that it has also been twelve years since his death.

[105]  Cf. E. J. Burns, 'The Doubled-Question Test: Mystic Discourse in Chrétien's *Perceval*', *Romance Notes* 23.1 (1982), 57–64; and Maddox, *Once and Future Fictions*, pp. 111–13.

[106]  See, for example, 'The Strange Story of Thomas of Elderfield' whose testicles are

walks again and rules his lands, will Perceval be shoved back into the position of the infantilized child? The Grail service contains a complete realization of the fantasized and ambivalent relation to the father so powerfully evoked in Freud's reading of the Oedipus myth. *Do you kill the father or do you sustain him? And at what price?*[107]

Another reading unfolds from within this one. We have observed how the Anglo-Norman use of castration in a political context is tied to the imperatives of conquest. As we reflect on the role of gender in this legal history, we realize that in fact the *Conte du Graal* teems with allusions to sexual violence set against the backdrop of Arthur's own unfinished conquest. Inevitably, these reminders of rape harken back to the lawlessness of war and to a time of fear which has not yet receded into the past. Indeed, allusions to frontier rebellions, clan rivalries and a traffic in refugees are scattered throughout the romance. The hapless female victims whom Perceval and Gauvain each encounter on their quests show clearly enough that it is not safe to be out and about in the countryside. Gauvain's encounters near the *Bornes de Gauvoie*, the frontiers of Scottish Galloway, serve as a potent reminder of how central sexuality is to the romance's concern for justice and the rule of law. Greoreas seeks vengeance against Gauvain, who made him eat with the dogs for a month as punishment for having raped a girl (vv. 7077–91). The Proud Maid of Logres has lost every aspect of herself except for her anger. Traumatized by the murder of her beloved and then by the murderer Guiromelant's forced affections (vv. 8879–911), she bears the name of the country from which she was abducted – abducted during the very same wars through which Arthur secured his imperium.

> Trop est male et desdeigneuse,
> Et por ce a non l'Orguilleuse
> De Logres, ou ele fu nee,
> Si an fu petite aportee. (vv. 8589–92)

> (She is very wicked and full of scorn; that is why she is called the Proud Maid of Logres, where she was born and whence she was brought as a child.)

Perceval's defence of Blancheflor likewise inscribes itself in this fused logic of military and sexual conquest. Clamadeu des Illes (Clamadeu *of the Isles*) besieges the town with an army that grows daily (v. 1996);

---

miraculously restored by St Wulfstan. The Internet Medieval Source Book, http://www.fordham.edu/halsall/source/wulftrans.html, accessed 5 January 2012.

[107] Cf. C. Méla, '*La Lettre tue*: cryptographie du Graal', *Cahiers de civilisation médiévale Xe-XIIe siècles* 36.3 (1983), 209–21 (p. 217).

his seneschal Aguingeron refers to his lord's siege and past aggressions against Blancheflor's father and uncle as part of 'this war' ('An cest guerre li ocis', v. 2275).[108] Clamadeu seeks to possess both the maiden's lands and her body (vv. 2003–11; v. 2169), while Perceval's triumph over this attacker earns him the right to take possession of them himself (vv. 2083–6).[109] It can be stated without hesitation that the quest for a viable social order in the *Conte du Graal* pivots on the institutionalization or institutionalized prohibition of sexualized violence.[110]

This observation brings us once more into dialogue with myth. The misfortunes of Oedipus's family begin long before Oedipus sires children in his own mother's womb. They begin with another transgression, with Laius's abduction and rape of Chrysippus.[111] To the quest for knowledge, the transgressive libidinal dynamics of the family unit and the obsessing pursuit of origins, we add another layer to our understanding of this foundational narrative: the myth of Oedipus confronts the relations between sexual ethics and good governance.

Chrétien's romance presents Perceval with a long series of men to stare at, and in the mirror of whose example to contemplate his own reflection: the armoured, luminous knights of the opening scene; the withered father whom Perceval cannot remember; Gornement, who gives socially fastidious but spiritually uncertain lessons; Clamadeu des Illes, all battle fury and appetite; the Fisher King, waiting saint-like and passively at the edges of the world; and the forest hermit, avatar of a whole, but utterly chaste, father. Each of these encounters renews the dilemma first glimpsed when five knights entered the Waste Forest of the hero's childhood. 'What kind of man am I? What kind of man will I become?' Oedipus and his cursed line return to our consciousness: *Does each generation repeat the father's sins?* At its heart, Perceval's quest concerns the seemingly impossible

---

108    Like Perceval, Blancheflor appears to be one of the older, post-Uther war's orphans, now victim to a fresh cycle of violence.

109    Numerous other examples abound, but these incidents bring the *political* character of sexual violence to the fore.

110    See also Donald Maddox's judgement that the Tent Maiden and the Orgueilleuse 'together comprise a new and powerful critique of masculine aggression' (Maddox, *Once and Future Fictions*, p. 126). On sexual violence and Arthurian romance, cf. K. Gravdal, *Ravishing Maidens: Writing Rape in Medieval French Literature and Law* (Philadelphia, 1991). On the 'reconciliation of tensions necessary for the maintenance of a viable social order' (Sturm-Maddox, 'Lévi-Strauss in the Waste Forest', p. 94), see above.

111    Pelops, father of Chrysippus, adds further elements to the thematic coherence *mahaing* brings to the *Conte du Graal*. In the prologue to *Cligés*, Chrétien claims to have translated 'la morsure de l'épaule', that is, the tale of Pelops and the bite (the wound with a missing piece) which (like the Fisher King's) does not heal.

task of a mature and ethical masculinity, neither impotent nor ravaging, worthy of the kingdom to be inherited.

## Epilogue: Signifier/Signified, Redux

Lévi-Strauss's writings about Perceval placed the Grail tradition in the cross-hairs of contemporary intellectual debate. The *Conte du Graal* became a privileged site for medievalists' exploration of theory, but also one around or through which philosophers and critics from Jauss to Derrida articulated their own ideas about the ways that meaning is produced in the literary text. It is in this light that one of the more subtle consequences of Lévi-Strauss's inverted Oedipus theory throws off a long shadow.

Early in this essay, I remarked that the origins of the Grail dish long formed the object of Grail scholars' quest.[112] Chrétien's medieval inheritors transformed his strangely bright Grail 'trestot descovert' (v. 3267) into a cauldron of plenty, as in this passage from the *Quête du Saint Graal*.

> Adonc entra leenz li Sainz Graal covert d'un blanc samit. [...] Et maintenant qu'il i fu entrez fu li palés empliz de si bones odors come se totes les especes terrienes i fussent espandues. Et il ala par mi le palés d'un part et d'autre tot entor les dois. Et tout einsi com il trespassoit par devant les tables, estoient maintenant les tables raemplies endroit chascun siege de tel viande com chascuns chevaliers pensa.[113]
>
> (Then the Holy Grail entered where they were, covered by a white silk cloth. [...] And when it had entered the palace was filled with such delicious aromas as if every worldly spice had been spilled forth. And it went about the palace from one end to the other and all around the dais. And wherever it passed in front of the tables, the tables were immediately filled in front of each seat with whatever meats that knight was hungry for.)

The perfume of the Grail, for both the medieval characters who pursue it on horseback and for a century of philologists, tantalizes with the promise of fullness and satisfaction. The Grail's alimentary plenty enacts the transcendent transparency of the sign in material terms. The Grail dish,

---

[112] Already in 1891, philologist Moses Gaster could write of how, though 'many a scholar' had 'tried to solve the problem of its origin', 'in the history of mediaeval romances there is none so complicated' ('The Legend of the Grail', *Folklore* 2.1 [March 1891], 50–64 [p. 50]).

[113] *La Quête du Saint Graal*, ed. F. Bogdanow, trans. into modern French by A. Berrie (Paris, 2006), p. 112. My translation.

covered or revealed, becomes a symbol of the plenitude, satisfaction and wholeness of meaning itself.[114]

In another medieval response to the *Conte du Graal*, Wolfram von Eschenbach's *Parzifal*, Anfortas is afflicted by a gangrenous genital wound which will not close and cannot be healed.[115] Reactions to Lévi-Strauss's theory shifted scholarly attention away from the Grail dish and towards the Fisher King and his wasted kingdom. Previously scholars had asked, 'What is the origin and meaning of this Grail dish, this cauldron of plenty?' Now the question increasingly heard became, 'What is the origin and meaning of the lame King's affliction?'

In Chrétien's romance, the Grail ceremony brings together signifiers of fullness (the dish) and lack (the crippled man who presides, the absent father whom it serves). The shift in critical attention from Grail dish to Fisher King's body enacts a shift from a symbol of transcendent whole-ness to a metonymy of radical, absolute lack. The phallic presence of the Grail is displaced by the total vacuum of the castrated father. This shift in attention from the Grail to the Fisher King's body is not just a shift from metaphor to metonymy. It is a shift that neatly reprises the history of the twentieth century's philosophy of literature, a kind of *translatio imperii et studii* – a passage between two unreconciled views of literature and meaning themselves, from the promise of an answer, as it were, to the unassuaged malaise of a knowledge which is always and ever incomplete.

---

[114] Cf. Bloch, *Etymologies and Genealogies*, p. 210: 'In the achievement of the Grail Quest, Galahad transcends paternal and linguistic difference, penetrating – beyond language – to "that which can neither be thought nor said" ("ce que langue ne pourroit descrire ne cuer penser")'. One useful essay on medieval sign theory which considers the Grail, Lévi-Strauss and lineage is G. B. Ladner, 'Medieval and Modern Understanding of Symbolism: A Comparison', *Speculum* 54.2 (1979), 223–56. Cf. Miranda Griffin's psychoanalytic reading of Eucharist scenes in the Vulgate cycle, in *The Object and the Cause in the Vulgate Cycle* (London, 2005), pp. 140–50.

[115] See also A. Klosowska, *Queer Love in the Middle Ages* (New York, 2005), chapter 1: 'Grail Narratives: Castration as a Thematic Site', especially pp. 30–2.

## II

## MALORY'S THIGHS AND LAUNCELOT'S BUTTOCK: IGNOBLE WOUNDS AND MORAL TRANSGRESSION IN THE *MORTE DARTHUR*

### Karen Cherewatuk

The most familiar wound in medieval romance is not literal but metaphor-ical: the wound of love. The conceit imagines the heroine (consciously or not) penetrating the knight's heart – either through her image or gaze – and inflicting a wound that only she can heal. Romance writers such as Chrétien and Guillaume de Lorris adopted the metaphor from the trouba-dours.[1] By the time Chaucer's Troilus passes Criseyde in the temple and is 'Right with hire loke thorough-shoten',[2] the entire audience would be familiar enough with the motif to wonder whether the lady would serve as the knight's physician or agent of death. In contrast to Chaucer, Malory shows little interest in the lover's malady.[3] Rather, it is physical injury – cuts, slashes, stabs and punctures – that Malory reports, usually under the single noun 'wound'.

Malory treats these injuries realistically. Wounds are staunched to stop the flow of blood, searched, cleansed – on one occasion with 'whyghte wyne' to prevent infection (234.18–19) – and 'salved'.[4] 'Rest' or 'repose'

---

[1] Chrétien de Troyes, *Lancelot, ou le chevalier de la charette*, ed. J. C. Aubilly (Paris, 1991), ll. 1335–42; Guillaume de Lorris and Jean de Meun, *Le Roman de la Rose*, ed. F. Lecoy, 3 vols. (Paris, 1965), I, ll. 1679–1718.

[2] Geoffrey Chaucer, 'Troilus and Criseyde', in *The Riverside Chaucer*, ed. L. B. Benson, 3rd edn (Oxford, 2008), I: 325. I cite the *Morte Darthur* from E. Vinaver, ed., *The Works of Sir Thomas Malory*, 3rd edn, rev. P. J. C. Field, 3 vols. (Oxford, 1990).

[3] In *Vision and Gender in Malory's Morte Darthur* (Cambridge, 2010), M. Martin analy-ses vision and its intersection with courtly love and gender construction, but she never discusses the metaphorical wound of love nor have I located it anywhere in Malory's text.

[4] 'Staunched' (260.13 and 21, 326.4, 334.18, 336.4, 1076.12, 1086.28, 1132.1) or 'stanch' (230.23); 'serched' (148.24–5, 279.26, 383.12–13, 385.3–4, 626.12, 642.4, 1145, 20, 1145.20, 1146.13, 1150.33, 1152.30 and 32) or 'serche' (40.12, 384.25, 1149.01, 1152.06); 'ransacked' (885.28, 1152.27); and 'salved' (1218.10, 1232.28)

is required so that the injured man may be made 'hole' or 'healed', his injury 'well eased' or 'well amended'.[5] Yet wounds in the *Morte Darthur* can bear more than literal meaning. Chivalry demands martial display and, as Andrew Lynch claims in his seminal study, blood is 'the basic currency of fights and quests'; its display literalizes noble status.[6] Thus blood that flows from male-on-male violence and the resulting wounds prove a knight's worth, sometimes even when he loses the battle, as for La Cote Male Tayle (473.15–32). Injuries can represent a knight's honour and function, in Laurie Finke and Martin Shichtman's witty phrase, as 'symbolic capital'.[7] Arguing against a tendency of gender critics to assess all wounds as feminizing, Kenneth Hodges analyses the positive role wounds play in educating knights and creating community, stating that 'the injuries sustained give weight and worth to the abstract issues being fought about'.[8] Through wounds and their trace in scars, Malory writes upon a knight's body the honour he has gained in battle.

Intriguing to me, however, are the wounds that mark not honour but dishonour, and the ways they are interpreted by the injured knight within the tale and the audience outside it. By 'audience', I refer to the medieval audience that Malory inscribes within his tales. Malory sometimes signals this group, his social context for reception, in 'we-' phrases – including himself among 'men of worship' or the gentry, the class from which he came (e.g. 375.23–9, 484.18–22). Because aural tags within the *Morte Darthur* indicate that Malory anticipated that his audience would hear the tale read (e.g. 375.16) rather than read it silently, I prefer the term 'audience' to 'reader' as I turn to three scenes of wounding:[9] Percivale's

---

or had salves – 'salff', 'salve' or 'salvys' – applied (52.6–7, 234.4, 462.13, 1193.2, 1194.4, 1232.29). These treatments often appear in sequence, as steps in a process: 'The ermyte serched the kynges woundis and gaff hym good salves' (52.6–7); Lyonett 'unarmed' Bewmaynes 'and searched his woundis and staunched the blood' (326.4–5); Guenevere has her knights 'searched, and softe salves were layde to their woundis' (1130.19–20). In *Malory's Book of Arms: The Narrative of Combat in* Le Morte Darthur (Cambridge, 1997), A. Lynch refers to Malory's 'practical acquaintance with wounds' and cites Trevisa's *On the Properties of Things* for the idea that 'Wine is used to wash wounds and drunk to counteract blood-loss' (p. 74 n. 48). Lynch cites Malory's use of wine to heal wounds at 234.18–21, 473.29–32 and 1076.9–13.

5   'Wound' occurs with 'rest' or 'repose' at 475.27–8, 619.20–1, 475.27–8 and 619.20–1; with 'hole' at 393.2–3; with 'healed' at 10.31 and 1152.1; with 'eased' or 'amended' at 162.14–15 and 52.4–9.

6   Lynch, *Malory's Book of Arms*, pp. 60, 62.

7   L. Finke and M. Shichtman argue that violence undergirds 'a hegemonic masculinity based on martial prowess' in 'No Pain, No Gain: Violence as Symbolic Capital in Malory's *Morte d'Arthur*', *Arthuriana* 8 (1998), 115–34 (p. 118).

8   K. Hodges, 'Wounded Masculinity: Injury and Gender in Sir Thomas Malory's *Le Morte Darthur*', *Studies in Philology* 106 (2009), 14–31 (p. 16).

9   For a fuller description of the social context of Malory's medieval audiences, see

self-wounding in the thigh, Gareth's injury to the thigh and Launcelot's wound in the buttock.

In each of the scenes of ignoble injury, the knight receives the wound not in public combat but in private encounter, and not from a male opponent but from a woman or her agent. Percivale stabs himself in the thigh after an encounter with a she-devil, and Gareth receives a similar puncture wound from an automaton-like knight controlled by Lady Lyonett. In contrast, Launcelot endures a wound to the buttock from the arrow of a female huntress. While the scene of Percivale's wounding derives from a French source, Gareth's and Launcelot's injuries show Malory either radically altering sources or producing original scenes, and thereby creating narrative continuity via the same romance motif or meme.[10] Through specific verbal echoes, these sexualized wounds become 'texts' that comment on each other.[11] Ignoble injury thus occupies a middle ground between the symbolic and the real, functioning symbolically yet requiring real treatment. Most interestingly, the wounds require the knights within the tale and the audience outside it to 'read' or interpret their moral meaning from the plot. The thigh wounds of Percivale and Gareth suggest the threat of castration as punishment for lost virginity, while Launcelot's buttock wound reflects a similar threat of emasculation as well as a feminized objectification of the hero. Launcelot's ignoble injury further points – possibly through adaptation of the myth of Diana and Actaeon – to the way in which the greatest hero both wounds and is wounded though his sexuality. Whether influenced by Ovidian myth or not, the huntress episode illustrates how Malory engages his audience in the dynamic of reading morality from context.

K. Cherewatuk, *Marriage, Adultery and Inheritance in Malory's* Morte Darthur (Cambridge, 2006), pp. xii–xvi; J. Coleman, 'Reading Malory in the Fifteenth Century: Aural Reception and Performance Dynamics', *Arthuriana* 13 (2004), 48–70; and the other essays in *Arthuriana* 13, a special edition on 'Reading Malory Aloud, Then and Now'. In using the term 'audience', I do not pretend that there was a single, ideal audience for reception. Rather, I use the singular to refer to a single possible interpretation resulting from hearing or silent reading, the plural to multiple interpretations or 'readings'.

[10] According to H. Cooper, *The English Romance in Time* (Oxford, 2004), p. 3, 'meme' in this sense means 'a romance motif ... that proves so useful, so infectious, that it begins to take on a life of its own' and is able 'to replicate faithfully and abundantly, but also on occasion to adapt, mutate and therefore survive'. In this essay I argue that Malory has consciously replicated the ignoble wound.

[11] I borrow the phrasing of M. Leitch in her study of Malory's bloody bedsheets, '(Dis) figuring Transgressive Desire: Blood, Sex, and Stained Sheets in Malory's *Morte Darthur*', *Arthurian Literature* 28 (2011), 21–38 (p. 33).

## Percivale's Wound to the Thigh

The most clearly symbolic of the three ignoble wounds, Percivale's, harkens back to didactic religious texts. Malory's source for the scene, *La Queste del Saint Graal*, explicitly delineates the values of earthly versus heavenly chivalry (*chevalerie terrienne* vs. *chevalerie celestial*). Malory softens that distinction, yet his 'Sankgreal' presents a semi-allegorical landscape that requires ethical conduct. While other tales focus on the honour gained through external action, the Grail adventures require sinlessness and sexual purity. As noted by Robert L. Kelly, knights who possess moral self-awareness avoid sin and wounding, but those who have not made the turn towards interiority and act on the values of externalized chivalry are injured.[12] Thus, celestial Galahad remains impenetrable, the earthly Gawain is wounded and Launcelot lies in a coma, suggesting his middle moral state. For Percivale, the self-inflicted wound in the thigh indicates both his sin and its correction; for Malory's audience, it affirms their ability to read temptation from a context that recalls the penitential tradition.

In the scene a woman, later revealed as the 'mayster fyende of helle' (920.4), joins Percivale in the wasteland. Although she arrives on a ship covered in black silk, 'saylyng in the see as all the wynde of the worlde had dryven hit', Percivale sees only 'a jantillwoman of grete beauté' (915.32–3, 916.1). He interprets their conversation literally, missing all hints at demonic identity: her knowledge of his name (916.10), the thinly disguised tale of her disinheritance by the 'grettist man' and her appeal for aid to Percivale's sense of chivalric honour (917.11–30). She serves a marvellous meal and the strong wine makes him 'chaffett' – heated – 'a lityll more than he oughte to be' (918.8–10). The fiend-lady resists Percivale's offer of love 'for cause he sholde be the more ardente on hir' (918.9–10, 16). Only after he is 'well enchaffed' and has promised his allegiance does she finally consent, laying down 'unclothed' and Percivale 'by her naked' (918.16–25, 27, 29). Malory's scene of temptation unfolds

---

[12] In 'Wounds, Healing and Knighthood in Malory's Tale of Launcelot and Guenevere', in *Studies in Malory*, ed. J. Spisak (Kalamazoo, 1985), pp. 173–98, R. Kelly writes, 'In Malory's Sankgreal, humility and healing are repeatedly associated with true knighthood, and pride and wounding (or being wounded) with false knighthood' (p. 179). In 'Warfare and Combat in *Le Morte Darthur*', in *Writing War: Medieval Literary Responses to Warfare*, ed. C. Saunders, F. Le Saux and N. Thomas (Cambridge, 2004), pp. 169–86, K. S. Whetter offers the caveat that the association of injury and sin holds only partially, even in the Grail quest (p. 170). Hodges comments that 'the Grail quest transforms the lessons of wounds from practical to spiritual' and that 'injuries are used to punish sin but also to point the way to moral restoration' ('Wounded Masculinity', p. 21).

at a quicker pace than that of the French source, with fewer words of narrative and dialogue. In the *Queste* the fiend asks, 'Le me creantez vos ... come loiaux chevaliers?' and Percivale answers, 'Oil' ('Do you promise this as a loyal knight?' 'Yes'.)[13] In the only place where Malory expands rather than contracts the source, Percivale answers, 'Yee, ... fayre lady, by the *feythe* of my *body*' (918.22, emphasis mine). Percivale is stopped from copulating with a devil only when he spies the 'rede crosse' on his pommel and reflexively blesses himself (918.29–31). Tension erupts: the pavilion turns upside-down, dissolving in a cloud of black smoke, and the fiend 'wente with the wynde, rorynge and yellynge', the water burning behind her. As the audience had realized from the start but the knight had not, in this encounter faith and the body are the issues at risk.

In dramatic reproof, Percivale punishes the 'fleyssh' that would be his 'mayster' and 'rooff hymselff thorow the thygh' so that that his blood ran or 'sterte' (918.33–919.10, 11–12, 14–15). Connecting his illicit desire to the need for self-mastery, Percivale wounds himself in a stroke of symbolic castration. The site of his self-inflicted injury recalls the Hebrew tradition in which the thigh functions as a euphemism for male genitalia.[14] In Christian scripture castration serves as an ideal of high calling: 'For there are eunuchs, who were born so from their mother's womb: and there are eunuchs, who were made so by men: and there are eunuchs, who have made themselves eunuchs for the kingdom of heaven. He that can take, let him take it' (Matthew 19. 12). Analysing the influence of the Christian ideal of spiritual castration on the French Grail legend, Jed Chandler observes that the men of the Grail family are marked by their wounds and literal or figurative castration – among them the Grail King, the Fisher King and King Mordrain.[15] Their state as figurative eunuchs aligns them with the female custodians of the Grail and explains the virgin effeminacy of the hero Galahad. According to Chandler, the Grail quester achieves union with God rather than the lady of romance. For Malory's Percivale, the sword emasculates him through symbolic castration and effeminizes him through penetration – the flow of blood warning against the breaking of chastity.[16] 'Penetrator

---

[13] *La Queste del Saint Graal*, ed. A. Pauphilet (Paris, 1967), 109.25–6. I cite the English translation from *Lancelot-Grail: The Old French Arthurian Vulgate and Post-Vulgate in Translation*, ed. N. J. Lacy, 5 vols. (New York and London, 1993), IV. 36, sect. 31. Henceforth I cite this edition by volume, section and paragraph numbers.

[14] See, for example, Genesis 24. 2, 24. 9, 47. 29, all passages concerned with procreation, purity of the bloodline and trust. Throughout this essay, I cite the Douay-Rheims translation of the Bible.

[15] J. Chandler, 'Eunuchs of the Grail', in *Castration and Culture in the Middle Ages*, ed. L. Tracy (Cambridge, 2013), pp. 229–54 (pp. 238–40, 233, 230).

[16] Chandler, 'Eunuchs', p. 244.

and penetrated', Percivale becomes both and neither male nor female, as does the fiend whose gender changes grammatically with the revelation that 'that jantillwoman' was the 'mayster fiend of helle' (920.4 and 9). According to Kathleen Coyne Kelly the scene represents 'a well-known and well-documented misogynist intertext in which female desire is demonized – here literally'.[17]

Percivale's ignoble wound both reveals and corrects his moral deficiency. In committing the sex act mentally rather than physically, Percivale flirts with a 'sin of intent'. According to St Thomas Aquinas, this type of sin 'includes the deliberate intention to realize or gratify the desire' and 'has the same malice' as the intended action.[18] When the fiend disappears in a puff of smoke, Percivale grasps his sinful intention. He prays, 'Fayre swete Lorde Jesu Cryste, ne lette me nat be shamed'. However, he manifests this humiliation physically when the good man, his spiritual counsellor, arrives and Percivale, 'sore ashamed', swoons (919.10 and 26). The details of Percivale's pierced thigh, flowing blood and swoon coalesce to suggest to the audience the deposition of the cross, aligning the knight with both the suffering Christ and his mother swooning at the foot of the cross. In a very literal way, then, when Percivale wounds himself, he follows the precept of Paul 'to be made conformable to the image of His Son' (Romans 8. 29). Percivale's prayer voices new spiritual understanding: 'take thys in recompensacion of that I have myssedone ayenste The, Lorde!' (919.16–17). Outside 'The Sankgreal', Malory's knights experience shame as lost honour. Within the holy adventure, however, 'shame' expresses grief and guilt, emotions that medieval audiences probably associated with compunction: piercing pain at the recognition of one's own sin and acceptance of responsibility. This is a stage through which every penitent must pass.[19] Physical satisfaction, such as Percivale's thigh wound, allows the sinner to achieve conformity with the suffering human Christ, whose 'woundis wyde' – according to Malory's reformed Guenevere – offer healing and salvation (1252.14).

By wounding himself and miming castration, Percivale arrives at the interpretative strategy which the audience outside the tale had already brought to their interpretation of this most Christian of Malory's tales. As when reading Scripture or a penitential text, the audience relies on

---

[17] K. C. Kelly, 'Menaced Masculinity and Imperiled Virginity in Malory's *Morte Darthur*', in *Menacing Virgins: Representing Virginity in the Middle Ages and Renaissance*, ed. K. C. Kelly and M. Leslie (Newark, DE, 1999), pp. 97–114 (p. 102).

[18] *The Summa Theologica of St. Thomas Aquinas*, trans. Fathers of the English Dominican Province, 2nd edn (Westminster, 1920), Ia IIae Q12; http://www.newadvent.org/summa/.

[19] I have illustrated Malory's use of the stages of Penance in 'Malory's Launcelot and the Language of Sin and Confession', *Arthuriana* 16 (2006), 68–72.

authorities to supply assumptions that undergird interpretation. Percivale voices one of those assumptions when he recognizes that if he had lost his virginity, he could never recover (919.20–1). The 'good man' who comes to Percivale and instructs him to 'beware and take this for an insample' represents religious authority (920.12). He affirms the audience's and the knight's reading of the episode. Thus Percivale's self-wounding teaches an almost sacramental lesson in repentance. The ignoble wound allows the knight to catch up to the audience's level of understanding, after which he stops the flow of blood with a piece of his shirt (919.22–3), the narrative returns to the literal level and Percivale – now a careful reader of the scene in which he finds himself – gets on with the spiritual adventure.

## Gareth's Bleeding Thigh

The images from Percivale's wounding – the pierced thigh, the flowing blood and the swoon – appear together earlier in the arc of the narrative in 'The Tale of Sir Gareth'. Rather than religious, however, the context of 'Sir Gareth' is social and comic, ending with the knight winning his lady and with marriage, as in Shakespearean festive comedy. Since the tale lacks a known source and may be Malory's invention, it is striking that the motif of ignoble injury is doubled. In a first scene Gareth suffers penetration by sword while attempting to have intercourse, and in a repeated scene the wound reopens. As in 'The Sankgreal', the thigh wound represents castration and lost virginity, but Malory removes the penitential sting even as the injury offers correction to a knight who, like Percivale, strays beyond the bounds of licit sex. Because this straying occurs between Sir Gareth and Lady Lyonesse's pledging of trouth (or engagement) and their wedding (332.35 and 333.9), the ignoble wound preserves custom and ensures social stability by leading the couple into marriage. The audience outside the tale interprets the wound as a none-too-subtle warning against pre-marital sex.[20] It takes the hero within the tale repeated injury and interpretation to come to an understanding of the social ramifications of illicit relations.

In this 'Fair Unknown romance', the young lovers Gareth and Lyonesse reach an understanding. Separately he has proven his prowess

---

[20] Much of my argument derives from two earlier pieces: 'Pledging Trouth in Malory's "Tale of Sir Gareth"', *Journal of English and Germanic Philology* 101 (2002), 19–40; and *Marriage, Adultery, and Inheritance*, pp. 1–23. C. Francis develops similar observations in 'Reading Malory's Bloody Bedrooms', *Arthurian Literature* 28 (2011), 1–19 (pp. 5–6).

by freeing her from the Red Knight and she has determined his social status and suitability as a husband. Together they decide 'to abate their lustys secretly' (332.37–333.1).[21] Through 'subtyle craufftes' Lyonesse's sister, Lyonett, forces the couple to delay the 'delytes untyll they were maryed' (333.11–13). Lyonett's magical craft involves the prophylactic injury to the thigh that twice halts consummation. In the first scene the attacking knight, serving at Lyonett's behest, strikes Gareth 'with a foyne thorow the thycke of the thygh, that the wounde was a shafftemonde brode' (333.31–3). Gareth decapitates his attacker, but as a result of this penetrating 'foyne' (a thrust), Gareth 'bled so fast that he might not stond, but so leyde hym downe upon his bedde' and 'sowned and lay as he had bene dede' (334.1–3). As with Percivale, the sword emasculates Gareth through symbolic castration and effeminizes him through penetration. Gareth loses so much blood that he collapses on the bed, presumably staining the linen. In the romance tradition, from Béroul's *Tristan* to Malory's 'Knight of the Cart', the bloodied bed indicates illicit sex, read in blood drops on a floured floor or soiled sheets.[22] It is this meme that Malory invokes when Mellyagaunce discovers Guenevere in bed and charges her with committing adultery with one of the wounded knights (1131.26–1132.22). An audience versed in the romance tradition accordingly interprets the scene in 'Sir Gareth' as rife with sexual connotations: the bloodied bed, the attacker's missing head and Gareth's pierced thigh threaten castration to a knight whose intentions push the boundaries of socially acceptable behaviour. As Christina Francis observes, in the *Morte Darthur* 'it is generally the male body, and not the female body, that registers the illicit nature of the encounter'.[23] Thus Gareth's wound warns against penetrating the virgin's hymen and the resulting flow of blood. Like Percivale, Gareth takes on the qualities of both female and male, penetrated and would-be penetrator.

The immediate purpose of Gareth's thigh wound, then, is to prevent consummation. Its ultimate purpose, however, is social: to restore the hero's honour after ignoble injury. Kenneth Hodges has argued that wounds imposed upon a knight rather than willingly hazarded on the field bring shame.[24] Gareth fought on the field in the first half of the romance, to establish an identity which had been hidden under the sobriquet

---

[21] Right before the attempted consummation, Lyonett has her brother Sir Gryngamour kidnap Gareth's dwarf and learns from him her lover's 'noble house', name and kin (331.36–332.2 and 332.30–2).

[22] Cherewatuk, *Marriage, Adultery, and Inheritance*, pp. 15–16; Francis, 'Reading Malory's Bloody Bedrooms', pp. 5, 8, 10–12; Leitch, '(Dis)-Figuring Transgressive Desire', pp. 21–30, 35–6.

[23] Francis, 'Reading Malory's Bloody Bedrooms', p. 5.

[24] Hodges, 'Wounded Masculinity', p. 27.

'Beawmaynes'. In the midst of proving his prowess, Gareth also demonstrates his moral worth when he refuses to sleep with the nameless virgin
daughter of a vanquished opponent. Gareth explains to the girl, 'God
deffende me ... that ever I sholde defoyle you to do sir Persaunte such a
shame!' Upon learning of Gareth's reaction, her father exclaims 'Truly ...
whatsomever he be he is com of full noble bloode' (315.9–10, 19–20).
For Sir Persaunte, Gareth's sexual restraint and social decorum mark
him as a nobleman. Gareth nearly loses his moral standing, however,
when he gives in to his private passion and attempts to sleep with an
all-too-willing Lyonesse. Her sister Lyonett explains to Gareth that she
acted out of concern 'for your worshyp and [that of] us all' (334.33–4).
'Us all' includes Lyonesse, whose status as a woman worthy of marriage
would be diminished, as would her family's position, should she yield too
lightly her virginity. Class issues elide with conservative sexual values,
for Gareth ranks higher than Lyonesse. In fact, he is not simply noble
but royal, and her family closes around the impetuous couple to ensure
that Gareth takes her as wife rather than mistress.[25] To rein in the hot and
hasty lovers – to preserve Lyonesse for a marriage from which can issue
legitimate offspring, to ensure that Gareth remains a nobleman in the full
sense of the term – the attacking knight penetrates Gareth's thigh and
interrupts the tryst. In Malory's most happy tale, however, fear of social
dishonour and physical danger are muted. The couple's private meeting
opens up to additional actors: the sister, the brother and the attacker who
illuminates the bedroom scene 'with many lyghtes aboute hym' (33.25).
That knight loses his head, but not Lyonesse her maidenhead nor Gareth
his genitals. After the threats of deflowering and castration, the audience
enjoys the comic relief of the attacker's head being reattached 'in sight
of them all' (334.21).

Although the would-be lovers flout conventions of courtship, these
are not nearly as fixed in this romance context as are religious morals in
'The Sankgreal'. No spiritual authority, no 'good man', enters to explain
the episode. Rather, the narrator prefaces the encounter by noting that
Gareth and Lyonesse 'were but yonge bothe and tendir of ayge' and 'a
lytyll overhasty' (333.5, 8). The narrator leads the audience – inscribed
as wiser and more experienced than the lovers – to nostalgic empathy. In
contrast, Sir Gryngamour shows less concern for his sister's chastity than
for the assault that a royal guest suffers in his hall – 'that this noble knight
[Gareth] is thus dishonoured' (334.7). Grynagamour's attitude might res-
onate with those who have to maintain good relations or rely on the
patronage of social superiors. For her part, Lyonesse is eager to engage in

---

[25] Cherewatuk, *Marriage, Adultery, and Inheritance*, pp. 8–14.

relations with 'her lord', referring to Gareth by a title that a wife uses with her husband and perhaps suggesting that their troth-plighting constitutes a private marriage.[26] Lyonesse's frank admission of female desire might prove refreshing to both men and women in Malory's audience. Lyonett, however, is so concerned about her sister's integrity and public 'worship' that she directs the attack on Gareth, an act that preserves the status quo and accords with moral and social conservatism. The characters within the tale – the narrator, Gryngamour, Lyonesse and Lyonett – offer variant readings of the events surrounding Gareth's wounding. Their various views grant freedom to the audience for multiple interpretations.

However varied the audience members' reactions, they read in the wound a warning that the hero within the tale chooses to ignore. He instead attempts a second tryst. The same pattern unfolds, with heightened comedy. Gareth does everything necessary to protect Lyonesse, except avoid sex. He takes his armour to bed and, when attacked, continues to fight even after 'the olde wounde brast ayen on-bledynge'. In fact, Gareth 'was so hote and corragyous' that he 'toke no kepe' of his loss of blood (335.5–6, 15–16). The hero strikes down the attacker, decapitates him and 'hew the hede upon an hondred pecis', tossing the 'gobbettis of the hede' out of the window into the castle moat. This done, Gareth can hardly ('unnethis') stand 'for bledynge' and falls down in a swoon (335.19–24, 32). The reopening of Gareth's thigh illustrates two senses of blood, literally as the liquid life force and metaphorically as bloodline or kin. According to the then-prevailing Galenic view of medicine, sperm was a rarefied form of blood, heated by the male's heart; excess desire would lead to a display or discharge of blood. Thus Andrew Lynch interprets this episode as a letting of Gareth's 'hot blood, saving his energies for the field and for procreation of legitimate offspring'.[27] The second time around, Gareth learns to read castration in his ignoble wound: the injury warns against casual sex by rendering the hero temporarily impotent; it thus saves his blood for marriage and the legitimate continuity of his line.

In this double-tiered version of a Fair Unknown romance, the hero's success in the opening adventures leads to the two unsuccessful trysts and the ignoble wound to the thigh. These bedchamber scenes cast momentary doubt on the hero. Gareth, the characters within the tale and the audience outside it may interpret the attack and the thigh wound in different ways,

---

[26] Cherewatuk, *Marriage, Adultery, and Inheritance*, p. 16.

[27] Lynch, *Malory's Book of Arms*, pp. 66–7; Cherewatuk, *Marriage, Adultery, and Inheritance*, p. 17, both citing D. Jacquart and C. Thomasset, *Sexuality and Medicine in the Middle Ages*, trans. M. Adamson (Princeton, NJ, 1988), pp. 52–60. Similarly Francis, 'Reading Malory's Bloody Bedrooms', pp. 3–4.

on a spectrum ranging from deadly serious and potentially emasculating, to expedient, humorous or even hilarious. After the second attack, Lyonett reprises her earlier role as healer and repairs the attacker's head, reminding Gareth of 'your worshyp' and that of 'us all'. Doctors or 'lechis' then attempt to staunch 'his bledynge', warning Gareth that 'no man that bare the lyff sholde heale hym thorowly of his wounde' but the one who 'caused the stroke by enchauntemente' (336.3 and 5–6). Presumably this is Lyonett, but in a larger sense Gareth himself possesses the ability to overcome his ignoble injury. Returning from the symbolic to the literal level of action, he wins honour in a staged public display, a tournament, and with it the hand of his bride. The hero and the audience ultimately arrive at the same moral: that desire subordinated to social mores leads to social stability for 'us all'. In 'The Sankgreal', religious morals and Christian mysticism are joined in Percivale's wound to illustrate a penitential teaching. In 'Sir Gareth' the symbolic, magical and scientific elide to reinforce social, rather than religious, concerns. The site of the wound is the same for the two heroes, but the context of the thigh injury leads Percivale and his audience to an inner, spiritual lesson, and Gareth to a public, social moral.

## Launcelot's Buttock and Echoing Wounds

The question of social and even gender stability is marked by the third wound, the injury Launcelot endures in his buttock. Oddly but descriptively, Malory uses that noun in the singular.[28] This injury comes when a 'huntresse' misses her intended prey – a barren hind – but hits Launcelot who rests at a 'welle', that is, a spring or fountain with running water (1104.4 and 17).[29] All three of Malory's knights render themselves vulnerable by acting heedlessly in their encounters with women. Yet compared to Percivale who was tipsy during his tryst with the fiend and Gareth who was otherwise occupied with his lady, Launcelot is injured when his guard is most down – that is, he is sound asleep, outdoors, in open space. At this moment Launcelot seems innocent of sexual entanglement, yet he is the only one of the three knights wounded directly by a woman rather than through an encounter with one. Launcelot's wound 'in the thycke

---

[28] In Middle English as in modern, the plural 'buttocks' is used far more commonly in reference to human anatomy, although the singular does appear (*MED*, 'buttok' n., 1a). The singular 'buttok' appears most familiarly with Nicholas in Chaucer's 'Miller's Tale': 'And out his ers he putteth pryvely, / Over the buttok, to the haunche-bon' (I.3802–3).

[29] A 'welle' can mean either a natural water source, such as a spring, pool or stream, or 'a man-made fountain or conduit' (*MED*, 'wel(l)e' n., 1. a and 1. b.)

of the buttok' recalls Percivale's injury 'thorow the thigh' as emasculating punishment; more specifically, through verbal repetition it suggests Gareth's wound 'thorow the thycke of the thigh' as a warning against violating social mores. Yet how do the hero within the tale and the audience outside it read a wound in such a humiliating place, the buttock?

There are two recognized analogues for this scene in the Vulgate cycle – one from *La Mort Artu* and the other from the Prose *Lancelot*. Neither of them is particularly close to Malory's version of events, and in both French texts the knight is penetrated in the usual place, *la cuisse* (the thigh).[30] In contrast, an injury in the buttock is unusual and troubling: Launcelot is penetrated in a sexual manner, and not by a man but by a woman whose sex Malory emphasizes in doubled phrases, such as this 'lady, the huntresse'. She effectively unhorses Launcelot with her arrow, for he may 'nat sytte in no sadyll' (1104.11, 1105.14–1106.3). After unspecified treatment (1106.10), Launcelot smites fifty of Arthur's men at the Great Tournament and afterwards describes the wounding to the king and queen. Hence, two narratives of the wound are offered and these frame the tournament: the narrator's diegetic narration and Launcelot's own retelling. Through diction and detail the two accounts of Launcelot's wound echo back, recalling past injuries, and project forward, associating the hero with future events. The sheer number of echoic references opens the audience to multiple interpretations of Launcelot's buttock wound. Yet this most graphic of Malory's three ignoble injuries, and the one twice told, the hero refuses to read.

While Percivale's injury has religious associations and Gareth's resonates with the romance tradition as well as marriage customs, the strikingly specific details of Launcelot's wound suggest previous episodes within the *Morte Darthur*. This would especially be the case for audiences who knew the text through repeated hearings or readings. According to the narrator, the lady's 'arow smote sir Launcelot in the thycke of the buttok over the barbys' (1104.28–9). To follow one chain of associations,

---

[30] Vinaver suggests episodes from *La Mort Le Roi Artu* and the Prose *Lancelot* as possible sources (p. 1591 and n. 1145). In *La Mort Artu*, ed. J. Frappier (Geneva, 1954), 64.27–52, a sleeping Launcelot is struck in the thigh by an archer from Arthur's household who had aimed at a deer. In the Prose *Lancelot*, ed. A. Micha (Geneva, 1980), V, 88.6 and L-G III.226, not Lancelot but another knight is hit in the thigh. He explains his injury as follows: chasing a knight he had wounded, the knight spies two women bathing in a spring, one of whom wounds him in the thigh to protect the injured knight. Now the knight narrating can only be healed by the best knight in the world, that is Lancelot. In 'Malory's Lancelot and the Lady Huntress', in *On Arthurian Women*, ed. F. Tolhurst and B. Wheeler (Dallas, 2001), pp. 245–57, M. McInerney carefully works through the differences in plot between the two possible analogues and shows how the implications of these injuries differ from the wound to the buttock (pp. 246–7).

the lady's arrow recalls the tusk of a boar that had hurt Launcelot in his state of madness: 'The bore rove hym on the brawne of the thyghe up unto the howghe-boone' (821.18–19).[31] In terms of syntactic categories, the sentences use parallel phrasing: noun–verb–direct object [i.e. Launcelot/hym]; prepositional phrase; prepositional phrase; prepositional phrase; prepositional phrase. Beyond the rhythm of the sentences, the players and place of the two scenes overlap. For the boar's wound, a hermit had treated Launcelot, but the deranged knight fled his care. Launcelot arrives at Castle Corbyn, falls asleep by 'a welle', is discovered by Elaine and restored to sanity by the Grail (822.13–15; 823.15–16; 824.20–7). Launcelot's healing had been necessitated by both the physical wound caused by the boar and the earlier psychological injury caused by Guenevere. She had competed for Launcelot with the same Elaine who rescues him at the well. The huntress's arrow brings to mind this earlier episode, mostly by way of contrasts. Rather than Launcelot being discovered by the woman at the well and then healed, it is there that he suffers the huntress's arrow. And rather than bearing both physical and psychological wounds, Launcelot suffers only in his fleshly bottom. It is he who had earlier caused psychological damage – namely to Elaine of Ascolat who, like her namesake, Elaine of Corbyn,[32] had vied with Guenevere and failed in the competition for the hero. The women involved in the two episodes are doubling for each other. Furthermore, to describe the injury of the boar, the thigh wound that anticipates the buttock wound, Malory chose the verb 'rove', meaning 'pierce'.[33] Diction cues an attentive audience to notice the parallels and to move from literal to symbolic interpretation: to realize that in his relationships with women – past and present – Launcelot is both wounded and wounding.

The huntress's injury is not only deep, it is also described by measurement. When the hero narrates how he was shot 'in the buttok wyth a brode arrow, and how the wounde was at that tyme six inchys depe and inlyke longe' (1114.4–7), his description echoes Gareth's 'foyne thorow the thycke of the thigh' that measured 'a shafftemonde brode' (333.31–2). Since 'a shafftemonde brode' means six inches wide,[34] an audience familiar with wounds and scarring would associate Launcelot's injury in the buttock with Gareth's in the thigh. Gareth's scene of wounding

---

[31] According to the *MED*, 'hough' could refer to the '?haunch, ?groin, or ?hipbone', at any rate a sensitive and sexualized part of the human body.

[32] For parallels between the two Elaines, see Cherewatuk, *Marriage, Adultery, and Inheritance*, pp. 56–74.

[33] *MED*, 'rouen' v. 4. B.

[34] *MED*, 'shaftmonde' n. 'A measure of length based upon the distance from the end of the extended thumb across the width of the palm, equivalent to about six inches.'

thus becomes the backstory for Launcelot's, instructing again by contrasts. In the earlier episode, Gareth had sustained his injury after his near violation of Lyonesse's chastity; in the present, Launcelot receives his wound after his refusal to violate Elaine of Astolat's virginity. In fact, after recovering from a wound received at the Assumption Day tournament, Launcelot departs Ascolat not with Elaine as wife or 'paramour' (1090.4) but with her brother as companion. Lavayne's passion equals his sister's, as he explains: 'but she doth as I do, for sythen I saw first my lorde sir Launcelot I cowde never departe frome hym, nother nought I woll, and I may follow hym' (1091.11–14). On her deathbed Elaine describes such devotion as 'oute of mesure' (1094.1), herself echoing Launcelot's confession of his passion for 'a queen unmesurabely and oute of mesure longe' (897.16). Yet another detail of that Assumption Day tournament involves Lavayne digging out of Launcelot's side the spearhead left by Bors who had not recognized his disguised kinsman (1072.4–5, 1074.1–14).[35] Fearing Launcelot's imminent death, Lavayne brings the hero to a hermit for healing. In the present narrative, Launcelot attempts to remove the arrow himself, but he 'leffte the hede style in hys buttok, and so he *wente waykely* unto the ermytage, *ever more bledynge*' to find Lavayne (1105.7–9, emphasis mine). This time it is the hermit who cuts out the arrowhead, but blood loss renders Launcelot incapable of riding and threatens his chivalric status (1105.14–1106.3). The links to Gareth and to Elaine and Lavayne associate Launcelot's buttock wound with the theme of precipitous, unmeasured passion.

So layered are these echoes, however, that they also recall the wound of Percivale and raise for the audience the issue of illicit sex. At the level of word-choice, Launcelot's bleeding buttock associates him with Percivale who 'wente … wakely' after punishing himself for immoderate desire (919.28). Launcelot, however, does not see any links with earlier wounds or read any warnings about the future and his relationship with the queen.[36] Launcelot literally cannot see his buttock wound. In fact he does his best to ignore the wound, fighting with excessive violence at the Great Tournament and setting out to overcome injury through a hyper-display of masculinity. For Launcelot, the lady's wound presents not ignoble injury but the opportunity for ennobling action. His attacks on Gawain's clan, however,

---

[35] Lavayne's battlefield ministrations to Launcelot anticipate his sister's nursing of the hero in the hermitage (1085.11–16). R. Kelly notes that in removing the truncheon from Launcelot's side, Lavayne takes on the role of healer accorded to Launcelot in the Prose *Lancelot* ('Wounds, Healing and Knighthood in Malory's Tale of Launcelot and Guenevere', pp. 175–6 and 185–6).

[36] Launcelot does not learn from his wounding at Wynchester to avoid disguise and battle against any member of the Round Table. Instead he takes to the Great Tournament Guenevere's advice of not fighting against kin while in disguise (1103.20–2).

lead the king to exclaim, 'A, sir Launcelot ... this day ye have heted me and my knyghtes!' (1113.32–3). Because of the verbal associations with episodes past and future and with the sexualized wounds of both Percivale and Gareth, Launcelot's buttock wound reminds the audience of his sexual misconduct in the affair with Guenevere. The audience hears the king's warning as anticipating Launcelot's fracturing of the Round Table into the two great affinities of the civil war. As such, the hero's measured wound suggests the way his own unmeasured passion penetrates the body politic.

Still other audience members would associate Launcelot's wound with those of Sir Urry, which are the only wounds in the *Morte Darthur* said to fester (1145.18). Launcelot cries after Urry's miraculous healing, 'as he had bene a chylde that had bene beatyn!' (1152.36). His tears are as open to interpretation as his buttock wound. Catherine Batt notes that the passage places responsibility on Malory's audience: 'The description of Launcelot's weeping in response to the act of grace ... is also the signal of, and means to, authorial and reader creativity – it is we who have to "explain" why Launcelot should cry like a child.'[37] Both bodily markers – the tears and the wound – are physical texts for audiences to interpret. They indicate the hero's isolation and separation from community and mark him as both an insider and outsider at court. The episode following his ransacking of wounds undermines Launcelot's status as 'beste knyghte of the worlde' (1145.19–20): outside the queen's chamber Launcelot lays 'twelve of hys felowys' down 'colde to the erthe' and wounds the thirteenth, Mordred (1168.20–3). From this moment forward Launcelot metes out wounds and even death to the knights of Arthur's fellowship and suffers their injury in turn. Audiences now read his transgression with the queen as a festering wound that, left untended, will destroy them all. Tragically, the hero within the tale refuses to read his multiplying injuries in light of past warnings, to accept the present affirmation of community offered by Urry's healing, or to interpret the looming tragedy of war.

Although Kenneth Hodges sees Launcelot's buttock injury as 'unhappy' rather than feminizing,[38] the multivalent associations of the buttock wound lead to a destabilizing of gender. First, by penetrating Launcelot, the lady

---

[37] C. Batt, *Malory's* Morte Dathur: *Remaking Arthurian Tradition* (New York, 2002), p. 158. In an earlier psychoanalytic reading, entitled 'The Hand of the Huntress', in *New Feminist Discourses, Critical Essays on Theories and Texts*, ed. I. Armstrong (London, 1992), pp. 263–79, C. LaFarge suggests that in the Urry episode, Lancelot comes face-to-face with his double (p. 271): 'Lancelot cries because he is Urry and not Urry, massively unwhole and yet, for no good "reason" ... able to heal ... He is uncomfortable with the public acclaim which, inside, he knows he does not match. Wholeness, a state verbally linked with the desired unity and completeness of the male fellowship, "all wholly tydydirs", is the conceit in Malory around which revolves all sense of self'.

[38] Hodges, 'Wounded Masculinity', p. 17.

places him in the object position of the sexually vulnerable female rather than in the subject position typically associated with the male. The wound thus signifies Launcelot's powerlessness as the object of female desire. That desire may be the queen's, although women other than she and the two Elaines have pursued Launcelot. His reciprocated passion for Guenevere leads him to compromise his loyalty to Arthur, while other women's desire renders Launcelot vulnerable. Secondly, the buttock wound suggests that Launcelot's charisma intensifies even homosocial relations, triggering in Lavayne homoerotic desire. Lavayne was involved intimately with each of Launcelot's penetrating injuries and remains as devoted to him as any female would-be lover. Some audience members may resist a queer reading as more modern than medieval, yet Lavayne at the very least functions as a cipher for all characters, male or female, who are overwhelmed by passion for Launcelot. These include the members of Launcelot's affinity who remain with him in right or wrong. Depending on whether the wound resonates with male or female desire, audiences may interpret the hero as feminized, emasculated or simply disruptive to community.

Etymology opens yet another possible reading. The noun 'buttock' derives from the Old English, but the Old French 'butt' is a term from archery meaning 'target'. Bilingual audiences may hear an aural pun across languages: the hero's buttock literally stands in as the 'butt' or 'mark' for the huntress's archery practice.[39] Modern historians report that before the Battle of Crécy (1346), English longbow archers had struck Norman soldiers who had mooned the English, only to be nailed 'in the back with an arrow'.[40] Earlier in the *Morte Darthur*, in 'The Tale of Sir Launcelot', Malory rendered Launcelot the object of humour when the young knight panics at the desire of the four queens, crawls into bed with Sir Belleus and then over-reacts, and eventually finds himself unarmed and up a tree (257.35–258.10, 259.27–260.4, 282.34–283.27). The buttock wound is a more pointed humiliation then these jests at Launcelot's youthful inexperience. Maude McInerney argues that in the episode of the lady huntress we witness Malory turn against his beloved hero: Malory erupts with 'scorn and disgust' because he cannot 'undo' the adultery plot which

[39] *MED* but (also 'butt(e)') n.1. 2.a 'a target for archers' or 'the mound against which the target was set'; *OED*, butt n. 4.II. 'a mark for archery practice'. Definition 5 indicates that the meaning of butt as 'object of scorn or ridicule' came into use in the seventeenth century, and the phrase 'butt of a jest' or joke in the eighteenth. *Green's Dictionary of Slang* (e-book, Oxford, 2011), *butt* 1a. indicates that the noun was slang for the posterior by 1675, a date too late for Malory but nonetheless a suggestive association.

[40] R. J. Jarymowycz, *Cavalry from Hoof to Track* (Westport, CT, 2008), p. 46, citing J. Burke, *Connections*, BBC Television, 'Longbow', hhtp://www.liquidnarrative.csc.ncsu.edu. I have not been yet been able to track this story to a medieval source.

he would experience as 'a personal betrayal' of chivalry.[41] While this claim goes too far in my view, following the work of Michelle Camille, McInerney's convincingly links marginal images in romance manuscripts to mockery of the chivalric actions described within a text. One manuscript of the Prose *Lancelot* shows archers shooting naked knights in the buttocks.[42] In particular, folio 220r of Beinecke Library MS 229, a text of the *Queste of the Saint Graal*, describes Percivale getting into the ship with the beautiful she-demon and illustrates that scene with a miniature. A naked knight standing atop the miniature is struck with an arrow in the rear. The page brings together the scene of Percivale's temptation with the punishment Launcelot receives at the hand of the huntress. Malory seems to have brought an image from memory of a celebrated English military victory or from the margin of one of his sources to the fore of his imagination. I am inclined to think that audience as well as author derived pleasure from seeing Launcelot humiliated – just once. Of course, in Malory's inventive scene the sex of the archer is notably female.

## The Point of the Huntress

Malory's audience thus cannot ignore this 'lady, the huntress', in part because of the singularity of her presence in the *Morte*. There is no other figure, human or divine, who so clearly derives from classical tradition as she who 'dwelled in that foreyste' and 'ever she bare her bowghe with her, and no men went never with her, but allwayes women', with 'many good doggis' (1104.4–9). Malory may have known the Graeco-Roman Diana, goddess of chastity and the hunt, through her romance mutations. Diana appears, for example, in the Old French Prose *Lancelot* with a euhemeristic explanation. In the Old French non-cyclic Prose *Lancelot*, a lake takes its name from Diana, a queen of Sicily with a passion for hunting. Queen Diana's subjects mistakenly assumed that she was a goddess:

---

[41] McInerney, 'Malory's Lancelot and the Lady Huntress', p. 254. Her argument merits quoting: 'For Malory, who has fallen as thoroughly in love with Lancelot as everyone else in *Le Morte Darthur* does, from Guenevere to King Bagdemagus's daughter to Gareth to Sir Belleus, Lancelot's inevitable fall because of his love affair with the queen is not just a moral lapse or lesson; it is a personal betrayal. Therefore, what the attack by the lady huntress reveals, finally, is the erotic charge of the gaze the author casts upon his hero ... It is only the humiliation of the one by the other which allows Lancelot to re-emerge, in the rest of the last two books, as a tragic and beloved figure' (p. 255).

[42] McInerney, 'Malory's Lancelot and the Lady Huntress', p. 250, citing M. Camille, *Images on the Edge, The Margins of Medieval Art* (Cambridge, MA, 1992) on the 'arrow in the hindquarters motif' (p. 106). See Camille, illus. 50 and 55 of MS New Haven, Beinecke Lib. 229, fol. 39v and 220r.

Li lais estoit apelez, des lo tens as paiens, li lais Dianez. Diane fu reine de Sezile et regna au tans Virgile, lou bon autor, si la tenoient la fole genz mescreanz qui lors estoient por deesse. Et c'estoit la dame del monde qui plus amoit deduit de bois et tote jor aloit chacier, et por ce l'apeloient li mescreant la deesse del bois.

(The lake has been called the lake of Diana, since pagan times. Diana was queen of Sicily and reigned in the time of the good author Virgil, and the foolish pagan people of that time believed that she was a goddess. She loved the pleasures of the forest more than any woman in the world, and would go hunting all day long, and for that reason the pagans called her the goddess of the woods.)[43]

This passage appears nearly verbatim in the cyclic Prose *Lancelot*, with the only change being that the lady would spend 'every day' ('toute iour') rather than 'all day long' ('tote jor') hunting (*Lancelot*, vol.VII., III.8; *L-G* II.5.11). The authors of the Prose *Lancelot* and of the cyclic version make no mention of Diana's female companions and associate her with Virgil rather than Ovid, but these passages show clear references in two of Malory's source texts to the classical Diana – albeit references that explain away her divine status. The phrasing of the cyclic Lancelot ('toute iour') comes closer to Malory's 'dayly' although Diana is still missing the accompanying women, dogs and bows and arrows that she has in the *Morte Darthur*.

The classical goddess, however, is clearly invested with supernatural power, including the ability to protect a spring from male violation.[44] In Ovid's *Metamorphoses*, for example, Callisto is driven from attending Diana (here called Cynthia) when bathing in a sacred spring reveals the nymph's pregnancy: '"I procul hinc" dixit, "nec sacros pollue fontis!"/ Cynthia deque suo iussit secedere coetu' ('"Begone! And pollute not our

---

[43] *Lancelot do Lac, The Non-cyclic Old French Prose Romance*, ed. E. Kennedy (Oxford, 1980), p. 7.1–6; English translation taken from *Lancelot of the Lake*, trans. C. Corley (Oxford, 1989), p. 10.

[44] C. LaFarge points out that both *Lancelot* authors associate the pagan Diana with the Lady of the Lake: when she abducts the infant Lancelot, the Lady of the Lake jumps into Diana's lake ('The Hand of the Huntress', pp. 266–7). See Prose *Lancelot*, ed. Kennedy, p. 15.26–30, Corley p. 21; Micha vol. VII, IIIa.8; *L-G* IV.9.28. However, when LaFarge refers to 'the fairy Diana of Arthurian romance' she elides two references: the Diana of the *Lancelot* is neither a goddess nor a fairy but a human queen, while the Lady of the Lake or Niniene/Ninianne is clearly a fairy (Prose *Lancelot*, ed. Kennedy, p. 21.11–12, Corley, p. 25; Micha vol. VII, V.1; *L-G* IV.11.38). Despite my small correction, I draw inspiration from LaFarge's larger argument that the appearance of these figures 'in Malory's own literary tradition and direct sources can only lend support to a reading of Lancelot's wounding as having a particular relevance to his gender, his knighthood and his relations with women, and to gender and wholeness in Malory generally' (p. 267).

sacred pool"; and so expelled her from her company'; *Met.* 2.464–5).[45]
More typically, the victims of Diana's wrath are men, punished for violating a follower's chastity or intruding upon the goddess. In Ovid's
*Metamorphoses* this is the fate of Actaeon (*Met.* 3.155–255) whose situation oddly parallels Launcelot's, and this myth creates for the audience
a new context of echoic association.

Central to Ovid's episode, as to the scene of Launcelot's wounding,
is the presence of the male intruder at a spring, his unintended violation,
the dogs, the prey of the deer, the female hunter and the ironic reversal in the man's punishment. A devotee of hunting, Actaeon chances
upon the goddess, who was wearied from the chase ('fessa venatu',
*Met.* 3.163) and was bathing in a spring for refreshment. When Actaeon
enters her secret grove, Diana's nymphs cannot hide the goddess from
his gaze. Lacking arrows, she instead flings at the intruder 'avenging
drops' of water ('ulticibus undis', *Met.* 3.190). His head sprouts horns,
his body hide and the hunter is transformed into a stag. Not knowing
whether to return to the palace or hide in the wood, torn between fear
and shame, Actaeon is beset by his own beloved hunting dogs. The
first, Melanchaetes, reaches Actaeon and 'fixes his fangs in his back'
or literally 'makes a wound in his back' ('in tergo vulnera fecit', *Met.*
3.232).[46] Actaeon's violation involves seeing, his punishment feeling, as
the unrecognized hunter becomes the quarry of his own dogs and is cut
down by his own men. The moral of the episode is a haunting lack of
one, for the audience members must decide whether Actaeon merits the
goddess's punishment (*Met.* 3.253–5).

It would be unusual for Malory to draw upon a classical text. Yet
echoic details link the episode of Launcelot's wounding to Actaeon's.[47]
Only Ovid offers a scene in which the male trespasser is wounded not in

---

[45] I cite Ovid in Latin and English translation from the Loeb edition, *Metamorphoses*, 2
vols., trans. F. J. Miller (Cambridge, MA, 1972). For violations of Diana's spring, see
also *Met.* 5.618–22, 14.229–332, 15.547–51.

[46] With characteristic wit, the Ovidian narrator observes, 'Well indeed, he might wish to
be absent, but he is here; and well might he wish to see, not to feel, the fierce doings of
his own hounds' ('vellet abesse quidem, seb ades; velletque videre, / non etiam sentire
canum fers facta suorum', 3.247–8).

[47] Earlier critics have drawn a connection between the huntress and the classical goddess.
E. Reiss discusses the huntress as a Diana-figure but interprets Guenevere as the
guilty party represented by the barren hind in *Sir Thomas Malory* (New York, 1966),
pp. 166–8. R. Kelly cites Reiss's argument but sees the wound as 'a judgment upon
and warning to Lancelot' ('Wounds, Healing and Knighthood in Malory's Tale of
Launcelot and Guenevere', p. 186). E. R. Anderson asserts that Malory adopted the
Diana-figure from Chaucer's 'Knight's Tale' in 'Malory's "Fair Maid of Ascolat"',
*Neuphilologische Mitteilungen* 87.2 (1986), 237–54 (pp. 244–5). Two additional articles that fully treat the huntress, her relation to Diana and the implication of the wound

the thigh, but in the back (*Met.* 3.232, cited above). If the *Metamorphoses* does serve as an analogue to the *Morte Darthur*, however distant, Malory's blurring of distinctions – male and female and divine–human–beast – proves richly ironic. First, Malory has reversed the sex of the one who rests at the spring. Both the weary goddess and Launcelot are drawn to running water, she to bathe in the spring that babbles ('fons sonat', *Met.* 3.160), he to 'ly downe by the welle and se the well sprynge and burble' (1104.1–2). The locations of the springs, the grotto at Gargaphie and the 'welle by the ermytayge', should be single-sex enclaves. Diana's spring certainly was until Actaeon stumbled upon it, and so presumably was the hermitage to which Launcelot had retreated, but perhaps not the well where he habitually rests. That spring is 'by the hermitage' and apparently in the path of the deer pursued by 'the grete hunteresse' who 'spyed hym' at the well (1104.1, 3–4, 25). When wounded, Launcelot takes on the superior tone of the goddess suffering transgression, an attitude he several times strikes in the *Morte Darthur* when he finds himself the object of unwanted female desire.[48] But while assuming the part of the goddess whose spring has been violated, Launcelot also behaves like the wearied beast: he makes himself vulnerable by lying down at the spring, as had the exhausted hind 'that went to soyle', that is, 'lay in the shallows of the stream' (1104.20 and n.).[49] Malory thus places into the scene a feminized version of Actaeon's stag. More details than the prone position connect Launcelot to this prey. Astutely analysed by Maude McInerney, the passage's pronouns render gender unstable and link Launcelot to the female quarry. The hind is both 'he' and 'she' in a single sentence; the 'hym' that the huntress spies could refer (ungrammatically) to the female hind or (grammatically) to the sleeping knight (1104.19, 21, 25).[50] Since 'he' in Middle English can mean 'she', the confusion might be scribal, but the text as it stands suggests that Malory elides gender. He thus cues the audience to consider that the lady purposefully wounds Launcelot. At the very least, when she overshoots the hind and injures the hero, she disdainfully offers an explanation but no apology: 'I saw you nat but as here was a barayne hynde at the soyle

are those of LaFarge and McInerney, cited above (nn. 37 and 30). As far as I am aware, I am the first to draw a connection between Launcelot and Actaeon.

48 See, for example, Launcelot's dialogue with the four queens at 257.20–258.10.
49 McInerney, 'Malory's Lancelot and the Lady Huntress', p. 265 n. 5, explains that, according to the rules of hunting, hunters may legally take a barren hind. Hunters are forbidden to take pregnant or lactating does, limiting the hunting of the female to the autumn, as is the case in the opening of the *Awyntyrs off Arthur*, l. 7 in *Sir Gawain: Eleven Romances and Tales*, ed. T. Hahn (Kalamazoo, 1995), p. 178.
50 McInerny, 'Malory's Lancelot and the Lady Huntress', p. 248.

in thys welle. And I wente I had done welle, but my hande swarved' (1105.3–5). The episode lacks a literal metamorphosis and the Ovidian vocabulary of transformation, yet the traits of the wounded deer accrue to Launcelot. In Malory's revision of the Actaeon episode, the man rests at the well, exposed and vulnerable; the huntress arrives armed, retaining the vengefulness the goddess of chastity has for men; and she inflicts punishment at the well or spring on a man who receives the wound destined for a deer. The shifting of roles and gender renders a Launcelot who is both hunted and hunter: like Diana, he is trespassed against and godlike in his disdain; like Actaeon, he is self-absorbed and ignorant of the pain he inflicts; like Actaeon's stag and the barren hind, he is sought after, weary and too big to miss.

Most important, like Actaeon, Launcelot is made to feel the bite of the punishment. In this scene of Anglicized classicism, rather than a dog wounding the transformed man-stag in the back (*Met.* 3.232), the huntress's arrow cuts Launcelot 'in the thycke of the buttok over the barbys' (1104.28–9). The visceral description makes even modern readers wince. Launcelot responds to the wound with shock, pain or perhaps anger: 'he whorled up woodly, and saw the lady that had smytten hym' and said 'Lady, or damesell, whatsomever ye be, in an evyll tyme bare ye thys bowe. The devyll made you a shoter!' (1104.30–5). Launcelot's unusually colloquial exclamation recalls the folk tradition of the devil as hunter, seen for example in Chaucer's 'Friar's Tale' (III.1380–3), as well as the anti-feminist linking of female sexuality and demons seen in Percivale's encounter with the fiend. From Launcelot's point of view, he is the undeserved victim of a suspect hunter and her errant arrow. However, in addressing the huntress as 'lady or damesell', Malory uses titles appropriate to a married woman and a virgin and thus reminds the audience of those he has victimized through his sexual appeal. Launcelot injures one married lady – the queen – in the very next episode, 'The Knight of the Cart'. The huntress's wound – caused when her 'hande swarved' – anticipates Launcelot's self-wounding when, eager to enter Guenevere's bed, he pulls the window out from the stone wall so that 'one the barres of iron kutte the brawne of hys hondys thorowoute to the bone' (1131.23–5). Like Gareth's wound in the thigh, Launcelot's hand bloodies the bed and confirms the illicit encounter. In fact, this is the only scene in the *Morte* which confirms Launcelot and Guevenere's adultery. Unfortunately for the queen, the episode does not end as it had for Gareth's lady, in marriage and the comic resolution; instead it initiates a chain of events that eventually lead Guenevere to the stake, stripped of her smock and her honour (1177.9–10 and 18). Launcelot has also injured 'damesells', particularly Elaine of Corbyn whose love he refuses even though he has taken her virginity (inadvertently), and Elaine of Ascolat whose death he incites.[51] The huntress's arrow thus exacts a contrapasso-like wound on the knight who has unwittingly transgressed female integrity. Malory leaves the audience to judge the appropriateness of Launcelot's punishment for the unintended consequences of his actions.

Perhaps it was from Ovid that Malory learned how to open up space for audience interpretation. Actaeon's story begins with the Ovidian narrator summarizing it for his grandfather, Cadmus, then asking 'For what crime had mere mischance?' ('quod enim scelus error habebat?", *Met.* 3.141–2). By questioning Cadmus, the narrator also invites the audience to consider whether Actaeon is responsible for a mistake ('error') or a crime ('scelus'). The narrator then closes the episode by creating an audience within the tale who actually engage in debate: 'Common talk wavered this way and that: to some the goddess seemed more cruel than was just; others called her act worthy of her austere virginity; both sides found good reasons for their judgement' ('Rumor in ambiguo est; aliis violentior aequo / visa dea est, alii laudant dignamque severa / virginitate vocant pars invenit utraque causas', *Met.* 3.253–5). By so framing Actaeon's story, Ovid creates internal audiences that model debate about ethical considerations for the external audience. Malory does not always inscribe internal audiences for his episodes of ignoble injury, but he always grants his external audience freedom to judge his characters. For half a millennium Malory's audiences and critics have debated Launcelot's culpability even as we recognize the author's protective affection for his hero. Malory's echoic treatment of the wound given by the huntress leaves us debating possible meanings as the hero 'wente waykely' away.

The *Metamorphoses* was a canonical grammar school text, taught as a model for poetry and in prose paraphrase as a source for mythography, but it is impossible to prove that Malory knew it.[52] Ovid had an extraordinary influence in the Middle Ages, increasingly so for vernacular writers as his myths became known through the courtly tradition.[53] Many English writers before Malory cite Ovid, and they seemingly accept the interpretative freedom offered in the Actaeon episode. In the 'Knight's Tale'

---

[51] Anderson argues that Launcelot's wound serves as 'symbolic retribution' for the death of Elaine of Ascolat; 'Malory's "Fair Maid of Ascolat"', pp. 244–5.

[52] If Malory enjoyed a grammar school education, he could have encountered the *Metamorphoses*, since it was used in English schools to teach Latin grammar from the early Middle Ages through to Milton. P. J. C. Field reminds us, however, that 'Malory's style suggests that his mind was strikingly unacademic', in *The Life and Times of Sir Thomas Malory* (Cambridge, 1993), p. 172.

[53] R. Hexter, 'Ovid in the Middle Ages: Exile, Mythographer, Lover', in *Brill's Companion to Ovid*, ed. B. Weiden Boyd (Leiden, 2002), pp. 413–42 (pp. 424–32); and R. Cormier, '*Ovide moralisé*', *Approaches to Teaching the Works of Ovid and the Ovidian Tradition*, ed. B. Weiden Boyd and C. Fox (New York, 2010), pp. 18–22.

Chaucer's Emelye cites Actaeon as a victim of Diana's vengeance when she prays to the goddess to be allowed to remain chaste (I.2302–3),[54] while in *Confessio Amantis* John Gower explains the hunter's fate as 'an ensemple touchende of mislok' – that is, a warning to the lover not to look where he shouldn't.[55] In contrast, Christine de Pisan's *Epistle of Othea*, translated into English by Stephen Scrope (1450), draws from the episode two different ethical lessons: in the gloss, Actaeon as hunter warns against abandoning oneself to idleness and wasting wealth on the pursuit of game; and in the allegory, Actaeon as stag represents a man once bound to the flesh who has taken on penance.[56] Christine's pattern of double interpretation and her moral readings derive from the *Ovide moralisé* (*c.* 1300–30), which is the single most important work for transmitting Ovidian mythography to later medieval writers. The Franciscan author of the *Ovide* translated the poem into short poetic narratives, followed by allegories which in fact are designed to limit – not open up – the audience's response to the Roman poet's ethical ambiguities.[57] The *Ovide moralisé* offers variant interpretations, but actually directs the audience how to read. In fact, the passages cited above from Chaucer, Gower and Christine all show the influence of the *Ovide moralisé*.

The *Ovide moralisé* author interprets the Actaeon episode in two ways, first as a warning against the dangers of hunting (*OM* 3.371–603). An illumination from the Rouen manuscript shows a very human-looking stag suffering as he is bitten in the haunch.[58] This miniature indicates that a manuscript's visual programme sometimes emphasizes details of the Latin original that the French poem and allegories ignore, such as Ovid's emphasis on the wound in the back or backside ('in terga vulnera', *Met.* 3.232). Secondly, the author deals with the problem of Ovidian change by interpreting Actaeon's transformation as a sign of the Incarnation,

[54] Analysing the scene with the huntress, Norris argues that Malory was influenced by references to Diana from Chaucer's 'Knight's Tale' or 'Franklin's Tale' and that the depiction of Emily as a huntress in the 'Knight's Tale', ll. 1683–7, might explain Malory's 'otherwise puzzling change of the gender of the hunters in his major sources' (p. 130).

[55] 'Confessio Amantis', in *The Complete Works of John Gower*, ed. G. C. Macaulay (Oxford, 1902), vol. II, Liber Primus, 1.333 and 380.

[56] Christine de Pizan, *The Epistle of Othea*, trans. S. Scrope, ed. C. F. Buhler, EETS o.s. 264 (Oxford, 1970), pp. 84.15–17 and 23–7.

[57] M. Desmond, 'The Goddess Diana and the Ethics of Reading in the *Ovide moralisé*', in *Metamorphoses: The Changing Face of Ovid in Medieval and Early Modern Europe*, ed. A. Keith and S. Rupp (Toronto, 2007), pp. 61–76 (pp. 63–4). Although a new edition of the *Ovide moralisé* is in preparation, the standard edition remains *Ovide moralisé: Poème du commencement du quatorzième*, ed. C. de Boer, 5 vols. (1915–38; reprint Wiesbaden, 1966). I cite vol. 1, which translates and expands the *Metamorphoses*' third book, as *OM* by book and line numbers.

[58] Desmond, 'The Goddess Diana', fig. 3.3, from MS Rouen, Bibl. Mun. 04 (1315–20).

with the Actaeon-stag revealing the sacrificial suffering of the Son (*OM* 3.604–70).[59] This allegorizing hermeneutic contradicts Ovid's own championing of open-ended interpretation, but it was the mode that established his medieval reputation as the 'ethical Ovid' (*Ovidius ethicus*).[60] The Christological reading of the stag proved too much for Malory's publisher, William Caxton. In his 1480 translation of the *Ovide moralisé*, Caxton turned the warning against hunting into an economic lesson: 'Actaeon so entremeted of huntynge [concerned himself] ... whyche amynusshed [reduced] hys goodes and empowered hym'.[61] Caxton probably never printed his translation of Ovid.[62] He may have felt a conflict between the Christian practice of didactic interpretation and an early humanist attraction to classical texts. Given his reading of Actaeon and his business acumen, it seems more likely that Caxton decided that a moralized Ovid would not sell. 'Ovid's Metamorphoses English'd by Caxton' nonetheless shows that Malory's printer was seriously engaged

[59] Desmond explains that the Trinity was one of the means by which the *Ovide moralisé*'s author integrated Ovid's polytheism into monotheistic Christianity. In the Actaeon story Diana becomes the naked essence of God and the transformed Actaeon the Son (*OM* 3.604–70, esp. 635–43). The most extensive (and wildly) allegorical reading of the Actaeon episode appears in the Latin prose *Ovidius moralizatus* (early 14th c.) of Pierre Bersuire (Petrus Berchorius). In Bersuire's hands, the spring becomes the carnal delights into which women dip themselves, Diana is both Avarice and the Virgin Mary, and Actaeon the victim of his own dogs (who represent the Jews) and a figure of the Incarnation (W. D. Reynolds, 'The Ovidius Moralizatus of Petrus Berchosius: An Introduction and Translation' [unpublished dissertation, University of Illinois, 1971], pp. 186–9). Malory offers a different interpretation of the white hart as Christ at 999.26–30. Here Malory is influenced not by moralized interpretations of Ovid, but by the patristic interpretation of Christ as a life-renewing stag.

[60] The term derives from the *accessus* or academic prologue preceeding the *Ovide moralisé*. Desmond, 'The Goddess Diana', p. 64.

[61] *The Metamorphoses of Ovid, translated William Caxton*, 2 vols. (New York, 1968), Bk. 3, cap. 7. The manuscript and facsimile lack numeration.

[62] Caxton's version of the *Ovide moralisé* is a very literal translation of a book he came across while working with the scribe and printer Colard Mansion in Bruges (a text of which is BL MS Royal 17.E.q). Caxton's translation exists in a unique manuscript that was split into two volumes. The second volume, the Pepys Manuscript, contains books 10–15. It was bequeathed to Magdalene College in 1703 by the diarist, Samuel Pepys. The first volume, the Phillips Manuscript, contains books 1–9. It was discovered in 1964 and purchased by Magdalene College in 1966. According to R. Lyne, 'Ovid in English Translation', in *The Cambridge Companion to Ovid*, ed. P. Hardie (Cambridge, 2002), pp. 249–63, the manuscript 'resides in two libraries even though the volumes share one display case, thanks to rigorous rules governing the Pepysian Library at Madgalene College Cambridge' (p. 250). Based upon the Preface to the *Golden Legend*, in which Caxton lists the *Metamorphoses* among his works 'Parfourmed and accomplished', Lyne argues that the work was printed (p. 250), but W. Kuskin takes the stand that it was 'apparently unprinted'; *Symbolic Caxton: Literary Culture and Print Capitalism* (Notre Dame, IN, 2007), p. 241.

with a textual descendant of the *Metamorphoses* just before he prepared the *Morte Darthur* for print (1485). And if Ovid engaged Caxton, perhaps a version of the *Metamorphoses* – perhaps in French, perhaps illustrating the wound in Actaeon's haunch – influenced Sir Thomas Malory. All of the didactic versions of the *Metamorphoses* discussed above, including Caxton's, ignore the conflict of a man's unwilled error and painful punishment – the very issue Ovid left his audience to ponder. In contrast, Malory seems to direct his audience to precisely this ethical issue through the huntress's arrow.

When does a wound in the *Morte Darthur* signify honour and when moral loss? The answer seems to reside in the circumstances of the wounding, whether the injury derives from honourable combat or sexual behaviour. No simple moralist, Malory suggestively links the thigh or buttock with illicit sex, illustrating the plight of knights whose morals dishonour them. In 'The Sankgreal', Christian teachings on chastity undergird the adventures; audience and hero bring those assumed values to bear on Percivale's temptation, thigh wound and repentance. Percivale's self-wounding reveals a symbolic castration that replaces sexual temptation with spiritual honour. In 'The Tale of Sir Gareth' social conventions prove more flexible than the Grail quest's sexual proscriptions, so that the audience brings multifaceted readings to Gareth's wound: they may be tickled by the foolishness of the lovers or relieved by their marriage, but they never feel a threat like the prospect of sex with a devil. Gareth's wounding by the male intruder, controlled by a woman, protects both male and female honour and sends the couple into socially sanctioned marriage. Additionally, both Percivale and Gareth learn to read the warning of their wounds and take appropriate measures to undo injury. In the case of Launcelot, the buttock replaces the wounded thigh, and its injury suggests the way Launcelot's sexual charisma pricks female chastity and threatens the male fellowship while it objectifies the hero. Additionally, Launcelot's own passion for the queen punctures his personal sense of chivalry. The hero is unwilling to interpret his ignoble injury as moral transgression, but the audience might read the injury as analogous to Launcelot's wounding of the social body, unseen but festering.

# III

# WEEPING, WOUNDS AND WORSHYP IN MALORY'S
## *MORTE DARTHUR*

### *K. S. Whetter*

There are a lot of wounds and a lot of weeping in Sir Thomas Malory's
*Le Morte Darthur*. This is hardly surprising given that armed combat 'is
Malory's favourite topic'.[1] Yet despite the popularity and longevity of the
*Morte*, combat has not always proven to be equally beloved by Malory's
critics. Roger Ascham famously condemned the *Morte*'s excessive reliance on 'open mans slaughter, and bold bawdrye', and in doing so he
initiated what would become a long-standing critical refrain.[2] Recent
scholarship on Malory's *Morte Darthur* emphasizes the supposed somatic
anxieties of Malory's text, the ways in which various characters feel pain.
Emotions, too, are sometimes said to be fractured in the *Morte*, especially
in relation to violence in the text and even, for some scholars, for Malory
himself outside the text. It is my contention that both of these lines of rea-
soning misrepresent the complexity and unity of Malory's *Morte Darthur*.
   Wounds and weeping are omnipresent in the *Morte*, but not as a negative cause-and-effect binary. Malory makes abundantly clear that seeking
after *worshyp* by 'taking the adventure' involves some form of bodily
hazard, usually fighting, and also that combat can have bloody and painful

---

[1]  E. Vinaver, ed., *The Works of Sir Thomas Malory*, 3rd edn, rev. P. J. C. Field (Oxford,
1990), p. xxxiii. The most sustained study of Malorian combat is Andrew Lynch's
masterly *Malory's Book of Arms: The Narrative of Combat in Le Morte Darthur*
(Cambridge, 1997). For a qualification of some of Lynch's views, see my 'Warfare
and Combat in *Le Morte Darthur*', in *Writing War: Medieval Literary Responses to
Warfare*, ed. C. Saunders, F. Le Saux and N. Thomas (Cambridge, 2004), pp. 169–86.
For helpful comments, advice and occasional criticism, thanks are due to the audience
of the 2013 International Congress on Medieval Studies in Kalamazoo, where my
argument was first aired.
[2]  Ascham, *The Scholemaster*, in *The English Works of Roger Ascham*, ed. W. A. Wright
(Cambridge, 1904), p. 231.

as well as worshipful consequences. Concomitantly and paradoxically, public recognition of success in combat is the surest means of winning worship, and worship is what all knights – and, as we shall see, at least one lady – strive for in the *Morte*. Nevertheless, a knight's acceptance of the interconnection of worship and wounds does not (*pace* Jill Mann) mean that he surrenders his free will 'to chance', nor do wounded bodies evoke Malory's own authorial insecurities about textual traditions and instability (*pace* Catherine Batt).[3] It does mean, however, that earthly worship is ultimately the more important factor, the prize for which all knights regularly risk bodily harm. '[W]orshyp in armys may never be foyled' (841.26), as Malory insists in the May Passage.[4] Although the narrative divisions and section breaks of most modern editions of the *Morte Darthur* obscure the connexion, the physical layout of the Winchester manuscript at this point in the narrative makes it clear that the May Passage and its praise of faithfulness in love *and worship* is meant to conclude the Great Tournament as much as it introduces the Knight of the Cart episode.[5] This thematic and codicological primacy of worship, I shall further suggest, is precisely why Launcelot weeps his famous tears

---

[3]   On adventure, chance and the arbitrariness of knightly fate, see J. Mann, '"Taking the Adventure": Malory and the *Suite du Merlin*', in *Aspects of Malory*, ed. T. Takamiya and D. Brewer (Cambridge and Totowa, NJ, 1981), pp. 71–91 (pp. 80–1); and Mann, 'Malory: Knightly Combat in *Le Morte Darthur*', in *Medieval Literature: Chaucer and the Alliterative Tradition*, ed. B. Ford (Harmondsworth, 1982), pp. 331–9 (p. 333). For relations between wounded bodies and Malory's fears of textual instability, see C. Batt, *Malory's Morte Darthur: Remaking Arthurian Tradition* (New York and Basingstoke, 2002).

[4]   All references to Malory's text are by page and line number to *Le Morte Darthur*, ed. P. J. C. Field, 2 vols. (Cambridge, 2013). Volume I is the complete text; Volume II is the complete apparatus and commentary.

[5]   Scholars have naturally focused their attention on Vinaver's edition (as in n. 1). Compare and contrast the layout and divisions of *Works* 1113–20 (Field's *Morte Darthur* 839–42) with *The Winchester Malory: A Facsimile*, intr. N. R. Ker (London, 1976), fols 434r–435v. For the sundry ways in which Vinaver's narrative divisions obfuscate Winchester's presentation of this passage and its themes and unity, see E. R. Anderson, 'Malory's "Fair Maid of Ascolat"', *Neuphilologische Mitteilungen* 87.2 (1986), 237–54; K. T. Grimm, 'Knightly Love and the Narrative Structure of Malory's Tale Seven', *Arthurian Interpretations* 3.2 (1989), 76–95 (pp. 85–7); Grimm, 'Editing Malory: What's at (the) Stake', *Arthuriana* 5.2 (1995), 5–14 (pp. 7–8); C. M. Meale, '"The Hoole Book": Editing and the Creation of Meaning in Malory's Text', in *A Companion to Malory*, ed. E. Archibald and A. S. G. Edwards (Cambridge, 1996), pp. 3–17 (pp. 15–16); and H. Cooper, 'Opening up the Malory Manuscript', in *The Malory Debate: Essays on the Texts of Le Morte Darthur*, ed. B. Wheeler et al. (Cambridge, 2000), pp. 255–84 (pp. 262–3). In contrast, Field maintains Vinaver's textual layout and offers a compelling textual-critical defence (see his headnote to Tale VII, *Morte Darthur*, II, 686–7).

after healing Urry, for despite his and Gwenyvere's adultery he remains the best and most worshipful knight of the world.

My reading of Malory's presentation of combat and the knights who partake of it runs counter to much contemporary scholarship of the Arthuriad. Although few Malorians share Ascham's vitriol, it is nonetheless true that the standard interpretation of the *Morte* sees Malory as ultimately interrogating or even rejecting earthly chivalry. Even readers more sympathetic to the complexities of Malory's art can be heard to complain, with R. T. Davies, of 'battle after tedious battle' and the accompanying necessity for the reader to 'dodge the cloven heads'.[6] Although pain and bloodshed are not always explicitly invoked, critics typically insist that the downfall of the kingdom in Malory's Arthuriad is due to sin; this is true even if such critics add that the religious deaths of Launcelot and Gwenyvere create a qualified happy ending. Thus, for Robert L. Kelly, Launcelot's wounds depict his fallibility and sins, an argument endorsed at times by Andrew Lynch.[7] Catherine Batt goes even further, arguing that 'Malory raises questions ... about how the Arthurian world functions', including how Malory fails to legitimize violence.[8] Batt sees connexions between bodily injury and authorial anxieties about textual stability and wholeness, so that, especially in the case of Launcelot, physical and textual anxieties reflect 'the vulnerability of the hero'. The correlation between injury and the hero's vulnerability or even feminization is a commonplace of gender criticism, and both Kathleen Coyne Kelly and Megan G. Leitch argue – in different ways – that the blood of male knights highlights bodily concerns and the subversion and 'critique' of knightly identity.[9] For both critics this is especially true of knights who bleed in the bedroom.

Bleeding, however, is not axiomatically a sign of weakness in the *Morte Darthur*. On the contrary, the text, the narrator and the characters all repeatedly associate wounds with worship: pain is obviously not

---

[6]   R. T. Davies, 'The Worshipful Way in Malory', in *Patterns of Love and Courtesy: Essays in Memory of C. S. Lewis*, ed. J. Lawlor (London, 1966), pp. 157–77 (p. 169).

[7]   R. L. Kelly, 'Wounds, Healing, and Knighthood in Malory's Tale of Lancelot and Guenevere', in *Studies in Malory*, ed. J. W. Spisak (Kalamazoo, MI, 1985), pp. 173-97; Lynch, *Malory's Book of Arms*, pp. 74–8.

[8]   Batt, *Remaking Arthurian Tradition*, p. xxi et passim. E. Scala, 'Disarming Lancelot', *Studies in Philology* 99.4 (2002), 380–403 (esp. pp. 382–6), makes a similar complaint.

[9]   K. C. Kelly, 'Menaced Masculinity and Imperiled Virginity in the *Morte Darthur*', in *Menacing Virgins: Representing Virginity in the Middle Ages and Renaissance*, ed. K. C. Kelly and M. Leslie (Newark, DE, and London, 1999), pp. 97–114 (p. 110); M. G. Leitch, '(Dis)figuring Transgressive Desire: Blood, Sex, and Stained Sheets in Malory's *Morte Darthur*', *Arthurian Literature* 28 (2011), 21–38. I am indebted to Amy S. Kaufman for the Kelly reference.

desirable, but it is accepted as a measure of chivalric attainment. To some extent, blood is simply a way of keeping score.[10] It is also an ever-present accompaniment to adventure. Indeed, as Jill Mann notes, whilst blood and the body are obviously key symbols of Christ's Passion and the Eucharist, 'body and blood are also the central elements of the knightly experience'.[11] Here I am in complete agreement with Kenneth Hodges, who rightly observes that injury was a commonplace of knighthood both in medieval literature and in medieval life.[12] As such, Arthurian authors and characters may not be as concerned with bodily integrity as we moderns think; this is especially true of Malory and the *Morte Darthur*. As D. S. Brewer astutely notes, the primary 'motivating force' for Malory's characters is *worshyp*, and *worshyp* is best won through fighting, whether in earnest or in play.[13]

Malory, of course, was well acquainted with both fictional and real-world violence. Much of the fighting in his Arthuriad is carried over from the sources, but since Malory was capable of rearranging, splicing and cutting across vast tracts of those sources at will, it is telling that he keeps as much fighting as he does. Malory also at times updates the fighting of his sources, rendering equipment or techniques (or both) more in keeping with fifteenth-century practice rather than the early thirteenth-century martial mores reflected in the prose Vulgate and Post-Vulgate cycles which comprise the core of Malory's French book.[14] This awareness of and focus on combat must reflect Malory's own interests and reading habits, but also, presumably, his own life experiences. Malory's marble tombstone (now sadly lost) recorded that he was *valens miles*, a

[10] Cf. Lynch, *Malory's Book of Arms*, p. 60; and K. Hodges, 'Wounded Masculinity: Injury and Gender in Sir Thomas Malory's *Le Morte Darthur*', *Studies in Philology* 106 (2009), 14–31 (pp. 16, 24, 27–8).

[11] J. Mann, 'Malory and the Grail Legend', in *A Companion to Malory*, ed. E. Archibald and A. S. G. Edwards (Cambridge, 1996), pp. 203–20 (p. 208). See also Mann, 'Knightly Combat', pp. 338–9. This is perhaps the most spectacular way in which knighthood managed to appropriate religious theology and teaching to its own purposes. For further examples and a cogent elucidation of the complex relationship between chivalry and the Church, see R. W. Kaeuper, *Holy Warriors: The Religious Ideology of Chivalry* (Philadelphia, 2009).

[12] Hodges, 'Wounded Masculinity', esp. pp. 14–16.

[13] D. S. Brewer, ed., Introduction to *The Morte Darthur: Parts Seven and Eight* (London, 1968), p. 25, reprinted in *Arthurian Literature* 26 (2009), 1–37.

[14] On Malory's sources, see especially the headnote to each Tale of the *Morte* in Vinaver's Commentary, the essays collected in P. J. C. Field's *Malory: Texts and Sources* (Cambridge, 1999), and R. Norris, *Malory's Library: The Sources of the Morte Darthur* (Cambridge, 2008). On the historical veracity of fighting in the *Morte*, see my 'The Historicity of Combat in *Le Morte Darthur*', in *Arthurian Studies in Honour of P. J. C. Field*, ed. B. Wheeler (Cambridge, 2004), pp. 261–70.

phrase testifying not only to Malory's knighthood but to his having some 'distinction in arms'.[15] Not only was Malory a knight, he was a knight – a fighter – during the bloodiest period in English history, a history, let us recall, that includes invasions by the Romans, the Angles, Saxons and Jutes, the Vikings and the Normans. Malory may have fought in France in the closing years of the Hundred Years War; he certainly fought in England on both sides of the Wars of the Roses, and his knowledge of the techniques of fifteenth-century warfare may well have extended to siegecraft. Certainly he was present on the Yorkist side at the 1462 siege of Bamburgh and other Lancastrian castles in the north.[16] When he was not fighting politically sanctioned battles Malory was also capable of finding his own fights, including the attack on Buckingham that helped land him in prison, and including breaking out of prison and acquiring weapons and fighting companions. In other words, Malory was extremely well-versed in the equipment, mechanics and consequences of chivalric (and no doubt not-so chivalric) fighting. Malory *may* have been moderately unusual for one of his class in so persistently falling in and out of favour with the powers that be, but his interests in warfare and combat are entirely of his age. As Catherine Nall affirms, 'the evidence of ownership of military treatises points to the widespread interest in the prosecution of war among fifteenth-century English readers'.[17]

In Malory's case, familiarity breeds practicality. Consequently, Malory's awareness of the contingencies of martial endeavour is evident on the several occasions in his 'Book of Sir Trystram' when it is emphasized by Trystram, by Malory himself and by Dynadan that even the best knight will at some point be overcome or injured by a weaker knight. The first occasion is when Trystram, at Mark's insistence, unfairly unhorses Lamorak in a tournament, and Trystram tries to appease Lamorak by insisting 'that knyght nother horse was never fourmed that allway may endure' (343.32–3). The second occasion is just after Trystram and Lamorak fight and then reconcile, and Palomydes suddenly rides up and 'smote' them both down – whereupon Malory as narrator invokes the same idea, although here the notion gets nearly buried by the introduction of the Questing Beast (378.27–379.8). The third occasion for the

---

[15] The tombstone epitaph is recorded in London, British Library, MS Cotton Vitellius F.xii, fol. 284r; the 'distinction' interpretation is from P. J. C. Field, 'Hunting, Hawking and Textual Criticism in Malory's *Morte Darthur*', in his *Texts and Sources*, pp. 103–13 (p. 103 n. 3).

[16] I repeat here some information from the opening of my 'Historicity'. For details of Malory's life, campaigns, imprisonments and prison breaks, see P. J. C. Field, *The Life and Times of Sir Thomas Malory* (Cambridge, 1993).

[17] C. Nall, *Reading and War in Fifteenth-Century England: From Lydgate to Malory* (Cambridge, 2012), p. 2.

K. S. WHETTER

sentiment is when Palomydes unhorses Trystram unfairly, and Dynadan observes 'here may a man preve, be he never so good yet may he have a falle; and he was never so wyse but he myght be oversayne, and he rydyth well that never felle' (408.4–7). The first and third of these ideas seem to be carried over from whatever version of the prose *Tristan* Malory was working from, but Malory's own interjection of 'Here men may undirstonde that bene men of worshyp that man was never fourmed that all tymes myght attayne, but somtyme he was put to the worse by malefortune, and at som tyme the wayker knyght put the byggar knyght to a rebuke' is 'largely' original.[18] If one accepts that the marginalia in the Winchester manuscript most likely derive from Malory himself, then it is significant that this narrative insistence on the vagaries of combat and the inevitable defeat of even the best knight is marked at Trystram's second unhorsing by a marginalium.[19]

It is, I think, noteworthy that these emphases on the contingencies of combat come in the thematically important 'Book of Sir Trystram'. Proleptically and thematically Malory thus reminds readers that nothing lasts forever, thereby preparing for the final destruction. But these references also emphasize that there is no shame in occasionally being bloodied or beaten. The silent but accompanying principle must therefore be that there is no automatic shame in being wounded. On the contrary, building on Lynch's observations, I contend that wounds in Malory's *Morte Darthur* frequently betoken nobility, not sin or failure.[20] Lynch also perspicaciously argues that prowess brings its own special goodness with it. Prowess, in fact, is the acme of chivalric endeavour, the chief means of winning *worshyp*. As Beverly Kennedy rightly notes, 'Late medieval treatises on knighthood are unanimous in making the desire for worship the *sine qua non* of a successful knightly career.'[21] Since in both medieval society and medieval literature armed combat was a sport (tournaments) and a reality (warfare), the winning of worship is primarily established through fighting. Fighting obviously has both good and bad consequences in the *Morte*, but consequences and ethics are not necessarily the same

[18] Vinaver, Commentary on 484.18–22 (Field's *Morte Darthur* 379.5–8).
[19] *The Winchester Malory*, folio 212v. Trystram and Lamarok's fight and reconciliation just before their unhorsing are also marked by a marginalium: folio 196v. Even if the marginalia are scribal, there is still a marked correlation between narrative text and theme and manuscript layout in these (and other) instances.
[20] Lynch, *Malory's Book of Arms*, esp. pp. 28–46, 76. Lynch's views – and now hopefully my own – are partly endorsed and magnified by Hodges, 'Wounded Masculinity', esp. pp. 15–17.
[21] B. Kennedy, *Knighthood in the Morte Darthur*, 2nd edn (Cambridge, 1992), p. 148. On the priority of winning worship through 'the demi-god prowess', see further R. W. Kaeuper, *Chivalry and Violence in Medieval Europe* (Oxford, 1999), pp. 129–60.

thing. It is for such reasons as these that I disagree with Lynch and Carol Kaske, each of whom claims that Malory in the *Morte* occasionally displays an ideological unrest about, or criticism of, violence and combat and their often bloody consequences.[22] Robert L. Kelly similarly argues for a 'double view of Lancelot', since (in Kelly's eyes) knights who heal are good, but knights who wound or are wounded are bad, and Launcelot both inflicts and receives wounds.[23] None of this, I think, is entirely accurate.

The association of worship, prowess and combat is evident throughout the *Morte Darthur*. Arthur himself, in Tale I, frequently embarks on adventure, including the joust with Pellynore. The notable thing about this encounter is that Pellynore praises Arthur's martial prowess (41.15–17) and, when the adventure becomes public knowledge, 'all men of worship seyde hit was myrry to be under such a chyfftayne that wolde putte hys person in adventure as other poure knyghtis ded' (45.10–12). The knights respect not merely that Arthur carries himself as *primus inter pares*, not merely that he too performs great deeds; equally important is the fact that Arthur 'wolde putte hys person in adventure'. No one actively seeks injury, but all men of worship, including the king, are willing to risk injury as the path to worship. For Malory and his characters, it is part of Arthur's greatness that he himself subscribes to this view. In light of my contention elsewhere about the close correlation between the narrative and manuscript of the *Morte Darthur*, about the manner in which Winchester's physical layout reinforces Malory's and the *Morte*'s principal themes, it is significant that Malory regularly refers to Arthur in the first tale as 'sir' as much as 'king'.[24] As Dhira B. Mahoney points out, Malory thus tries to indicate and distinguish between different facets of Arthur's character, including the fact that Arthur is as much warrior as monarch.[25] As for the priority of *worshyp* over weeping or wounds in the *Morte*, it is noteworthy that Malory takes pains here and elsewhere in the early tales of the narrative to emphasize precisely how much Arthur has to fight to secure and maintain his right to the throne. Arthur's kingship is

---

[22] A. Lynch, '"Thou woll never have done": Ideology, Context, and Excess in Malory's War', in *The Social and Literary Contexts of Malory's Morte Darthur*, ed. D. T. Hanks Jr and J. G. Brogdon (Cambridge, 2000), pp. 24–41; C. Kaske, 'Malory's Critique of Violence before and just after the Oath of the Round Table', in *Beowulf and Beyond*, ed. H. Sauer and R. Bauer (Frankfurt, 2007), pp. 259–70. For a more detailed refutation of the notion that Malory criticizes violence, see my 'Warfare and Combat'.

[23] Kelly, 'Wounds, Healing, and Knighthood', p. 191.

[24] See my 'Malory, Hardyng, and the Winchester Manuscript: Some Preliminary Conclusions', *Arthuriana* 22.4 (2012), 167–89. On the titles Malory gives his characters, including Arthur, see D. B. Mahoney, 'Narrative Treatment of Name in Malory's *Morte d'Arthur*', *ELH* 47 (1980), 646–56.

[25] Mahoney, 'Narrative Treatment of Name', pp. 651–2.

obviously a good thing in the eyes of Malory and most of his characters, and that kingship is – at times quite literally – based on Arthur's willingness to purchase worship with the odd wound.

The primacy of worship over wounds is also apparent in the tragic figure of Balyn. When told that the sword he has just won is cursed and that he must give it back, Balyn famously retorts that he 'shall take the aventure' (50.5). As Mann elegantly affirms, this notion of 'taking the adventure' is the dominant motif of the Balyn story (and indeed of the *Morte* as a whole), and the phrase itself is, in two of its three occurrences in this tale, original to Malory.[26] *Worshyp* is what motivates (and, for Mann, partially explains) adventure – though I do not agree with Mann's accompanying conclusions that Malory is uninterested in characterization or that the knight in seeking adventure must also automatically surrender his free will. The important thing, for my present argument, is that Balyn's dismissal of the sword-damsel's warnings clearly prioritizes worship over wounds. Balyn's adventure with Garnyssh of the Mownte similarly illustrates his prioritizing of honour over emotional pain, for when Garnyssh complains about Balyn's revelation of the infidelity of Garnyssh's lover, Balyn responds that he 'dyd none other but as I wold ye dyd to me' (70.16–17). For Balyn, both physical and emotional pain are superseded by *worshyp*, including public recognition of prowess and honour. This, of course, is why he keeps the doomed sword, for it both guarantees adventure and symbolizes his worshipful stature as 'a passynge good man of hys hondys and of hys dedis, and withoute velony other trechory and withoute treson' (48.1–3). Balyn's efforts at winning worship, moreover, succeed: hence Garnyssh's acclamation 'I know you well inowghe: ye ar the Knyght with the Too Swerdis, and the man of moste proues of youre hondis lyvynge' (69.21–2). Swords and prowess, smiting and worship, are clearly and continuously interwoven in the *Morte Darthur*.

That adventure leads to combat, a display of prowess and the winning of worship (albeit not necessarily happiness) is a leitmotif of the *Morte*, occurring even in the 'Tale of the Sankgreal'. Although Malory scholars regularly argue for a disconnect between Grail values and chivalric values in Malory's Grail quest and its source, it is significant that Bors, one of the Grail elect, considers the quest yet another opportunity to win 'much erthly worship' (731.10). As I have remarked elsewhere, it is arguably even more significant that Bors's eremitical interlocutor agrees with him.[27] Shortly hereafter Bors agrees to champion a dispossessed lady against her sister's champion. Despite the lady's accounts of the opponent knight's victories, the many dead men he has scored up and his status as

---

[26] Mann, '"Taking the Adventure"', pp. 80–1.
[27] See my 'Warfare and Combat', p. 175.

'the moste douted man of thys londe', Bors is happy to fight (733.3–22). Malory recounts how the two champions 'made grete woundis and depe, that the blode wente oute of hyre bodyes', and that 'there founde Sir Bors gretter deffence in that knyght more than he wente; for thys Sir Prydam was a passing good knyght and wounded Sir Bors full evyll, and he hym agayne' (735.7–11). Malory also takes care to inform readers or listeners that, as a result of Bors's victory, 'the yonge lady com to her astate agayne be the myghty prouesse of Sir Bors de Ganys' (735.27–8). Several pages later, Bors encounters an abbot who (naturally, in the Grail quest) informs him of the allegorical significance of this scene, how Bors and his prowess were really championing 'the newe law of Oure Lord Jesu Cryst and Holy Churche' (741.35–742.1). Nevertheless, despite the change to celestial values that, for many critics, the Grail quest is supposed to usher in, Bors clearly fights for earthly reasons, to reinstate a lady to her earthly property. By patristic standards, such lands and status should not matter. But Bors, however much he might be a Grail knight, is also still an Arthurian knight, and he champions the lady explicitly to reclaim her lands (732.28–733.24; 735.23–31). This defence of a lady, as the Round Table Oath enjoins knights (97.27–35), is precisely what he should do as an Arthurian hero. There is, moreover, no indication that what he does runs counter to Grail law. The abbot's subsequent lecture attempts to give this episode a more religious meaning than it had in its synchronic narrative moment, but Bors had no way of knowing this when he agreed to fight on the lady's behalf. Nor does Malory ever tell us that God fought through Bors or that Bors was secretly fighting for God. Instead, what is emphasized, especially since the battle comes after Bors's statement about winning earthly worship, is that Bors fights for honour, to defend ladies and the Round Table Oath and, we can safely assume, to win *worshyp* – as indeed he does. But as my quotation about the fighting itself reveals, this worship is achieved through the physical pain and bloodletting of Bors and his opponent. Bors, however, shows little concern. Indeed, far from being worried by somatic distress before the battle, Bors actively increases his bodily hardship by ignoring the lady's offer of 'supper with fleyssh and many deyntees' in favour of 'watir' and 'soppis' (732.19–22); likewise Bors insists upon sleeping 'on the floore' (733.25). Bors's diet and sleeping arrangements are unusual, and happen only in the Grail quest, but whether in 'The Sankgreal' or elsewhere in the *Morte*, the earthly worship justifies the painful bodily means.

The essential connection between wounds and worship is confirmed not only by male action throughout the *Morte*, but also by Percyval's Sister who, like Bors or Balyn or Arthur, explicitly wants to win *worshyp*. Although Galahad warns her that consenting to give up a dish of blood as is the custom of a particular castle will no doubt secure her death, she remarks, 'Truly, … and I dye for the helth of her I shall gete me grete *worship* and soule helthe, and *worship* to my lynayge' (767.23–4; my emphasis). Percyval's Sister effectively hazards her blood and her body to win worship, the same sort of action regularly undertaken by male knights in the course of countless secular adventures throughout the *Morte Darthur*.[28] Notably, for Percyval's Sister as for the male knights who more regularly take the adventure, the winning of worship negates any anxiety about somatic disruption. Like Balyn – or like Gawayne when fighting Launcelot in Benwick – she knows the bodily effects of this adventure. Both Galahad and she herself foretell her demise, but she pursues the adventure – and the fame – notwithstanding the risk. 'No pain, no gain', as Laurie A. Finke and Martin B. Shichtman remind us.[29] My point, then, is that, for Malory and his characters, *worshyp* is the highest concern. Significantly, *worshyp* is neither qualified nor negated by somatic injury.

Although Mann and Molly Martin each, in different ways, rightly argue that the values of the Grail quest are not as egregiously at odds with the rest of the *Morte Darthur* as critics often claim,[30] it is nevertheless true that, in this section of the *Morte* and only in this section, knightly things are not always what they have been. For obvious reasons, much criticism of Malory's 'Sankgreal' revolves around the question of how much or how little Malory adopts of the French *Queste*'s condemnation of Lancelot. Yet when Malory's Launcelot encounters a female recluse who explains his unprecedented defeat in the tournament of the white and black knights, Malory offers a clear indication that the values of the Grail quest are anomalous to the *Morte Darthur* as a whole. Launcelot's defeat in the tournament is traditionally interpreted as chastisement of his pride and evidence that Malory is implementing a new set of values. What is over-looked in this judgement is that Launcelot's desire to win earthly worship is of course entirely typical of knightly achievement and identity through-out the *Morte*. Even in the Vulgate or *Lancelot-Grail* cycle, as Sandra

[28] On Percyval's Sister and the winning of worship, see A. Lynch, 'Gesture and Gender in Malory's *Le Morte Darthur*', in *Arthurian Romance and Gender: Selected Proceedings of the XVII International Arthurian Congress*, ed. F. Wolfzettel (Amsterdam and Atlanta, 1995), pp. 285–95 (pp. 291–2); and especially L. Robeson, 'Women's Worship: Female Versions of Chivalric Honour', in *Re-Viewing Le Morte Darthur: Texts and Contexts, Characters and Themes*, ed. K. S. Whetter and R. L. Radulescu (Cambridge, 2005), pp. 107–18 (pp. 115–16).

[29] L. A. Finke and M. B. Shichtman, '"No Pain, No Gain": Violence as Symbolic Capital in Malory's *Morte Darthur*', *Arthuriana* 8.2 (1998), 115–33.

[30] Mann, 'Malory and the Grail Legend', p. 209; M. Martin, *Vision and Gender in Malory's Morte Darthur* (Cambridge, 2010), pp. 118–47. Martin offers a thorough overview of the principal scholarly approaches to Malory's Grail quest.

Ness Ihle reminds us, Lancelot always chooses to fight on the losing side to increase his worship, 'and in the pre-*Queste* world such behavior would have been magnanimous'.[31] This is equally true of Malory's Arthuriad before and after 'The Sankgreal'. Ihle thus goes on to point out how, in Malory's version of Grail events, Launcelot's sins are greatly reduced and his 'prowess is a virtue if used rightly and without vainglory, whereas in the *Queste* he is constantly adjured by hermits to rely only on God and not to trust his own prowess'.[32] Malory, however, goes even further than this in exonerating Launcelot, for there is a subtle acknowledgement of the normality of this desire for worship in the recluse's explanation that 'in *thys* queste God lovith no such dedis' (722.2–3; my emphasis). That pronoun is a telling qualification.

If the supreme importance of worship intrudes even into the Grail quest, it is hardly surprising to see its status overwhelmingly reaffirmed in the closing tales of the *Morte Darthur*, particularly in the series of combats and tournaments that dominate 'The Book of Sir Launcelot and Queen Guenevere' (Tale VII). Edmund Reiss caustically complains that 'to return to worldly aims after glimpsing higher purposes and values is for man to be either frustrated or deceived into thinking that he is still leading a good and worthwhile life'.[33] For Reiss and others, the Arthurian fondness for earthly chivalry – including winning earthly *worshyp* – exemplifies the sinful wrongheadedness that helps destroy the Arthurian dream and that highlights the inadequacies of chivalry. As Mark Lamberts rightly asserts, however, Reiss's complaint ignores Malory's tone and diction in Tales VII and VIII, especially the 164 uses of the word *noble* in these final tales versus the three appearances of the word *noble* in 'The Sankgreal': 'Clearly "noble" is a word Malory associates with earthly, Arthurian chivalry but not with … religious chivalry.'[34] What Reiss's complaint also overlooks is the reason for the prominence of winning earthly adventure and earthly worship in Malory's Arthuriad. Far from confirming failure and inadequacy, Tale VII returns us to the world of 'noble knyghtes' and 'taking the adventure', returns us, that is, to the Arthurian norm, at least in this version of the story. Such a world is hazardous, but it is also, for Malory and his characters alike, a valid and worshipful world. As P. J. C. Field puts it, 'noble knyghtes' is 'the most important thematic phrase of

---

[31] S. N. Ihle, *Malory's Grail Quest: Invention and Adaptation in Medieval Prose Romance* (Madison, WI, 1983), p. 86.

[32] Ihle, *Malory's Grail Quest*, pp. 151–2.

[33] E. Reiss, *Sir Thomas Malory* (New York, 1966), p. 158.

[34] M. Lambert, *Malory: Style and Vision in Le Morte Darthur* (New Haven, CT, and London, 1975), pp. 140–2.

the *Morte Darthur*'.[35] It is important in part because the idea is consistently valorized, not interrogated. Launcelot's renewed victories throughout this section of the *Morte* thus partly create suspense and heighten the pathos when everything is later destroyed; but partly, too, his victories reinforce the winning of earthly worship at the price of bodily pain.

At the close of the Poisoned Apple episode the poisoned knight Patryse is buried in one of the *Morte*'s many prominent tombs (803.14–24). As Vinaver notes, Malory at this point changes the source (the French *Mort le roi Artu*) to record on the tomb that Patryse was poisoned by Sir Pynell le Saveaige, not by the queen as was the accusation by Madore that instigated the adventure.[36] Given Launcelot's role in rescuing Gwenyvere and his insistence that the tomb should make 'no mencion … that ever Quene Gwenyvere consented to that treson' (801.31–3) – that the tomb should not, in fact, record precisely what the sources do record – we might see this tomb functioning as a monument to one of Launcelot's many adventures as well as to Gwenyvere's innocence. Batt perspicaciously reveals how the '*Morte* concentrates, in its accounts of burials, on the *commemorative* power of inscriptions'.[37] This excellent insight deserves further scrutiny, but for my current purposes what is notable about Patryse's tomb is not the ways in which it might memorialize Patryse's wounds or body or death, but rather the way in which Malory translates the tomb into a prominent commemoration of the manifest worship and love of the *living* Launcelot and Gwenyvere. Although, as Patryse's dead body makes clear, there is throughout the *Morte Darthur* an ever-increasing body count that repeatedly testifies to that love, the focus here is not on the wounds but the result: 'Than the knyghtes of hys bloode drew unto hym, and there aythir of them made grete joy of othir. And so cam all the Knyghtes of the Table Rounde that were there at that tyme and welcommed [Launcelot]' (802.30–2). There *are* tears involved, but Gwenyvere weeps not at Launcelot's or Patryse's physical injuries, but rather at Launcelot's worshipful and magnanimous behaviour: that he would champion her even after she had 'shewed hym grete unkyndenesse' (802.28–9). Weeping, at least in this instance, *acknowledges* worship. Prowess, love and worship once again trump somatic disruption or anxiety.

[35] P. J. C. Field, *Romance and Chronicle: A Study of Malory's Prose Style* (London, 1971), p. 75. See also Lambert, *Style and Vision*, pp. 140–1 and n. 22; P. E. Tucker, 'Chivalry in the *Morte*', in *Essays on Malory*, ed. J. A. W. Bennett (Oxford, 1963), pp. 64–103 (p. 65); and Mann, 'Knightly Combat', p. 332.

[36] Vinaver, Commentary on *Works* 1059.26–31. Malory's other major source here, the stanzaic *Morte Arthur*, follows the French: see *Le Morte Arthur: A Critical Edition*, ed. P. F. Hissiger (The Hague, 1975), vv. 872–901.

[37] Batt, *Remaking Arthurian Tradition*, p. 174; my emphasis. Cf. Lambert, *Style and Vision*, pp. 136–7.

Indeed, Launcelot's worship, as the opening of the 'The Noble Tale of Sir Launcelot du Lake' makes clear, is proven over and over again by his 'prouesse and noble dedys ... in all turnementes, justys, and dedys of armys, [where] both for lyff and deth, he passed all other knyghtes' (190.6–10). Crucially, neither Launcelot nor Malory nor any of Malory's other major characters are under any illusions about the potentially violent consequences of winning a reputation through armed combat.[38] One notable illustration of this theme comes with Launcelot's evoking of the 'olde-seyde sawe [that] there ys harde batayle theras kynne and frendys doth batayle ayther ayenst other, for there may be no mercy, but mortall warre' (820.35–821.2). The axiom is all the more apt for being evoked after Launcelot has been injured in a tournament by Bors when Launcelot managed an overly successful disguise by wearing Elayne of Ascolat's sleeve and fighting too earnestly against his own kin. But awareness and anxiety are not the same thing. When Launcelot is accidently wounded almost to death by Bors at the Winchester tourney, Launcelot and Lavayne seek out a hermit, Bawdwyn of Bretayne, to heal Launcelot's wounds. Bawdwyn is sought because of his skill as 'a full noble surgeon and a good leche' (812.8), and Lavayne is quick to stress to Bawdwyn that Launcelot's wounds reflect the performance of truly marvellous 'dedys of armys' (812.30–1). Continuing the emphasis on prowess, adventure and worship, Launcelot identifies himself to Bawdwyn as 'a knyght aventures that laboureth thorowoute many realmys for to wynne worship' (813.12–14). There *is* emotional anxiety surrounding Launcelot's physical injuries here, but the point of such anxiety is not that bodily injury is itself cause for alarm, but rather that Launcelot's injuries might prevent him from winning further worship by preventing him from competing in further tournaments and thus giving and receiving further worshipful injury. Likewise, Gawayne laments 'that the good knyght be so sore hurte', calling it a pity; but crucially for my purposes, 'hit ys gret damage and pité *to all thys londe*, for he ys one of the nobelyst knyghtes that ever I saw in a fylde handyll speare or swerde' (814.23–6). Although no one wants the victorious knight to be excessively injured, the real crisis here is not (the unrecognized) Launcelot's somatic suffering, but rather that the kingdom might be denied the fellowship of so worshipful and martially proficient a knight. For Malory and his characters (as for Homer and his) injury is an undesirable but probably necessary step to glory.

If wounds truly undermined heroics or gender in the *Morte* we might expect a clearer exposition of such a thesis. Equally, if heroic deeds and violence were genuinely undermined or negated or problematized by the

---

[38] See my 'Warfare and Combat', pp. 169–86.

anxiety of somatic disruption, that too we would expect to see manifest. Instead, the pattern that emerges is (as Mann notes) taking the adventure to win *worshyp*. When characters do display anxiety over wounds it is not out of fear of physical instability, but rather because wounds might interfere with worship. Lambert contends that, in contrast to other sections of the *Morte*, there are no major Arthurian characters killed in 'Launcelot and Guenevere'.[39] This is true to an extent, especially if one accepts Lambert's argument that Elayne of Ascolat is an Arthurian liminal and thus not one of the central characters. On the other hand, this trope of wounds getting in the way of worship occurs repeatedly in the *Morte*, and it becomes especially prominent in the opening episodes of Tale VII. Repeatedly in these episodes there is emotional pain, but the distress stems not from Launcelot's injuries, but rather from the possibility that Launcelot's injuries will prevent his participation at sundry tournaments. Hence the wound given to him by Bors, discussed above. Hence the reopening of that wound in a vain attempt to train for the new tournament between Arthur and the King of North Galys called for 'Allhalowmasse Day, besydes Wynchestir' (821.32–823.28). Hence too the famous buttock-injury, where Launcelot's concern is not with any punishment of sin, nor with the possible ignominy of the wound, but again only 'that he myght nat sytte in no sadyll' (834.11–12)!

This episode of the female huntress and the accompanying tournament is largely Malory's invention, though the originality seems to exacerbate rather than unify scholarly debate. Throughout these scenes there is no eremitical lecture about the superiority of celestial living or the dangers of fighting, merely a recognition that honourable knights will seek *worshyp*. I noted earlier that blood is sometimes simply a way of keeping score. Similarly, far from subverting knightly identity, wounds more often become badges of office that can help signify a character's identity and worship. Bawdwyn, for instance, recognizes Launcelot 'by a wounde on hys chyeke' (813.15–16), and Launcelot whilst recovering informs Lavayne that Bors would probably seek him out and that Lavayne would recognize Bors 'by a wounde in hys forehede' (819.34–5).[40] Malory scholars frequently argue that wounds in general, and the buttock-wound in particular, betoken punishment for sin.[41] Launcelot, in sharp contrast

---

[39] Lambert, *Style and Vision*, p. 139.

[40] Hodges, 'Wounded Masculinity', pp. 27–8, also cites these wound-recognitions, and at pp. 18–21 and 27–8 makes an argument that complements my own (and, I hope, vice versa).

[41] Thus for Reiss, *Thomas Malory*, p. 166, the buttock injury denotes Gwenyvere's sins, with Launcelot partly also at fault; Kelly, 'Wounds, Healing, and Knighthood', pp. 186–7, considers the wound 'as a judgment upon and warning to Launcelot'; for Anderson, 'Malory's "Fair Maid of Ascolat"', pp. 244–5, the wound symbolizes

to the critics, is worried only because 'I may calle myselff the moste unhappy man that lyvyth, for ever whan I wolde have faynyst worshyp there befallyth me ever som unhappy thynge. Now, so Jesu me helpe, ... and if no man wolde but God, *I shall be in the fylde on Candilmas Day at the justys, whatsomever falle of hit*' (834.13–18; my emphasis). As that last 'whatsomever falle of hit' elucidates, for Launcelot, earthly glory quite clearly trumps religion or bodily pain or textual anxiety.[42] Far from being invalidated by blood, knighthood, as Hodges perceptively points out, 'is proven through the willingness to bear wounds'. This, Hodges continues, is one reason 'why, when Launcelot runs mad, those who find him treat him well: [for] "whan they sawe so many woundys uppon hym, they demed that he had bene a man of worshyp"'.[43] Blood and wounds, as I argued above, frequently chart chivalric success and identity, not anxiety about textual, bodily or heroic legitimacy.

My final example of the dismissal of pain in favour of the greater good and greater *worshyp* comes with the person and adventure of Sir Urry. Batt claims that the 'Urry episode ... reconceptualizes chivalric violence', and that Urry himself 'painfully embodies the effects of violence'.[44] If true, this would help to reinforce the movement away from traditional martial values which many scholars trace from the Grail quest onwards in the *Morte*. But there is, in fact, no change in the perception and significance of either violence or knighthood in this episode; just the opposite. What we see in the healing of Sir Urry is a pronounced reification and celebration of standard chivalric values and life in the *Morte*.[45] Urry is maimed because the mother of a man he killed in combat – another great fighter, it seems – curses his wounds so that 'Sir Urry shulde never be hole, but ever his woundis shulde one tyme fester and another tyme blede, so that he shulde never be hole untyll the beste knyght of the worlde had serched hys woundis' (861.16–18). The wounds stay fresh and festering for seven years. Then Urry arrives at Arthur's court where, 111 attempts later, he is

---

Launcelot's punishment for Elayne of Ascolat's death. Karen Cherewatuk reads ignoble wounds as warnings against sexual transgression (see her essay in this volume). All of these critics take the sylvan-dwelling, female-companioned huntress as a Diana-figure; this mythical identity strikes me as a more certain interpretation than her possible moral significance.

[42] *Contra* Batt, *Remaking Arthurian Tradition*, passim. The focus on earthly knights in the Winchester manuscript at this point is evident by the fact that the names of Launcelot and his fellows are several times rubricated on this folio (431v), whereas Launcelot's invocation of 'Jesu' and 'God' are not rubricated. In telling contrast to knightly names, divine names are in fact never rubricated in Winchester.

[43] Hodges, 'Wounded Masculinity', p. 18, quoting *Works* 822.32–4 (Field's edition 648.21–2).

[44] Batt, *Remaking Arthurian Tradition*, pp. 153–4.

[45] Cf. Lynch, *Malory's Book of Arms*, pp. 45–6.

75

healed by Launcelot.[46] And as soon as Urry is healed, Arthur celebrates the cure and the knights by holding another tournament, reminding us of the pre-eminent significance of martial endeavours in the winning of worship throughout the *Morte Darthur*. Were Malory advocating a cessation of earthly chivalry or violence, Urry could have been maimed or even left out of the story altogether. Instead, Malory creates an episode that reiterates and celebrates earthly Arthurian chivalry and fellowship by having Urry healed by Launcelot – thereby confirming that Launcelot remains on the eve of destruction what he was in the wake of the Roman War: patently the best and most worshipful knight in the world.

Although critics agree that the Urry episode is, possibly excepting 'The Tale of Sir Gareth', Malory's longest original episode in the *Morte Darthur*, this originality is about all that we do agree on in this instance. Nowhere is there less interpretative unity than over the question of why Launcelot weeps after the healing. The phrase 'And ever Sir Launcelote wepte, as he had bene a chylde that had bene beatyn' (868.1–2), like the imagery created by such specific diction, suggests severe (albeit perhaps unwarranted) punishment. In this context, argues Batt, 'fifteenth-century language of human-divine relations … interestingly illuminates Launcelot's condition as a special child whom God chastises'.[47] Launcelot's chastisement would thus be 'an act of love' and a 'redemptive' experience. Corey Olsen argues that Launcelot's tears are in fact 'the clearest [interpretative] cue that Malory provides his readers' in this scene, accepts Batt's idea of Launcelot as a 'beloved' but wayward 'child of God', and concludes that this religious connection 'seems inevitable'.[48] For Olsen, and perhaps Batt, the tears thus signify divine judgement and grace, but also Launcelot's awareness of his lack of worth. Leaving aside the fact that, by this account, the tears might signify displeasure at the redemptive but corrective love and that refusing to accept God's grace is itself a sin, there is, I believe, another interpretation open to us, one that does not require us to read Malory and the *Morte* as typical exponents of the basic religious character of late medieval society, or necessitate reading the *Morte* through biblical teachings. I propose instead that the most relevant and important context for the healing of Sir Urry is the *Morte Darthur* itself, and that we

---

[46] That is, the 'hondred knyghtes and ten' (866.7) who fail the healing, plus Launcelot himself. Malory does not actually list 110 names, despite his claim to do so.

[47] Batt, *Remaking Arthurian Tradition*, p. 157.

[48] C. Olsen, 'Adulterated Love: The Tragedy of Malory's Lancelot and Guinevere', in *Malory and Christianity: Essays on Sir Thomas Malory's Morte Darthur*, ed. D. T. Hanks Jr and J. Jesmok (Kalamazoo, MI, 2013), pp. 29–55 (p. 47). Olsen does not acknowledge this, but the view that the tears signify Launcelot's awareness of his own sinful failings goes back to C. S. Lewis, 'The English Prose *Morte*', in *Essays on Malory*, ed. J. A. W. Bennett (Oxford, 1963), pp. 7–28 (p. 20).

should first prioritize the evidence of the major themes of the *Morte* and the obvious interests of its author; only thereafter can we turn to the often very fruitful interpretative aids supplied by social, political, religious or even literary contexts.

This alternate interpretation that I am proposing centres around the marked disconnect in this scene between words and image on the one hand, versus textual and thematic meaning on the other hand. Given the very public revelation of Launcelot's worship that is enacted through the healing, as well as the restoration of bodily wholeness to a knight long injured and suffering with a septic wound,[49] it is impossible to read the healing as the chastisement of Launcelot initially suggested by the language and imagery of the beaten child. We must accordingly find meaning in the episode's thematic and narrative contexts and symbolism. What these contexts reveal is public affirmation of Launcelot's continued and unrivalled stature as 'beste knyght of the worlde' (the one necessary to heal Urry: 861.18) and paragon of the Round Table fellowship. Hence the tears are not tears of religious joy or contrition, but rather tears of earthly emotion, principally relief and gratitude. Not, as R. M. Lumiansky would have us believe, relief that Launcelot has passed the test which Arthur has somehow cleverly contrived out of Urry's situation to discern whether or not Launcelot and Gwenyvere have been unfaithful to him.[50] There simply is no such test. Nor can I accept that Launcelot feels gratitude for being divinely chastised but nonetheless loved, or that being allowed to heal Urry after all else have failed and after the one episode in the entire *Morte* where Launcelot and Gwenyvere do explicitly consummate their relationship somehow signifies failure.[51]

Earl R. Anderson perceptively links Launcelot's tears to a widespread motif common to tales of warriors and heroes: sympathy for the hero's injuries. In this sense, argues Anderson, 'so far as Malory is concerned, weeping is part of the tradition in healing episodes and perhaps is a form

---

[49]  As Cherewatuk points out elsewhere in this volume, Urry's is the only long-festering wound in the *Morte Darthur*.

[50]  R. M. Lumiansky, '"The Tale of Lancelot and Guenevere": Suspense', in *Malory's Originality: A Critical Study of Le Morte Darthur*, ed. R. M. Lumiansky (Baltimore, 1964), pp. 205–32 (pp. 229–31).

[51]  That the healing and tears somehow highlight Launcelot's failure or 'unworthiness' is a common critical refrain, though critics differ as to whether the lack of worth is primarily chivalric or spiritual (or both): I quote 'unworthiness' from Lumiansky, '"Tale of Lancelot and Guenevere"', p. 231, but for similar views see Lewis, 'English Prose *Morte*', p. 20; Reiss, *Sir Thomas Malory*, pp. 170–2; S. C. B. Atkinson, 'Malory's "Healing of Sir Urry": Lancelot, the Earthly Fellowship, and the World of the Grail', *Studies in Philology* 78.4 (1981), 341–52 (p. 349); and D. T. Hanks Jr, '"All maner of good love comyth of God": Malory, God's Grace, and Noble Love', in *Malory and Christianity*, ed. Hanks and Jesmok, pp. 9–28 (p. 17).

of "sympathetic medicine"'.[52] Given the prominence of combat and its bloody consequences both in Malory and in heroic literature more generally, this is no doubt partially true. Together with the tears, I suggest, Malory's focus on chivalric bodies and blood, sympathetic healing and celebratory tournaments, actively reinforces Launcelot's heroic stature. He feels relief and gratitude not because he is unworthy, but precisely because he is still the preeminent knight of the world and still the yardstick of Round Table chivalric achievement and fellowship. The fact that earthly chivalric fellowship and values are still paramount at this point in the Arthuriad is even more apparent in the response of Urry himself to the healing. For Urry, who might understandably be thought to have had enough of potential injury through combat, is happy to celebrate his own healing by risking himself in yet another tournament. As Mann observes, the knightly body is a 'testing ground' used to establish worship, fellowship and – *pace* Mann – even character.[53] Knights undertaking adventure do – again *pace* Mann – possess free will, though they are also subject to chance, fate and other characters' actions. More importantly for my current argument, in following adventure, knights willingly accept wounds in exchange for worship. To reinforce the priority of earthly chivalric prowess and identity, Malory makes Urry one of the two victors of this tourney. As a result of their prowess in this tourney, moreover, Urry and Lavayne, the other victor, are elevated to the ranks of the Round Table (868.12–30). Neither Arthur's proposed tourney nor Urry's willingness to joust and fight immediately after being healed should surprise us. After all, as Percyval says to his mother, knights (including her husband, brothers and sons) cannot stay safely at home, or avoid violent adventure, for the simple reason that 'hit ys oure kynde to haunte armys and noble dedys' (637.8).

In a recent elucidation of Malory's biblical language and themes Lawrence Besserman reminds us that 'mortal man-to-man combat is a motif to be found in the Bible' as well as in heroic poetry or medieval romance. For Besserman, such 'Biblical precedents ... cannot make

---

52 Anderson, 'Malory's "Fair Maid of Ascolat"', p. 249 n. 24. Although he does not necessarily weep, Walewein in Dutch Arthurian romance often appears as healer as well as knight nonpareil: see, e.g., *Dutch Romances Volume I: Roman van Walewein*, ed. [and trans.] D. F. Johnson and G. H. M. Claassens (Cambridge, 2000); and D. F. Johnson, '"Men hadde niet Arsatere vonden alsoe goet": Walewein as Healer in the Middle Dutch Arthurian Tradition', *Arthuriana* 11.4 (2001), 39–52. On the literary tradition of painful emotion, sleep and swooning in and behind the *Morte*, see further Megan G. Leitch's essay in this volume.

53 Mann, 'Knightly Combat', p. 338. The argument that accepting adventures negates free will, contested in my next sentence, comes from Mann's '"Taking the Adventure"' and 'Knightly Combat'.

this violence [of the *Morte* or the Jewish Worthies] seem wholesome or just'; yet Besserman allows that Arthur and Launcelot and company are partially ennobled by such biblical echoes.[54] I argue that we can and should go beyond this recognition. Repeatedly throughout the *Morte Darthur* Malory emphasizes combat and worship and fellowship and love, as well as the tragedy that can result from conflicts amongst these four principal values. But the tragedy, as I have suggested elsewhere, does not negate the heroism, prowess or achievement of Malory's characters.[55] Wounds and weeping in the *Morte* are likewise not used to advocate peace, the perils of bodily injury or the inferiority of earthly chivalry. On the contrary, as we see with the catalogue of knights prefacing Urry's healing, Malory instead renders his entire Arthuriad into a tomb enveloping, valorizing and memorializing earthly Arthurian chivalry. This valorization perforce extends to the giving and receiving of wounds that are a staple feature of chivalric and heroic existence. But if the Bible offers some precedents for assessing wounds and violence in Malory's Arthuriad, it is more germane to seek precedents from amongst knightly practitioners.

Despite the claims still made by some scholars that knighthood was by definition innately religious, we must remember that knighthood was, first and foremost, a martial endeavour. Although it has been claimed that Malory himself 'would have seen his vocation as armed godliness',[56] the literary and historical and even biographical evidence all suggests otherwise. As *The Book of the Ordre of Chyvalry* puts it, 'Thoffyce of a knyght is to mayntene and deffende his lord worldly or terryen.'[57] Needless to say, both in literature and in life such protection took the form of smiting one's enemies. The Church did make considerable efforts to control knightly smiting, but we should be under no illusions: this was often little more than a stop-gap measure. As both Maurice Keen and Richard W. Kaeuper authoritatively illustrate, chivalry was quite adept at appropriating Church doctrine to its own quite earthly and martial purposes.[58] This was true in general terms, and it was even more certain in warfare, where 'knights

---

[54] L. Besserman, *Biblical Paradigms in Medieval English Literature from Cædmon to Malory* (New York and London, 2012), pp. 114–21 (pp. 118 and 120).

[55] See my 'Warfare and Combat', pp. 169–86, and my *Understanding Genre and Medieval Romance* (Aldershot, 2008), pp. 99–149.

[56] D. T. Hanks, Jr and J. Jesmok, 'Introduction', in *Malory and Christianity*, ed. Hanks and Jesmok, pp. 1–8 (p. 3).

[57] *The Book of the Ordre of Chyvalry: Translated and Printed by William Caxton from a French version of Ramón Lull's 'Le Libre del Orde de Cauayleria'*, ed. A. T. P. Byles, EETS o.s. 168 (London, 1926), p. 29.

[58] M. Keen, *Chivalry* (New Haven, CT, and London, 1984), pp. 44–63 (esp. p. 57); Kaeuper, *Chivalry and Violence*, pp. 45–51.

seem to have paid scant heed to the Church's strictures on conduct'.[59] The long-standing knightly insistence on the validity and enjoyment of tournaments in the face of equally long-standing clerical denunciation further reveals the independence of chivalric and clerical ideologies.[60] Given Malory's fondness for narrating feats of prowess in both tournament and warfare, it is safe to conclude that his views on violence and honour were fairly prosaic and realistic; he clearly belongs to the martial camp.[61] Furthermore, martial prowess for Malory and his characters is itself 'a moral quality'.[62]

Since fighting dominates the *Morte Darthur*, wounds are ever-present; but wounds are also always acceptable as a necessary accompaniment to *worshyp*. In this Malory is but of his age and profession. As Keen judiciously reminds us, 'the middle ages were, throughout, violent and warlike times, and that is why chivalry flourished'.[63] The Middle Ages also, of course, bequeathed to the modern world parliament and universities, but chivalry was not pacifist and it cannot be made to cohere with modern pacifist thought. Nor should it be forcibly conjoined to modern somatic theory. To quote Keen again, 'Chivalry was quintessentially bellicose, setting the fighting man on a pinnacle of honour.'[64] As Kaeuper observes in his pithy epitome of Geoffroi de Charny's views on violence and honour,

> Skillful, courageous, hands-on violence, the bloody and sweaty work of fighting superbly at close quarters with edged weapons is the glorious

[59] M. Strickland, *War and Chivalry: The Conduct and Perception of War in England and Normandy, 1066–1217* (Cambridge, 1996), p. 34.

[60] For details of this debate and a judicious insistence on the complexity of the two positions, see Kaeuper, *Holy Warriors*, pp. 66–8.

[61] Nall, *Reading and War*, pp. 139–58, looks not at literary or biographical reasons for Malory's fondness for describing fighting, but rather political ones. She argues that Malory's changes to the location and ending of the Roman War in Tale II of the *Morte* reveal his support for the view, common to many in fifteenth-century England, that foreign war could actually help secure domestic peace and prosperity. War also held considerable financial attractions for the nobility: see K. B. McFarlane, *The Nobility of Later Medieval England: The Ford Lectures for 1953 and Related Studies* (Oxford, 1973), pp. 19–40. Both of these positions buttress my own stance.

[62] I quote D. Brewer, 'The Paradoxes of Honour in Malory', in *New Directions in Arthurian Studies*, ed. A. Lupack (Cambridge, 2002), pp. 33–47 (p. 38); but see also Tucker, 'Chivalry in the *Morte*', pp. 64–8. Tucker's own opening insistence on chivalric worship should refute his later conclusion (pp. 98–100) that earthly chivalry is eventually superseded in the *Morte*.

[63] M. Keen, 'War, Peace and Chivalry', in his *Nobles, Knights and Men-at-Arms in the Middle Ages* (London, 1996), pp. 1–20 (p. 19).

[64] Keen, 'War, Peace and Chivalry', p. 18. Cf. Kaeuper, *Holy Warriors*, p. 6; and Kaeuper, *Chivalry and Violence*, pp. 161–88.

means of securing honor, which Charny (in company with all professional fighting men in all ages) knows is well worth purchasing at the price of mere pain, mutilation, or even death … [Bodily s]uffering is good because it is bonded to the prowess that secures honor.[65]

The problem for Malory and his characters, I suggest, is therefore not individual injury, but communal damage. A notable feature of the closing tales of the *Morte* is how the wounds of the principal characters become more severe as the narrative draws to its bloody and tragic conclusion. As Robert L. Kelly observes of Launcelot specifically, in four of the five episodes comprising Tale VII Launcelot is 'gashed in the thighs by Mador de la Porte [801.21–3], speared in the side by Bors [809.35–810.2], shot in the buttocks by the huntress [833.20–6], and cut severely in the hand as he tears out the bars of a window to Guenevere's bedroom [852.14–17]'.[66] Likewise the battles and tournaments of which Malory is so fond become more severe after the Grail: Gwenyvere is repeatedly threatened with burning, Gareth is killed, civil war occurs, the Round Table is 'disparbled'. For Kelly, Launcelot's wounds symbolize his sinful relapse and knightly decline before the healing of Urry. For Batt, as noted above, the wounds reveal anxieties about violence and about bodily and narrative stability. I argue contrariwise that there is no condemnation of Launcelot or the chivalric way of life he epitomizes. Nor is there any anxiety about bodily pain. There is only the tragic destruction of a noble fellowship and a cessation of opportunities for winning *worshyp*.

In Geoffrey of Monmouth's *Historia Regum Britanniae*, Stonehenge is erected by Merlin as a memorial to dead Britons.[67] Merlin likewise erects or engraves a great many tombs and memorials within Malory's *Morte Darthur*, but there is one notable memorializing tomb for the entire Arthurian fellowship and entire tragic narrative that has so far gone largely unremarked: that is the Winchester manuscript and its consistent rubrication of names, for the rubricated manuscript creates an elegiac memorial to Arthurian chivalry, Arthurian love and Arthurian adventure. By consistently drawing attention to the names, to the characters and deeds, this manuscript memorialization functions at several levels: synchronically as one reads or listens to the Arthuriad, but also diachronically and analeptically as one reflects back on the text. Most importantly for my argument,

---

[65] Kaeuper, *Holy Warriors*, p. 43.
[66] Kelly, 'Wounds, Healing, and Knighthood', p. 173. For consistency I have changed Kelly's citations from *Caxton's Malory* to Field's *Morte Darthur*.
[67] Geoffrey of Monmouth, *The History of the Kings of Britain: An Edition and Translation of De gestis Britonum [Historia Regum Britanniae]*, chapters 128–30, ed. and trans. M. D. Reeve and N. Wright (Woodbridge, 2007), pp. 170–5.

the rubrication's focus on knights and ladies pays heed to their pain, but also to the real purpose of such pain: the announcement, celebration and glorification of earthly Arthurian chivalry even – or especially – after its dismemberment.

# IV

# SLEEPING KNIGHTS AND 'SUCH MANER OF SOROW-MAKYNGE': AFFECT, ETHICS AND UNCONSCIOUSNESS IN MALORY'S *MORTE DARTHUR*

## *Megan Leitch*

In Malory's *Morte Darthur*, both sleep and swooning sometimes mark uncomfortable emotional states. For instance, when Guenevere reproaches Launcelot for sleeping with Elaine (a second time), the narrator reports that Launcelot:

> toke suche an hartely sorow at her wordys that he felle downe to the floure in a sowne. ... And whan sir Launcelot awoke oute of hys swoghe, he lepte oute at a bay-wyndow into a gardyne, ... and so he ranne furth he knew nat whothir, and was as wylde woode as ever was man.[1]

Here, although conscious (if crazed) perambulation is the more prolonged outcome, Launcelot's overwhelming sorrow has its more immediate manifestation in unconsciousness, in the form of a swoon. Moreover, like swooning, sleeping can also be the result of strong emotion: in the Tristram section, Launcelot reads the letter in which King Mark slanders Launcelot and Guenevere: 'And when he wyste the entente of the letter he was so wrothe that he layde hym downe on his bed to slepe' (617.25–7). When characters get so angry that they fall asleep, or so sad that they swoon, unconsciousness serves as a form of making emotion recognizable, of externalizing the authenticity of affect. To give just one further example for the moment, when Guenevere is put into her coffin and Launcelot swoons, a hermit construes the swoon as an indication of unbearable emotion:

---

[1] T. Malory, *The Works of Sir Thomas Malory*, ed. E. Vinaver, 3rd edn, rev. P. J. C. Field, 3 vols. (Oxford, 1990), pp. 805.31–806.7. Primary sources are cited first in full, and then by page and/or line number in the text. All italics and translations are mine unless otherwise stated.

And whan she was put in th'erth *syr Launcelot swouned*, and laye longe stylle, whyle the hermyte came and awaked hym, and sayd,

'Ye be to blame, for ye dysplese God with *suche maner of sorow-makyng.*'

'Truly,' sayd syr Launcelot, 'I trust I do not dysplese God, for He knoweth myn entente: for my sorow was not, nor is not, for ony rejoysyng of synne, but my sorow may never have ende.' (1256.21–5)

Launcelot hastens to inform the hermit that his sorrow is not for the loss of his relationship with Guenevere, which would be sinful, but rather for the loss of Arthur and Guenevere together, which is a sign of Launcelot's proper, undying loyalty to his sovereign. However, the hermit's diegetic reading of Launcelot's swoon as a sign of strong emotional response still holds; hermits are, after all, usually good at interpreting. Thus, while the affective core of this sort of somatic response goes unquestioned, the ethical valences are a matter for debate.

This essay addresses the way in which, in the *Morte Darthur*, sudden unconsciousness is read as a sign of something more significant. I use the term 'ethical' for the sphere of the practical pursuit of a moral life in order to distinguish it from morality as doctrine, though of course the two overlap.[2] In order to bring into focus the legible implications of sleep and swooning in Malory, I will adumbrate connections with other medieval literature and with explanations of these forms of unconsciousness circulating in medieval science and culture. Sleep in medieval literature has received relatively little critical attention. Swoons are rather less understudied; however, by approaching swooning from the perspective of medieval understandings of both sleep and swooning, this essay argues that the one form of unconsciousness can illuminate the other, and that unconsciousness has polyvalent intersections with affect and chivalric ethics in the *Morte Darthur*.

Sleep and swooning certainly overlap in medieval mentalities. To fall into a 'swoghe' or to 'swoon' in Middle English can mean either to faint or to fall asleep, as in the *Gawain*-poet's *Patience*, where Jonah effectively swoons into sleep: 'He swowed and slept sadly al ny3t.'[3] John Capgrave's mid-fifteenth-century *The Life of St Katherine* similarly testifies to the close links between sleep and swooning when specifying that 'Adam slepte in a swow.'[4] Furthermore, these texts, like Malory's *Morte Darthur*, were produced and received in a society whose prevailing sci-

---

[2] See J. A. Mitchell, *Ethics and Exemplary Narrative in Chaucer and Gower* (Cambridge, 2004), pp. 13–14; A. Blamires, *Chaucer, Ethics, and Gender* (Oxford, 2006), p. 8.

[3] *The Poems of the Pearl Manuscript*, ed. M. Andrew and R. Waldron (Berkeley, CA, 1979), *Patience*, l. 442.

[4] J. Capgrave, *The Life of St Katherine*, ed. K. A. Winstead (Kalamazoo, MI, 1999), 3.649.

entific paradigm, in Galenic medicine, invested the causation and consequences of sleep and swooning with implications beyond the bodily, as
discussed below. Medieval readers of romances and other literature also
read courtesy books and dietaries that offer instruction about sleep. Thus,
to suggest what reading for the ethics and affect of unconsciousness can
add to our understanding of Malory, I shall begin with what medieval
conduct manuals have to offer on the vexed subject of falling asleep.

*\*\**

As conduct manuals for young aristocrats, gentry and the aspiring middle
classes, late medieval courtesy books and dietaries offer behavioural
models for hospitality and mealtime comportment,[5] models that are
shared with romances, as has been demonstrated by Jonathan Nicholls
and Ad Putter.[6] What has been less well recognized is courtesy books'
and dietaries' related code of conduct regarding sleep, and the corresponding way in which sleep informs romance. Just as self-control was
fundamental to courteous speech, table manners and receiving or being a
guest for readers wishing to perform courtly behaviour, so self-regulation
was required with regard to sleep, particularly after a meal. As one such
conduct manual, Andrew Borde's *Regyment of Helthe*, explains:

> Whole men of what age or complexion so euer they be of, shulde take
> theyr naturall rest and slepe in the nyght: and to eschewe merydyall sleep.
> But and nede shall compell a man to slepe after his meate: let hym make
> a pause, and than let hym stande & lene and slepe agaynst a cupborde, or
> els let hym sytte upryght in a chayre and slepe.[7]

5   See R. F. Green, *Poets and Princepleasers: Literature and the English Court in the
    Late Middle Ages* (Toronto, 1980), pp. 9–10; R. L. Krueger, 'Introduction: Teach
    Your Children Well: Medieval Conduct Guides for Youths', in *Medieval Conduct
    Literature: An Anthology of Vernacular Guides to Behaviour for Youths, with English
    Translations*, ed. M. D. Johnston (Toronto, 2009), pp. ix–xxxiii (p. xii); M. A. Amos,
    '"For Manners Make Man": Bourdieu, de Certeau, and the Common Appropriation of
    Noble Manners in the *Book of Courtesy*', in *Medieval Conduct*, ed. K. Ashley and R.
    A. Clark (Minneapolis, MN, 2001), pp. 23–48 (pp. 45–6); K. H. Dannenfeldt, 'Sleep:
    Theory and Practice in the Late Renaissance', *Journal of the History of Medicine and
    Allied Sciences* 41 (1986), 415–41 (p. 420).
6   J. W. Nicholls, *The Matter of Courtesy: A Study of Medieval Courtesy Books and the
    Gawain-Poet* (Cambridge, 1985); A. Putter, *Sir Gawain and the Green Knight and
    French Arthurian Romance* (Oxford, 1995), esp. pp. 51–139; for an analysis of the
    prandial focus of one such conduct text, see C. Sponsler, 'Eating Lessons: Lydgate's
    "Dietary" and Consumer Conduct', in *Medieval Conduct Literature*, ed. Johnston, pp.
    1–22.
7   A. Borde, *Regyment of Helthe*, in *The Babees Book*, ed. F. J. Furnivall, EETS o.s. 32
    (London, 1868), p. 244.

The measures and postures prescribed here for unnatural but irresistible daytime or post-prandial sleep involve exerting – and visibly displaying – temperance. Moreover, even when sleeping *is* fully sanctioned – at night – correct procedures must be observed:

> To slepe grouellynge vpon the stomacke and bely is not good ... To slepe on the backe vpryght is vtterly to be abhorred: whan that you do slepe, let not your necke, nother your sholders, nother your hands, nor feete, nor no other place of your bodye, lye bare vndiscouered. Slepe not with an emptye stomacke, nor slepe not after that you haue eaten meate one howre or two after. In your bed lye with your head somwhat hyghe, leaste that the meate whiche is in your stomacke, thorowe eructuacions or some other cause, ascende to the oryfe of the stomacke.[8]

Sleep, then, was something that required a great deal of thought and care. Courtly persons needed to be conscientious about how they performed their loss of consciousness. Such principles are frequently expounded in late medieval courtesy books and dietaries.[9] While Borde's sixteenth-century *Regiment of Helthe* and some of the other extant courtesy books and dietaries post-date Malory's *Morte Darthur*, they continue the concerns of the less-frequently extant fourteenth- and fifteenth-century manuals.[10]

The conduct manuals further indicate that the consequences of failing to adhere to such standards of conduct were not merely bodily. For instance, in John Lydgate's early fifteenth-century version of these concerns in the *Dietary*:

> Suffer no surfytys in thy hous at nyght;
> Were of rere-sopers and of grete excese
> And *be wele ware* of candyll lyght,
> *Of sleuth on morow and of idelnes,*
> *The whych of all vyces is chefe, as I gesse.*
> [...]
> *After mete bewere: make not long slepe*;
> Hede, fete, and stomoke preserve from colde.[11]

---

8 Borde, *Regyment of Helthe*, p. 245.
9 For instance, see also 'A Diatorie', ll. 27–9 and ll. 37–8, W. Bulleyn, *Bulwarke of defence againste all Sicknes, Sornes, and Woundes*, p. 245, and H. Rhodes, *The Boke of Nurture*, all in *The Babees Book*, ed. Furnivall; J. Lydgate, *The Dietary*; W. Caxton, *Gouernayle of Helthe*; T. Elyot, *Castel of Helth*; L. Lemnius, *Touchstone of Complexions*; T. Cogan, *Haven of Health*.
10 As demonstrated by Nicholls, *Matter of Courtesy*, pp. 145–57. For an overview of the early modern dietaries' discussion of sleep, see Dannenfeldt, 'Sleep: Theory and Practice in the Late Renaissance'.
11 J. Lydgate, *The Dietary*, in *Codex Ashmole 61: A Compilation of Popular Middle English Verse*, ed. G. Shuffelton (Kalamazoo, MI, 2008), ll. 49–58.

Here, injunctions to avoid excess – in eating, drinking, etc. – are conjoined to injunctions not to do that to which festive excess leads – namely, sleep too long – because it would be not only bad for one's health, but also bad for one's soul. That this was a very popular didactic tradition is attested not least by the fact that fifty-seven manuscripts of the *Dietary* survive.[12] William Caxton also printed the *Dietary* with a longer, prose *Gouernayle of Helthe*, which circulated in England in Latin from the mid-to-late fourteenth century, and in English from the early fifteenth century (at the latest), and which similarly discusses sleep as an ethical event and focus of regulation.[13]

Penitential manuals used by preachers to prepare sermons corroborate this vexed association between sleep and sloth.[14] For instance, in Robert Mannyng's early fourteenth-century *Handlyng Synne*, the slothful are criticized for sleeping rather than attending Mass:

> *how sey þese men þat are þus slogh,*
> *þat oute of mesure slepe a throwe?*
> whan he heryþ a bel ryng,
> To holy cherche men kallyng,
> þan may he nat hys bedde lete
> But þan behoueþ hym to lygge and swete,
> *And take þe mery mornyng slepe.*[15]

The italicized lines – those which focus on sleep 'oute of mesure' – are not in Mannyng's French source, William of Waddington's *Manuel des Péchés*. The sinfulness of this sort of conduct is also underlined in a Middle English poem that laments late medieval churchgoers' inattentiveness, especially their sleeping, during sermons:

> Sum men at sarmones er to blame
> And war wele better be at hame:
> [...]
> Sum other unto sarmon cumes
> Bot in thaire brest no thing it blomes;
> *ffor slepe thai may no tent take,*
> (Bot at the taverne will thai wake.)

---

12  G. Shuffelton, 'The Dietary: Introduction', in *Codex Ashmole 61*, ed. Shuffelton, p. 528.

13  W. Caxton, *The Gouernayle of Helthe: With The Medecyne of the Stomacke*, ed. W. Blades (London, 1858), f. Bvi v–Bvii r.

14  S. Wenzel, *The Sin of Sloth: Acedia in Medieval Thought and Literature* (Durham, NC, 1960), p. 70.

15  *Robert of Brunne's 'Handlyng Synne'*, ed. F. J. Furnivall, EETS o.s. 119 (London, 1901), ll. 4253–9.

fful light thai er, ill laykes to lere,
And hevy sarmons for to here.
His hevide than may he noght hald up,
But wele he kepes the fendes cup.
*That the fendes cup, call I,*
*That makes tham slepe* and be hevy.[16]

To state that it is 'the fendes cup' that makes people sleep inappropri-
ately here highlights connections between sleep, sin and intemperance.
Monitoring sleeping habits, then, affected well-being on the three levels
associated with courtesy and ethics: somatic, social and spiritual. We
see these concerns combined in Lydgate's *Dietary* (above) and in Hugh
Rhodes' *Book of Nurture*, which instructs readers who wish to learn good
manners and avoid vice to:

Ryse you earely in the morning,
for it hath propertyes three:
Holyness, health, and happy welth. (ll. 57–9)

Sleeping at an inappropriate time or place, physically or metaphorically,
is viewed as unethical – or used to connote the unethical; it would, if
observed, affect one's social reputation, and it would also denote sinful
sloth.

In the *Morte Darthur*, sleep similarly interrogates proper conduct, as
when Launcelot sleeps at the beginning of 'The Tale of Sir Launcelot'.
Here, Malory states that 'the wedir was hote aboute noone, and sir
Launcelot had grete luste to slepe' (253.26–7). In Malory's French source,
the Prose *Lancelot*, it is explained that due to weariness and heat it was
*expedient* or *appropriate* for the knights to sleep until the heat of the day
passed.[17] This is rather different from Launcelot's 'great lust to sleep',
which implies a lack of temperance. Furthermore, Launcelot's declaration
that 'this seven year I was not so sleepy as I am now' (253.30–1) is not
in the French version.[18] Thus, the *Morte* emphasizes the way in which
giving in to this explicitly daytime sleep represents a lack of self-control
that the courtesy books would find reprehensible, and this seems to point
up Launcelot's responsibility for subsequent events. Significantly, during

[16] British Library, MS Harley 4196, fol. 88b; ed. G. R. Owst, *Preaching in Medieval
England: An Introduction to Sermon Manuscripts of the Period c.1350–1450*
(Cambridge, 1926), p. 174.
[17] Compare *Lancelot: Roman en prose du XIIIe siècle*, ed. A. Micha, 9 vols. (Geneva,
1978–83), VI.166: 'si furent si las et si travillié qu'il *les couvint* a reposer tant que li
chauz fust trespassez' ('they were so weary that it *befitted them* to rest until the heat
passed').
[18] Vinaver, Commentary, in *The Works of Sir Thomas Malory*, p. 1414.

Launcelot's unchivalric sleep, he fails his duty to his companion Lionel, who is captured by another knight. Furthermore, Launcelot's lack of vigilance is what allows the four queens to capture him (and to try to corrupt his fidelity to Arthur and Guenevere), since he is still sleeping when they approach him. Here, Malory's *Morte* registers the unethical connotations of inappropriate sleep, and it is by no means the only Middle English romance to do so.

While Middle English chivalric literature from *Sir Gawain and the Green Knight* to *Melusine* is informed by the courtesy books' sleep-related injunctions, perhaps most illuminating here as a touchstone for Malory's *Morte* is another Arthurian romance similarly translated and adapted from French, the early fourteenth-century *Ywain and Gawain*. Here, sleep is ethically loaded when King Arthur and Queen Guenevere fall asleep after a meal:

> After mete went the Kyng
> *Into chamber to slepeing,*
> And also went with him the Quene.
> That byheld thai al bydene,
> For *thai saw tham never so*
> *On high dayes to chamber go.*
> Bot sone, when thai war went to slepe,
> Knyghtes sat the dor to kepe.[19]

The knights' surprise registers the untoward nature of the monarchs' post-prandial sleep, reflecting the tenets of the courtesy books. Arthur and Guenevere transgress the norms of courtesy by retiring to sleep in the middle of the day, and this transgression produces a story about learning courtesy – since it is while they are asleep that, to pass the time, Colgrevance tells the tale that prompts Ywain's quest and the central narrative of the poem. The causal connection between the royals' feasting and their sleeping is less strong in the French source, Chrétien de Troyes' *Yvain*, where 'la reïne le detint' ('the queen detained') Arthur away from the feast for so long that he falls asleep, with rather more erotic insinuations than the Middle English version's ethical ones.[20] Thus, in the way that the when and how of falling sleep matters in the *Morte Darthur*, Malory's text takes part in a recognizable mode of exploring chivalric ethics that may be particularly – though of course not exclusively

[19] *Ywain and Gawain*, in *Sir Perceval of Galles and Ywain and Gawain*, ed. M. F. Braswell (Kalamazoo, MI, 1995), ll. 47–54.

[20] Chrétien de Troyes, *Le Chevalier au Lion (Yvain)*, ed. M. Roques (Paris, 1960); *The Knight with the Lion (Yvain)*, in *Arthurian Romances*, trans. W. W. Kibler (London, 2004), p. 295.

– insular. Like *Ywain and Gawain*, the *Morte Darthur* sometimes departs from its sources in order to construe sleep as a marker for a vulnerable or sinful state, a lack of perception, or a neglect of duties.

Falling asleep also has recognizable emotional connotations. We see this in an example with which this essay began, when Launcelot reads King Mark's revelatory letter: 'And when he wyste the entente of the letter he was so wrothe that he layde hym downe on his bed to slepe' (617.25–7). One notable difference between Launcelot's sleep here and the moment (earlier in the *Morte*) when he has 'grete luste to slepe' is that, in his anger-induced sleep, Launcelot sleeps in his bed rather than outdoors. One's bed is, of course, the proper place for sleep, while sleeping outside under a tree was considered dangerous – according to Galenic medicine and as witnessed elsewhere in romance by the ghastly fate that awaits Heurodis when she falls asleep outside under a tree in *Sir Orfeo*.[21] However, Malory specifies that the letter is read after morning Mass: 'as the kynge and the quene was at masse the varlet cam wyth the lettyrs, and whan masse was done the kynge and the quene opened the lettirs prevayly' (617.3–6), and then Guenevere 'sente the lettir unto sir Launcelot' (617.24–5). Given the great number of events, encounters and jousts that occur in the *Morte* without temporal tags, this seems a telling detail. It notifies the reader that, when Launcelot's anger prompts him to sleep in his bed, it does so in the middle of the day – the same time as when Launcelot and Heurodis fall asleep outdoors. Thus, even if Launcelot sleeps in the proper place when angry, he does not sleep at the proper time; the courtesy books would certainly disapprove.

Yet when considering these indicators regarding Launcelot's affective and ethical state when his anger produces sleep, it is worth observing that falling asleep due to some sort of distress is not unprecedented in medieval literature and may even have been an accepted practice. In Chardri's thirteenth-century Anglo-Norman version of the Life of the Seven Sleepers, uncomfortable emotion is likewise said to engender sleep. Chardri writes that:

> Ke par dolur, ke par penser
> Endormirent li set bacheler.
> Kar ceo avent, sachez, suvent
> Ke gent, quant il sunt trop dolent

---

[21] Dannenfeldt, 'Sleep: Theory and Practice in the Late Renaissance', p. 425; see *Sir Orfeo*, in *The Middle English Breton Lays*, ed. A. Laskaya and E. Salisbury (Kalamazoo, MI, 1995), pp. 63–82; and, for an overview of critical readings of the importance of the location of Heurodis's sleep, C. Saunders, *Rape and Ravishment in the Literature of Medieval England* (Cambridge, 2001), pp. 228–33.

Par pesance de lur penser,
Lur cuvent tost sumiller.[22]

(Whether out of distress or out of worry, the seven young men
went to sleep – for it often happens, you know, that when people
are very sad on account of the weight of their worries, it is natural
that they are prompt to slumber.)

This commentary is not paralleled in Chardri's Latin source, but is found
in Chardri's other saint's life, Josaphaz.[23] This suggests that Launcelot's
soporific rage would not have been as surprising to medieval (insular)
readers as it might be to modern ones. Such articulations of the way in
which emotions engender sleep speak to a particular cultural construction
of the emotions[24] – one which can be elucidated scientifically.

In Galenic medicine, which entered western Europe *c*. 1070–1300 via
Arabic medicine and, despite challenges, persisted through the sixteenth
century, sleep was considered one of the six 'non-natural' influences on
the body.[25] Significantly, sleep was understood to enable the restorative
transformation of food into the four humours. Given that emotions were
understood as imbalances in the humours – anger indicating a predominance of yellow bile, sorrow or melancholy a predominance of black
bile – this way in which sleep acts to restore the balance between the
humours makes sleep a legible response to a strong or uncomfortable
emotion. Here, sleep seems to serve as a way of pressing the 'reset
button'. As Marlowe's Dr Faustus would put it, it is a way to 'Confound
these passions with a quiet sleep'; and Galenic medicine was still the
prevailing scientific paradigm within which to interpret the passions,
or emotions, when Marlowe was writing (if only just).[26] In the holistic
understanding offered by Galenic medicine and by pre-Cartesian views

---

[22] Chardri, *La Vie des Set Dormanz*, ed. B. S. Merrilees, Anglo-Norman Text Society 35 (London, 1977), ll. 615–20; *The Works of Chardri: The Little Debate, The Life of the Seven Sleepers, and The Life of St Josaphaz*, ed. and trans. N. Cartlidge (Tempe, AZ, forthcoming, 2014).

[23] *The Works of Chardri*, ed. Cartlidge; see Josaphaz, ll. 1943–4.

[24] In approaching (medieval) emotions as culturally constructed, this article follows the work of scholars such as Sarah McNamer, in *Affective Meditation and the Invention of Medieval Compassion* (Philadelphia, 2010); and Barbara Rosenwein, in *Anger's Past: The Social Uses of an Emotion in the Middle Ages* (Ithaca, NY, 1998) and *Emotional Communities in the Early Middle Ages* (Ithaca, NY, 2006).

[25] The others are food and drink, inanition and repletion, air, exercise and the passions or emotions. Dannenfeldt, 'Sleep: Theory and Practice in the Late Renaissance', pp. 415–16; N. G. Siraisi, *Medieval and Early Renaissance Medicine: An Introduction to Knowledge and Practice* (Chicago, 1990), p. 101.

[26] C. Marlowe, *Dr Faustus*, ed. D. S. Kastan (New York, 2005), A-text 4.1.135 and B-text 4.4.25.

of the interrelations between mind and body, the idea of sleep as a reset button for the emotions – and perhaps especially for emotions produced by mental stress – has more grounding than it would today. We might refer to an angry person as being in an 'ill humour', but in late medieval mentalities this would be more than a metaphorical description.

This sort of causal relationship between the emotions and sleep also occurs elsewhere in Malory's *Morte* and other Middle English literature. Dream visions, perhaps unsurprisingly given their narrative necessity for slumber, offer various examples. For instance, the narrator of Chaucer's *Parliament of Fowls* describes his process of falling asleep:

> Berafte me my bok for lak of lyght,
> And to my bed I gan me for to dresse,
> *Fulfyld of thought and busy hevynesse*;
> For both I hadde thyng which that I nolde,
> And ek I ne hadde that thyng that I wolde.
> But fynally my spirit at the laste,
> For wery of my labour al the day,
> *Tok reste, that made me to slepe faste.*[27]

Here, by specifying that this narrator falls asleep not only after reading (as is also the case in other Chaucerian dream visions such as *The Book of the Duchess*),[28] but, moreover, when he is also 'Fulfyld of thought and busy hevynesse', Chaucer seems to suggest an affective dimension. 'Hevyness' can of course mean simply 'drowsiness' or 'weight', but 'thought and busy hevynesse' suggests the word's more affective implications of sorrow, anxiety or annoyance.[29] Not dissimilarly, but with more of an indication of the intertwining of such an affect-induced sleep with a negative ethical state, one of the dream visions in *Piers Plowman* is prompted when:

> Scripture scorned me and a skile tolde,
> And lakked me in latyn and li3t by me sette,
> And seide 'Multi multa sciunt et seipsos nesciunt.'
> *Tho wepte I for wo and wraþe of hir speche*
> *And in a wynkynge worþ til I weex aslepe.*[30]

[27]   G. Chaucer, *The Parliament of Fowls*, ll. 88–94, in *The Riverside Chaucer*, ed. L. D. Benson, 3rd edn (Boston, 1987).
[28]   As discussed by P. Boitani, 'Old Books Brought to Life in Dreams: the Book of the Duchess, the *House of Fame*, the *Parliament of Fowls*', in *The Cambridge Companion to Chaucer*, ed. P. Boitani and J. Mann, 2nd edn (Cambridge, 2003), pp. 58–77.
[29]   See *The Middle English Dictionary*, ed. H. Kurath et al. (Ann Arbor, MI, 1952–2001), 'hevyness', senses 4a, 4b, 5a, and 5b.
[30]   W. Langland, *Piers Plowman: The B Version*, ed. G. Kane and E. T. Donaldson (London, 1975), XI.1–5.

Here, when he is rebuked by Scripture (for his moral failure), Will's combined sadness and anger seem to precipitate his sleep. That the sleep that follows will be a contemplative sleep containing a dream with positive spiritual connotations does not detract from the fact that the sleep occurs when (and because) Will is in a condition where he could benefit from such a corrective vision. I would argue that this is also the case in *Pearl*, where again, although the dream to follow offers moral instruction, the dreamer's act of falling asleep when he 'slode vpon a slepyng-sla3te / On þat precios perle withouten spot' is itself dubious, because of the doctrinally inappropriate sorrow that produces it: that is, the *Pearl*-dreamer's sleep-inducing excessive grieving represents a lack of both spiritual and social decorum.[31] Such examples read as demonstrations of Chardri's maxim that 'the weight of worries' or emotions prompts people to slumber. While modern criticism may not customarily read Malorian romance in parallel with Ricardian dream visions, the occurrence of this idea in both genres seems to testify to its broader resonance in the cultural imaginary of the society for which Malory wrote.

In addition to Launcelot, Malory's Arthur also seems to fall asleep because of his cares, in a way that suggests an intertwining of affect and ethics. This occurs when Arthur is out hunting and witnesses the passing of the questing beast:

> therewith the beeste departed with a grete noyse, whereof the kynge had grete mervayle. *And so he was in a grete thought, and therewith he felle on slepe.* Ryght so there com a knyght on foote unto Arthure, and seyde, '*Knyght full of thought and slepy*, telle me if thou saw any stronge beeste passe thys way.' (42.16–21)

While the characteristically indeterminate parataxis of Malory's 'and so' here does not firmly locate the cause of the 'grete thought' that produces Arthur's sleep, the narrator presents two apposite circumstances. The most proximate is Arthur's sight of the questing beast, at which Arthur 'had grete mervayle'; however, we are also told that this hunting trip occurs the morning after Arthur has had a disturbing dream of 'gryffens and serpentes' that do 'grete harme' both to Arthur's people and to Arthur himself (41.23–30). This dream in turn directly follows the incestuous conception of Mordred when Arthur sleeps with his half-sister Morgause, and it is because Arthur is 'passynge hevy of hys dreme' (41.31–2) that he decides to go hunting. Thus, Arthur's midday, outdoor sleep brought on by worry or thought seems a testament to his ethical state following this adulterous union. Unlike Launcelot, Arthur is unaware of the extent of the

---

[31] *Pearl*, in *The Poems of the Pearl Manuscript*, ed. Andrew and Waldron, ll. 59–60.

sinfulness of his own adultery (since he does not yet know Morgause is his sister). However, both moments – the moment when a letter reminds Launcelot of the reprehensibility of his affair with Guenevere, and this scene in which Merlin appears to tell Arthur of his true identity and thus the way in which, for Arthur's incestuous adultery, 'hit ys Goddis wylle that youre body sholde be punysshed for your fowle dedis' (44.26–7) – both moments are marked by a similar sort of emotion-induced sleep. Moreover, in Malory's French source, *La Suite du Merlin*, Arthur does not fall asleep; the French Arthur is, instead, merely pensive.[32] Malory, then, adds the sleep, in a way that points up the parallels with Launcelot's angry sleep elsewhere.

Among the other moments in which sleep renders emotional and/or ethical states legible in the *Morte*, perhaps the most famous is Launcelot's sleep in 'The Tale of the Sankgreal' when the Grail makes an appearance. Here, after attempting but failing to enter a chapel, Launcelot is 'passyng hevy and dysmayed' (894.4) and falls asleep outdoors: 'And so he felle on slepe; and half wakyng and half slepynge he saw ... the holy vessell of the Sankgreall' (894.9–23). The narrator does mention that 'All thys [vision] sir Launcelot sye and behylde hit, for he slepte nat veryly' (894.13–14), but nonetheless, Launcelot's inability to entirely extricate himself from this sleep is narrated as a sign of his sin: 'he was overtakyn with synne, that he had no power to ryse agayne the holy vessell. Wherefore aftir that many men seyde hym shame' (894.35–895.2). Other characters corroborate a diegetic reading of Launcelot's sleep – a sleep preceded by uncomfortable emotions and dismay – as a sign of his negative ethical state: that is, an indication that Launcelot 'dwellith in som dedly synne' (895.10–11) or 'ys unhappy' (895.12–13). Thus, if not always in an entirely unambiguous fashion, Malorian emotions and ethics are repeatedly made manifest through sleep.[33]

Swooning likewise serves as an affective language, as when Launcelot swoons due to sorrow in the instances with which this essay began (when Guenevere reproaches him for his adultery and when Guenevere is buried) and as with sleep, the science of swooning is relevant here. Critical focus on swooning in Middle English literature has commonly been on swoons produced by love or other elevated emotions,[34] but recent articles by Judith

---

[32] Vinaver, Commentary, p. 1298.

[33] See also Percival's sleep when, during the Grail quest, his sorrow culminates in sleep (911.16–19); upon waking in the middle of the night, Percival sees a woman from whom he accepts a horse that turns out to be a fiend, suggesting, at the least, that he made a poor decision.

[34] See J. Mann's seminal article, 'Troilus' Swoon', *The Chaucer Review* 14 (1980), 319–35.

Weiss and Barry Windeatt have broadened the focus to include swoons generated by less hopeful emotions.[35] Windeatt demonstrates that Malory increases the frequency and intensity of swooning in the final two Tales of the *Morte* – 'The Book of Launcelot and Guenevere' and 'The Death of Arthur'.[36] For instance, when Launcelot is wounded in 'The Fair Maid of Astolat', Elaine swoons twice in pity at the sight of his pain and suffering:

> whan she saw hym ly so syke and pale in hys bed, she myght nat speke,
> but suddeynly she felle downe to the erthe in a sowghe. And there she lay
> a grete whyle; and whan she was releved, she shryked and seyde,
> 'My lord, Sir Launcelot! Alas, whyghe lye ye in thys plyte?'
> And than she sowned agayne. (1082.3–9)

At this point in the French *La Mort le roi Artu*, Elaine is certainly sad, but she does not swoon.[37] Likewise, while in Malory's French source Arthur weeps (but does not swoon) at the death of Gawain – and, in the alliterative *Morte Arthure*, with which Malory was familiar as the source for his earlier Tale II, Arthur's sorrow at his nephew's death results in one swoon – in Malory's *Morte* Arthur swoons not once but thrice: 'the kynge made great sorow oute of mesure, and toke sir Gawayne in hys armys, and thryse he there sowned' (1230.7–9).[38] Here and elsewhere in the final two Tales, as Windeatt puts it, 'Malory seems intent on out-swooning his sources'; and while such 'serial swooning' may seem 'comically improbable in "real" life', here in literature it 'betokens and accords value to an estimable intensity of feeling, whether in suffering or joy, love or loss'.[39] Malory also highlights ethical predicaments through his adjustments of swoons. For instance, whereas Malory's English source for the final two Tales, the stanzaic *Morte Arthur*, has the brother of the knight poisoned by the apple swooning over his sibling's tomb, Malory instead gives Guenevere a swoon when she is accused of having murdered the poisoned knight: here, Guenevere is 'so abaysshed that she cowde none other-wayes do but wepte so hartely that she felle on a swowghe' (1049.32–4). As Windeatt sensibly remarks, this is not a gendered translation in

---

[35] J. Weiss, 'Modern and Medieval Views on Swooning: The Literary and Medical Contexts of Fainting in Romance', in *Medieval Romance, Medieval Contexts*, ed. R. Purdie and M. Cichon (Cambridge, 2011), pp. 121–34; B. Windeatt, 'The Art of Swooning in Middle English', in *Medieval Latin and Middle English Literature: Essays in Honour of Jill Mann*, ed. C. Cannon and M. Nolan (Cambridge, 2011), pp. 211–30.

[36] Windeatt, 'Swooning in Middle English', p. 223.

[37] *La Mort le roi Artu*, ed. J. Frappier, 3rd edn (Geneva, 1964), p. 40.

[38] Compare *La Mort le roi Artu*, pp. 220–1, and the alliterative *Morte Arthure*, in *King Arthur's Death*, ed. L. D. Benson, rev. E. E. Foster (Kalamazoo, MI, 1994), l. 3969.

[39] Windeatt, 'Swooning in Middle English', pp. 224 and 213.

Malory's *Morte*; it is, rather, a way of making a swoon serve as an ethical marker as well as an emotional one, since it registers Guenevere's innocence.[40]

Physiologically, swooning was thought to have a variety of possible causes, some of which implicate the affective and ethical configurations of the swooning subject. According to John Trevisa's *On the Properties of Things*:

> of defaute of the herte and febilnesse of spiritis cometh swownynge that hatte comenlich *spasmacio*, and that cometh somtyme of accidentis of the soule, as of drede that closith the herte swithe, somtyme of grete ioye other of wrathe that openeth the herte to swithe, and so spiritis passith out by euaporaciuns, exsolaciouns, and schedinge. Somtyme it cometh of accidentis of the body, as of euel complexioun, of grete replecioun of mete and of drinke, of gret abstinence, of stoppynge of veynes and of pressinge and wryngynge of spiritis, and somtyme of to grete swetynge. And of this swownynge som dieth sodaynly.[41]

While pointing out that swooning sometimes has mundane causes such as over-eating or excessive fasting, Trevisa also indicates that swooning could be caused by emotions such as dread, great joy or wrath. Thus, like sleep, swooning was a recognizable, readable result of strong emotion, in medieval medicine as in Malory's *Morte*; and such emotion-induced unconsciousness often has ethical implications in Malory.

However, what about when Gareth swoons in Tale IV of the *Morte Darthur*? When Gareth is wounded by the magical knight and swoons, the implications are a little different than in the swoons of Tales VII and VIII discussed above. Gareth and Lyonesse plan to sleep with each other prior to their marriage, but Lyonesse's sister Lynet prevents this misstep by unleashing a magical knight whom Gareth defeats, but not before receiving a severe wound in the thigh. Gareth

> bled so faste that he myght not stonde; but so he leyde hym downe uppon his bedde, and *there he sowned* and lay as he had bene dede.
>     *Than Dame Lyonesse cryed alowde* that Sir Gryngamoure harde hit and com downe; and whan he sawe Sir Gareth so shamfully wounded he was sore dyspleased ... And there they staunched his bledyng as well as they myght, *and grete sorow made Sir Gryngamour and Dame Lyonesse*. (333.36–334.20)

---

[40]  Windeatt, 'Swooning in Middle English', pp. 222–3.

[41]  J. Trevisa, *On the Properties of Things: John Trevisa's Translation of Bartholomaeus Anglicus, De Proprietatibus Rerum*, ed. M. C. Seymour, 3 vols. (Oxford, 1975), vol. 1, Book 7, p. 378.

Here, Gareth's swooning is not – or at least not obviously – caused by sorrow; however, his swoon does cause sorrow in Lyonesse and Gryngamour. This somatic and affective cycle recurs in Gareth's and Lyonesse's second attempt to sleep with each other, when Gareth's wound reopens while once again defeating the magical knight:

> he was so faynte that unnethis he myght stonde for bledynge, and by than he was allmoste unarmed, he felle *in a dedly sowne* in the floure.
>
> *Than Dame Lyonesse cryed*, that Sir Gryngamoure herde her; and *whan he com and founde Sir Gareth in that plyght he made grete sorow*. And there he awaked Sir Gareth and gaff hym a drynke that releved hym wondirly well.
>
> But *the sorow that Dame Lyonesse made there may no tunge telle*, for she so fared with hirself as she wolde have dyed. (335.22–30)

In this second incident, the links between Gareth's swoon and Lyonesse's and Gryngamour's emotions are made especially clear: they make sorrow not just because Gareth is wounded, but rather because he swoons. Gareth's swoon shows them the gravity of his situation, the reason for their affect. Thus, whether it is the viewer of the wounded who swoons (as Elaine with Launcelot), or the wounded himself who swoons, swooning can both be a sign of sorrow and produce sorrow. It is a multivalent marker for moments of distress.

Yet what do his swoons indicate about Gareth himself? Gareth evidently swoons due to loss of blood, but this is not the only way to read his swoon. In addition to the emotive and physiological causes listed by John Trevisa (quoted above), Galenic medicine also interpreted swooning or fainting as a manifestation of hysteria, in both women and men; hysteria that 'was attributed to retained secretions, superfluous residues like menses and semen, which could be harmful to the body and indicated an inadequate sexual life'.[42] If a scholar as respectable as Judith Weiss can argue that Troilus's famous swoon before he sleeps with Criseyde occurs (in part) as a result of an unfulfilled sex life,[43] then I suggest that Gareth's swoons when he is prevented from sleeping with Lyonesse may carry similar connotations to a medieval readership. Of course Gareth's blood loss is a sufficient cause in itself; however, since sexual frustration (such as Gareth's here) was a recognized cause of swooning, this suggests a way in which one culturally legible discourse is bleeding into another. While Gareth's thigh wound can be read as a sexually legible sign (as in Karen Cherewatuk's essay elsewhere in this volume), his swoon can be

---

[42] Weiss, 'Modern and Medieval Views on Swooning', pp. 130–1.
[43] Weiss, 'Modern and Medieval Views on Swooning', pp. 133–4; see Chaucer's *Troilus and Criseyde*, in *The Riverside Chaucer*, III.1086–1127.

read in a similar way. Perhaps we can even see Elaine's swoons as a sign of deprivation in more than the emotional sense: that is, when she sees the wounded Launcelot and swoons, but more so when she discovers that Launcelot will not return her love. Here in the French version, she goes to bed and never gets up again; however, in Malory: 'she shryked shirly and felle downe in a swoghe; and than women bare hir into her chambir, and there she made overmuche sorowe' (1090.8–10).[44]

Thus, in the *Morte Darthur*, the implications of sleep and of swooning due to uncomfortable emotions are certainly not simple or unidirectional, but attention to the cultural discourses informing contemporary interpretation of such losses of consciousness can enrich our understanding of some of the ways in which the *Morte Darthur* anchors both emotions and ethics in the body.[45] The fact that this discourse often occurs in relation to Launcelot and Arthur, Malory's preeminent knight and king, suggests that the performative responses of sleeping and swooning cannot be dismissed as trivial when considering the ways in which modes of conduct are valorized or condemned in the *Morte Darthur*. Moreover, as we have seen, Malory increases emphasis on both sleep and swooning relative to his sources. Launcelot's swoon at Arthur's and Guenevere's tomb registers his emotion in a way that testifies to his ethical state: he performs the proper response to the loss of his king and queen. Arguably, his earlier swoon when Guenevere tells him off for his infidelity also reads on an ethical level, as a sign of his proper shame when his misconduct is brought home to him. However, Launcelot's sleep-inducing anger when he reads Mark's revelatory letter reflects less positively on him – it does not seem to be an indication of his repentance. Equally, Arthur's and Launcelot's troubled sleeps after the conception of Mordred and during the Grail quest, respectively, occur when they have yet to acknowledge or repent their sins.

This essay, then, has drawn attention to a mode of reading and moulding bodily performance; a mode of deploying and interpreting sleep and swooning that, in the *Morte Darthur*, often speaks to a character's ethical state. At the risk of oversimplifying, when the emotional input provoking a bodily response is anger or sorrow, swooning more often seems to register positive ethical states – or moral, remorseful responses to misconduct – while sleep more often marks negative ethical states. Palomydes rather

---

[44] Compare *La Mort le roi Artu*, p. 68; the contrast is noted by Windeatt, 'Swooning in Middle English', p. 223.

[45] See, for instance, J. Mann, 'Malory: Knightly Combat in *Le Morte Darthur*', in *The New Pelican Guide to English Literature*, ed. B. Ford, 9 vols. (Harmondsworth, 1982–88), I, Part I, 331–9; A. Lynch, *Malory's Book of Arms: The Narrative of Combat in 'Le Morte Darthur'* (Cambridge, 1997).

nicely sums up the connotations of daytime sleep for the chivalric subject when he is travelling with King Mark:

> Than they alyght and sette them downe and reposed them a whyle. And anone wythall kynge Marke fylle on slepe. So whan sir Palomydes sawe hym sounde on slepe he toke his horse and rode his way and seyde to them, 'I woll nat be in the company of a slepynge knyght.' And so he rode a grete pace. (591.1–6)

This also is not in Malory's French source.[46] Palomydes' decision to ride 'a grete pace' emphasizes the gulf between his chivalric virtue and Mark's by demonstrating the vigour of his conscious agency in contrast to Mark's unconsciousness. Here, Palomydes' pronouncement corroborates the way in which, in the *Morte*, unconsciousness often is – and is read as – an ethical and/or affective performance. For those who wish to 'doo after the good and leve the evyl',[47] it does not do to be a 'slepynge knyght'.

---

[46] Vinaver, Commentary, p. 1488: 'In *F* Palomides gives a different reason for parting company with Mark: *il ne m'est pas avis, au semblant que j'ay veü, que il ait gramment chevauchié.*'

[47] 'Caxton's Preface', in *Works*, p. cxlvi.7.

# V

# MIRRORING MASCULINITIES: TRANSFORMATIVE FEMALE CORPSES IN MALORY'S *MORTE DARTHUR*

## *Erin Kissick*

'Sertes, had nat this jantillwoman bene, I had nat come hyder at thys time.' So says Sir Galahad, when Percival's Sister leads him to the ship that announces itself as Faythe, joining him with the two friends who will accompany him for the journey out of the familiar world of chivalry and the community of the Round Table into the spiritual realm.

Sir Thomas Malory's *Morte Darthur* explores the nature of knighthood, creating a chivalric community in which the ideals of chivalry can be tested to their fullest extent.[1] Yet this chivalric community and its members are shown by the narrative to be, as Kenneth Hodges describes it, 'noble but fatally flawed, fatally unstable'.[2] By the end of the text the chivalric community must share the narrative with a newly formed spiritual community, comprised of former pillars of the chivalric community, so that the two communities must exist in tension with each other. I argue that this broader narrative is mirrored in the briefer narratives of Sir Pedivere's Wife and Sir Percival's Sister,[3] whose bodies

---

[1] This article uses Eugene Vinaver's edition of the *Morte*. T. Malory, *The Works of Sir Thomas Malory*, ed. E. Vinaver, 3 vols. (Oxford, 1947).

[2] K. Hodges, *Forging Chivalric Communities in Malory's* Le Morte Darthur (New York, 2005), p. 2. Jeffrey J. Cohen notes that, 'like any overarching ideology, chivalry promised a perfection that it could never in fact bestow. The accession to knighthood was continually represented as a straightfoward (in Frantzen's sense) *bildungsroman* in which a male body functioning as an overinvested site for communal suture moved quickly from the messy ambiguities of youth to a well-ordered adulthood. In fact, however, chivalry depended on a series of potentially open-ended becomings that did not necessarily fold ineluctably into predetermined contours. A tension between restrictive delineation and a multiplicity of possibility formed chivalry's conflicted heart.' J. J. Cohen, *Medieval Identity Machines* (Minneapolis, 2003), p. 47.

[3] I have chosen to borrow the capitalization of their 'names' (such as they are) from Roberta Davidson, who did so when referring to Percival's Sister and have extended

---

function as symbols prefiguring this broader transformation within a number of the knights who make up the chivalric community. These stories each function as what Kateryna Rudnytzky Schray refers to as a 'plot in miniature', that is, as single episodes that serve to map out the broader plot of the text in which they are situated.[4] By looking at these miniature narratives, we can see the ways in which these two women, who both lose their lives as a result of the expectations of the chivalric community, call for an alternative community in which the behaviours that cause their deaths will no longer be accepted. The narratives of the knights who encounter these bodies follow a pattern of failure, in which the corpse critiques the knight's behaviour and the code that has enforced it; penance, in which the corpse enacts some kind of discipline or punishment against the knight; and ultimately repentance and transformation, as the knight takes on a new role in a new community distinct from the demands of the chivalric community.[5]

## Corpses and Community

Before discussing the bodies of Pedivere's Wife and Percival's Sister, however, some groundwork is necessary. Their bodies cannot be read in isolation, as though their significance were self-evident and stood alone without reference to the other narratives in the text. Rather, their fullest significance only appears when they each are read as the climax of a building repetition of the same symbol within the other, otherwise unrelated, narratives that comprise the bulk of Malory's text,[6] including the

that practice to Pedivere's unnamed wife as well. R. Davidson, 'Reading like a Woman in Malory's "Morte Darthur"', *Arthuriana* 16 (2006), 21–33.

4  K. A. Rudnytzky Schray, 'The Plot in Miniature: Arthur's Battle on Mont St. Michel in the Alliterative "Morte Arthure"', *Studies in Philology* 101 (2004), 1–19.

5  Although in this essay I refer to 'the chivalric community' as though it were a monolith, Kenneth Hodges has rightly argued that it really is a collection of communities, each with varying definitions for chivalry. I am here treating it as a single community because, while they are distinct, they can still communicate their values clearly to each other and recognize each other as 'true knights'. The spiritual community, on the other hand, has priorities so foreign to the members of the chivalric community that those who truly embrace it often cease to be knights altogether.

6  As Edwards has noted, 'While the overarching plot concerning the rise, flowering and fall of Arthur's kingdom is evident, most of the narratives in this very long book do not serve that plot. Something recognisable as a unit of narrative takes usually no more than a few pages to recount. There is uniformity of pace, and of status; that is, narratives are not marked as more important than one another by either duration or stress. There is also frequently a dearth of causal and logical relations, an indeterminate sense of time and place, a limited set of narrative ingredients, and frequent repetitions of "the

first Lady of the Lake, decapitated near the beginning of Arthur's reign, and the infamous Fair Maid of Ascolat. These other female corpses do not have the same transformative power as Pedivere's Wife and Percival's Sister, but their stories are part of the same symbolic system that Malory uses to critique the male-dominated chivalric community.[7] In the absence of a broader narrative structure, Elizabeth Edwards shows that 'the most interesting and most basic method of structuration in the *Morte Darthur* is symbolic. That is to say that stories are generated by symbols and that the patterns of narrative resolution are symbolic.'[8] In order to drive the larger narrative and shape its parallel communities, Malory makes use of a series of symbols – that is, this series of female corpses – with each symbol's appearance in each narrative unit building on the previous appearances, so that the chivalric and spiritual communities, though distinct, share a common symbolic language as the broader narrative progresses.[9] While there are many other corpses in the text, including a number of dead knights, the female corpses are of particular interest because a dead lady outrages the rules of the chivalric community in a way that a dead knight does not.

This essay not only expands on the significance of these symbolic corpses but also further defines them into two symbolic types – the decapitated lady and the floating lady – in order to fully analyse their distinct yet related functions.[10] The decapitated ladies introduce and develop the concept that the corpse of a lady, whose death was caused by a knight dedicated to the service of ladies, indicates a profound rupture between the real and ideal within the text. The floating ladies appear later in the text, and build on the significance of the decapitated ladies by implicating the entire community of knights in their deaths. These two types, who for

same" or very similar incidents.' E. Edwards, *The Genesis of Narrative in Malory's* Morte Darthur (Cambridge, 2001), p. 3.

[7] Although there are also a number of fascinating male corpses and tombs in Malory's text, the critique offered by their corpses is distinct from that of the female corpses, due to the massive power differential between the two groups.

[8] Edwards, *Genesis*, p. 5.

[9] These symbolic corpses do not merely repeat the same meaning. Instead, they build on one another, each corpse's significance dependent both on the narrative of the preceding ones as well as on the new meaning it shapes in its own narrative. Neither do the symbols used in the text exist only as abstract symbols – they drift between story and symbology, each informed by the other, and cannot be read like a code that gives the reader a fixed meaning every time it appears. Rather, they are types, their readings all driving the narrative towards the final, most complete symbol.

[10] In her discussion of this process of narrative-shaping through symbol, Edwards hints at this pattern, noting the connections between Gawain's, Pellinore's and Balin's decapitated ladies, as well as a possible symbolic relationship to Elayne of Ascolat, but does not explore it in any detail. Edwards, *Genesis*, p. 3.

the majority of the text are firmly established within the chivalric community, are followed through the text to their respective fulfilments in the form of Pedivere's Wife and Percival's Sister. These two shift the narrative from its single-minded focus on the chivalric community to a broader vision encompassing two communities held in tension by the text – the chivalric and spiritual communities.

However, if one were to draw a Venn diagram of these two communities, there would be extensive overlap. After the collapse of the Round Table and the death of Arthur in the war with Mordred, a straggle of survivors form a small spiritual community headed by Sir Lancelot. After his death, four of them go on to the Holy Land and set up lands for themselves and battle enemies there, the way they had in England when they were members of the Round Table. The difference is that now these battles are 'upon myscreantes or Turkes' – that is, for moral or religious reasons – and in the end 'they died upon a Good Fryday for Goddes sake', rather than for the sake of Arthur or their own 'worship'.[11] Other versions of the Grail quest (such as Malory's source, *La Queste de Saint Graal*) have this alternative vision seize authority over the chivalric community. Martin Shichtman observes that the *Queste* 'suggests that if knights would abandon their corrupt ways and allow themselves to be directed by the [Cistercian] order's principles, they could begin to participate in the process of salvation' because of the religious community's concern over the perceived violence and decadence of the chivalric community.[12] However, Malory allows them to coexist in tension.[13] His text removes much of the interpretative certainty that had been provided by members of the spiritual community in the *Queste*, forcing his audience and the questing knights to regard these purported authorities with greater scepticism and to do their own interpretative work rather than depend on the priests and hermits they encounter.[14]

Malory does not expect his characters to fall into line and embrace the One True Community (whatever that may be), but instead allows these contrasting communities to be in conversation with one another.

---

[11] Malory, *Morte*, p. 1260.

[12] M. B. Shichtman, 'Politicizing the Ineffable: The *Queste del Saint Graal* and Malory's "Tale of the Sankgraal"', in *Culture and the King: The Political Implications of the Arthurian Legend. Essays in Honor of Valerie M. Lagorio* (New York 1994), pp. 163–79 (p. 166).

[13] Hodges, *Forging Chivalric Communities*, pp. 22–4.

[14] Shichtman, 'Politicizing', pp. 175–7. M. B. Shichtman, 'Malory's Gawain Reconsidered', *Essays in Literature* 11 (1984), 159–76 also demonstrates how Malory de-emphasizes Gawain's spiritual failings during the Grail quest and deletes much of the criticism from his sources, thereby reducing the power of spiritual and religious authorities to critique members of the chivalric community.

Rather than replace the chivalric community, the spiritual community exists alongside it, offering an alternative way for knights and ladies to relate to one another and to define themselves. Guenevere, for example, rejects the chivalric community that had rested so heavily on her and goes to Amesbury, where she becomes first a nun and later the abbess. When Lancelot comes to see her there, she rejects him:

> I requyre the and beseche the hartily, for all the lo[v]e that ever was betwyxt us, that thou never se me no more in the visayge. And I commaunde the, on Goddis behalff, that thou forsake my company. And to thy kyngedom loke thou turne agayne, and kepe well thy realme frome warre and wrake, for as well as I have loved the heretofore, myne [har]te woll nat serve now to see the.[15]

Lancelot's response is to reject the kingly duties within the chivalric community that she attempts to send him back to, claiming 'Nay, madame, wyte you well that shall I never do, for I shall never be so false unto you of that I have promysed. But the selff desteny that ye have takyn you to, I woll take me to, for the pleasure of Jesu, and ever for you I caste me specially to pray.'[16] After her death, he sings the Mass and buries her beside Arthur. After his own death, he is buried apart from her, although his corpse is carried in the same hearse as hers had been. The relationship between the two of them does not disappear, as both admit that there is still love between them. Rather, they choose a new way of relating to each other, through prayer and penance, which does not involve Lancelot deriving personal glory from his interactions with her.

The division between the two communities, then, is not absolute, and they share a symbolic vocabulary between them, so that the female body becomes a focal point for both communities, and the readings of the corpses defining the chivalric community deepen the readings of the corpses defining the spiritual community. In order to read the significance of these final two bodies – Pedivere's Wife and Percival's Sister – it is necessary to begin at the beginning of the thread and follow the narrative of the female corpses as it builds throughout the text until its fulfilment in the creation of the spiritual community. The primary narrative thread through which these bodies run is that of Sir Lancelot, who begins his story as the paradigm of chivalry, having 'the grettyste name of ony knyght of the worlde',[17] and ends it as the leader of a spiritual community. Yet though Lancelot's name will appear many times in this essay, my argument is not about him, but rather the symbolic thread that runs

[15] Malory, *Morte*, p. 1252.
[16] Malory, *Morte*, p. 1253.
[17] Malory, *Morte*, p. 287.

through his career as emblematic of Arthurian knighthood. His narrative is filled not only with women – a conclusion reached by many scholars – but particularly with dead women, especially dead women who have lost their heads or whose corpses travel over water. Moreover, the most famous of these dead floating women – the Fair Maid of Ascolat – is not the most significant corpse in this thread, and the appearance of her corpse at the end of the text marks the end of the dominance of the chivalric community. Rather, it is the corpse of Percival's Sister that escapes the chivalric community that has killed her, inviting the knights she encounters into a transformative journey from chivalry to spirituality.

The function of Malory's female characters in general has been fairly well established. As Dorsey Armstrong argues, in Malory the feminine is necessary to define masculine identity: traditionally, this means that the ladies serve to 'affirm [a knight's] masculine difference through courteous behavior', the powerless foils against which knights can define themselves as powerful and masculine.[18] This extends beyond individual knights to their broader community – how do knights decide who is a member of their community of knights and who is a 'false knight' who must be punished by the true members of the chivalric community? Their interactions with ladies are one key element of this boundary-drawing – do they obey the strictures of the Pentecostal Oath to 'allwayes to do ladyes, damesels, and jantilwomen and wydowes [sucour], stengthe hem in hir ryghtes, and never to enforce them, uppon payne of dethe', or are they like Sir Perys de Foreste Savage, the serial rapist slain by Lancelot and denounced as a 'false knyght and traytoure unto knyghthode'.[19]

I argue that it is not just the living damsels-in-distress who are used within the text to shape the chivalric community, their female bodies acting as foils for the male bodies of the knights and as a site for knightly self-definition. Rather, the dead female body has even greater power over the identities of the knights who encounter it and greater power to subvert the rules of the community to which they belong. In some ways, perhaps counter-intuitively, the lady corpses verify and reward the knights' masculinity. Death does not completely reverse the lady's function, and she continues to drive the knight to greater deeds of chivalry. However, the functions of the body of a living lady versus a dead lady, as far as their use for knightly self-definition is concerned, are not equivalent, for the abject bodies of the dead cut both ways. Once dead, a body becomes less stable

[18] D. Armstrong, *Gender and the Chivalric Community* (Gainesville, FL, 2003), p. 37. This 'masculine difference' which is affirmed by interaction with a lady mirrors the 'masculine sameness' affirmed by interaction with a fellow knight. This strict gender role binary is a key element of the construction of the chivalric community.

[19] Malory, *Morte*, pp. 120, 269.

and more disturbing to the community, so while some bodies in Malory's text continue to allow themselves to be used as a foil for knightly deeds for a period of time, these bodies inevitably begin to shift the boundaries of the community with them.[20] All of these corpses are surprisingly mobile, and this mobility allows them not only to escape the boundaries imposed upon them by the community but to draw new connections between previously unrelated locations, such as Camelot and Rome or Sarras.[21] They travel along with the itinerant members of the chivalric community, rather than being just another adventure for the knight to encounter and then continue past on the way to further adventures.

As persons-become-things, they retain a kind of agency, refusing to function the way they did while living. The community that they shape is therefore also different from that which they created when they were alive. Just as the women in Malory can be used as part of the construction of the chivalric community, their corpses can also deconstruct this community, subverting the expectations of the knights who depend on the female body for their masculine identities.[22] Knights who are merely boorish to their ladies lose status when the lady chooses to bestow herself on a different knight.[23] But a knight who violates the chivalric standard to the extent of causing a lady's death suffers more extreme consequences. His living lady becomes a decapitated lady and a symbol of failure, disrupting his career and signalling his doom. His status often does benefit initially as he valiantly overcomes the obstacles thrown in his way by the lady's corpse, yet the end of each knight's narrative shows that the original offence to the community's standard was never truly forgotten by the text, or the corpse. It is important to note, however, that these symbolic female bodies are not so transgressive that

[20] Corpses, as Julia Kristeva notes, cross boundaries by definition – 'the utmost of abjection … death infecting life'. J. Kristeva, *Powers of Horror: An Essay on Abjection*, trans. Leon Roudiez (New York, 1982), p. 4.

[21] This idea is explored in greater depth in the chapter entitled 'Trudging toward Rome, Drifting toward Sarras', in D. Armstrong and K. Hodges, *Mapping Malory's Morte: Geography and the Arthurian Legend in Fifteenth-Century England* (Basingstoke, 2014).

[22] 'Malory seems aware that chivalry is constructed, not discovered, and that therefore multiple, legitimate codes can coexist and coevolve … Thus the action in the book is not simply watching characters exemplify one ideal or waver among several, it is watching how the characters, the narrator, and his sources create and alter the ideals themselves' (Hodges, *Forging Chivalric Communities*, pp. 4–5.)

[23] Malory, *Morte*, p. 165. Later, when Gawain refuses to follow the directions of the damsel who has accompanied him specifically to show him adventures, she abandons him while he is distracted during combat and accompanies his opponent's companion instead. When they are reunited a year later, 'the damesell that Sir Gawayne had coude sey but lytyll worshyp of hym' (Malory, *Morte*, p. 178).

they defy the male-dominated text. Instead, they complicate (but do not rupture) the relationships between the male characters at the centre of the community by magnifying the hairline fractures that already exist, challenging the assumption that the community is noble and secure as is perceived. Though Lancelot's career is the one through which many of these subversive narratives run, other knights are also subject to this re-envisioning of their relationships with each other and their definition of masculinity. In this way the female corpses broaden the definition of masculinity allowed by the text beyond the dominant and highly regulated, but still extreme, violence of knighthood.[24]

While the majority of these female bodies leave those who handle their corpses within the chivalric community (albeit a problematized one), Pedivere's Wife and Percival's Sister posit an alternative community in which masculinity is no longer defined by a propensity for violence and ability to dominate the feminine. Furthermore, there is space for female agency within this new community – Hodges notes that although 'the women in the "Sankgraal" are excluded from one community, the apostolic fellowship of the Grail knights ... they are present and important in the larger religious community in which the Grail knights move'.[25] In spite of the many limitations still placed on them, '[w]omen [in Malory's spiritual community] can make their own religious choices', at least to a certain extent, like Guenevere, who bows out of the chivalric community altogether.

## Decapitated Ladies

The decapitated ladies lose their heads through the neglect or misconduct of one of Arthur's supposedly exemplary knights, so that after their deaths, their corpses, or at least their heads, are carried to Arthur's court by the knights responsible for their deaths. Each episode and each knight's failure succeed one another in increasing severity, from Balin's justified revenge to Gawain's carelessness and Pellinore's outright neglect, culminating in Pedivere's act of cold-blooded murder. The narrative thread of the decapitated lady and her body's travels begins with the Lady of the

---

[24] It is also notable that the violence inherent to knightly masculinity is directed towards other knights in a process of defeating and feminizing the opponent in order to take the masculine position in the encounter. Turning that violence against a lady, in other words, defeats the purpose of feminization through violence because the object is already feminine. See K. C. Kelly, 'Malory's Body Chivalric', *Arthuriana* 6 (1995), 52–71; and L. A. Finke and M. B. Shichtman, 'No Pain, No Gain: Violence as Symbolic Capital in Malory's *Morte Darthur*', *Arthuriana* 8 (1998), 115–34.

[25] Hodges, *Forging Chivalric Communities*, p. 125.

Lake, slain by Sir Balin in front of King Arthur and the first decapitated lady to appear in the text. As Balin is preparing to leave with the sword he has taken from the damsel, he sees the Lady of the Lake

> which by hir meanys had slayne hys modir; and he had sought hir three yere before. And what hit was tolde hym how she had asked hys hede of kynge Arthure, he wente to hir streyght and seyde, 'Evyll be [y]e founde: ye wolde have myne hede, and therefore ye shall loose youres!' And with hys swerde lyghtly he smote of hyr hede before kynge Arthure.[26]

At this point in the narrative, the chivalric community as constructed around the Round Table is still embryonic, lacking a codified set of expectations for the behaviour of knights. No knights have sworn the Pentecostal Oath to 'allwayes to do ladyes, damesels, and jantilwomen and wydowes socour'.[27] Furthermore, it becomes clear that Balin had been in the right in the conflict with the lady, after he reveals that she killed his mother, and Merlin later informs the audience that the Lady of the Lake had also been assisting in a revenge plot that was destined to kill Balin and his brother Balan.[28] Nevertheless, Balin's action shocks the court, which, even without the Pentecostal Oath and even given her crimes against Balin, recognizes that slaying a lady is absolutely inappropriate for a knight. Balin himself says that if it had not been for the 'grete damage' the lady did to him, he would have 'bene lothe as ony knyght that lyvith for to sle a lady'.[29]

Additionally, Balin shames the court by causing Arthur to fail to fulfil his duties to the lady and violate another, yet-uncodified, chivalric expectation – that knights 'allwayes fle treson', that is, keep their oaths and avoid committing deceit or betrayal of any kind under any circumstances. Although the lady was someone whom Arthur was 'much beholdynge to' and was visiting the court under his safe-conduct – his promise that she would be under his protection while in his court – Balin's actions cause Arthur's word to her to be broken. A king and knight who cannot protect his own guests should be ashamed, and Arthur is rightfully outraged at the damage done to his reputation, especially since that he had given his protection to Balin against the Lady of the Lake's demand for his head moments earlier.

---

[26] Malory, *Morte*, pp. 65–6.

[27] Malory, *Morte*, p. 120.

[28] It seems that the sword which Balin takes (against the damsel's advice) was infused with a curse intended to destroy someone else. Why she allows Balin to take it, even for a time, is a mystery.

[29] Malory, *Morte*, p. 69.

Balin is exiled from the court, but before leaving he 'toke up the hede of the lady and bare hit with hym to hys ostry',[30] while King Arthur buries the rest of her. The head then disappears, as does the grave, and the Lady of the Lake herself is replaced by her successor with hardly a hiccup and no comment. Compared to the other bodies seen later, the body of the Lady of the Lake is nearly invisible in the text. Furthermore, this is a voluntary action – while other knights are forced to carry the heads of the decapitated ladies, Balin picks hers up of his own accord. In spite (or because) of his deep hatred for her, he wants her head with him.

This odd and unexpanded detail of Balin carrying off her head signals the beginning of the symbolic thread of the mobile, disruptive female corpse, specifically the decapitated lady. The consequences of her death are dramatic, both for Balin and for the Round Table. Balin's exile sends him off into the Forest of Adventure where, at least initially, he achieves a level of fame that he might not have reached had he remained at Arthur's court. However, disaster follows Balin through his adventures. He causes the death of Lanceor's lady when he inadvertently slays Sir Lanceor and she kills herself, and later commits the Dolorous Stroke that destroys an entire castle, killing most of its inhabitants. Balin, though justified in beheading the Lady of the Lake,[31] nevertheless leaves a trail of destruction behind him ever after, ending in his own death and that of his brother, Balan.[32]

This first appearance of the decapitated lady is a warning: no matter how perfect the knight, some elements of the chivalric code are impossible to obey, simply because sometimes obeying one means defying another. Although the narrative condones, and even sometimes encourages, vengeance for kin, it was impossible for Balin to achieve this without committing an act that was forbidden to him as a knight. No matter how justified a knight is in slaying a lady, he will be punished by the narrative. Balin's failure was in spite of his own perfection as a knight and his narrative reads like a tragedy.[33] Subsequent appearances of the decapitated lady go

---

[30] Malory, *Morte*, p. 66.

[31] Malory, *Morte*, pp. 69, 85. Balin's right to take vengeance is not entirely unquestioned in Malory's text. Malory's treatment of Gawain's narrative and quest to avenge his father's death on Pellinore, for example, is ambivalent at best. Shichtman, 'Gawain', pp. 159–61.

[32] This sword of Balin's later reappears as part of the transition from the chivalric to the spiritual community, when it is taken up by Galahad before the commencement of 'The Sankgraal' (Malory, *Morte*, p. 501). See Hodges, *Forging Chivalric Communities*, pp. 22–3.

[33] Ralph Norris points out that in Malory's source text for the Balin narrative, the Post-Vulgate *Suite du Merlin*, Balin had originally been written as the doomed Evian set-up for Galahad's eventual triumphs, a much more direct indicator of the preferability of

further, revealing the deep flaws inherent in the code as well as in the knights who attempt to follow it.

The second decapitated lady appears shortly thereafter, as the chivalric community is beginning to become more formalized around Arthur and his court, though there is still no Pentecostal Oath. As part of the festivities for King Arthur's wedding, Sir Gawain (a brand-new knight on his first adventure) and his younger brother, Gaheris, are sent on a quest after a white hart. They successfully chase it down to a castle and kill it, with the assistance of Gawain's greyhounds. Then another knight, Sir Blamore, whose duty it had been to protect the hart, comes out of the castle and kills two of the greyhounds.[34] Naturally, Blamore and Gawain are enraged and a great battle ensues, until finally Blamore is forced to surrender. Still furious, Gawain refuses to grant the other knight mercy and prepares to behead him.

> Ryght so com his lady oute of a chambir and felle over hym, and so he smote of hir hede by myssefortune. 'Alas', seyde Gaherys, 'that ys fowle and shamefully done, for that shame shall never from you ...' So sir Gawayne was sore astoned of the deth of this fayre lady, that he wyst nat what he dud...[35]

That night, Gawain is preparing to disarm and go to sleep when four knights arrive, accusing him of having 'shamed thy knyghthode, for a knyght withoute mercy ys dishonoured. Also thou haste slayne a fayre lady, to thy grete shame unto the worldys ende.' They are about to kill Gawain when four ladies appear and ask that the knights give Gawain over to their charge instead.

Rather than killing Gawain, when the ladies discover he is Arthur's nephew and therefore very near the heart of the chivalric community, they choose to punish him and, as part of their function within the chivalric community, provide an opportunity for him to be brought more perfectly in line with the community standards he has broken: 'And than they delyverde hym undir thys promyse, that he sholde bere the dede lady with hym on thys maner: the hede of her was hanged aboute hys necke,

the spiritual community over the chivalric. However, Malory partially disentangles Balin's story from Galahad's, allowing him to be a tragic hero in his own right while still leaving Galahad and his party to pick up Balin's dropped narrative threads (including the sword mentioned above) and repair some of the damage caused by Balin's failed quest. R. Norris, 'The Tragedy of Balin: Malory's Use of the Balin Story in the *Morte Darthur*', *Arthuriana* 9 (1999), 52–67.

[34] Edwards uses Gawain's greyhounds as yet another example of Malory's use of symbol, as a given object (in this case, the greyhounds) shifts from symbol to ordinary dog and back.

[35] Malory, *Morte*, p. 106.

and the hole body of hys before hym on hys horse mane.'[36] Their sentence uses the other lady's corpse to mark Gawain as having shamed his knighthood and as a chance. When he returns, Guenevere sets a 'queste of ladyes' on Gawain and commands that he 'sholde never be ayenst lady ne jantillwoman, but if he fyght for a lady and hys adversary fyghtith for another'.[37] While Gawain's special duty towards ladies is ignored for the majority of the text – indeed, in Malory's account Gawain is never actually seen serving a lady at all – it nevertheless becomes a key factor in his ability to participate in deeds of knightly valour much later.[38]

As the Round Table (the ultimate symbol of the chivalric community) collapses into disunity and its members scatter, Gawain is killed in battle against Mordred. Several nights later, Gawain comes to Arthur in a dream to warn him about the upcoming battle against Mordred. He is surrounded by all the ladies whom he 'ded batayle fore in ryghteuous quarels', and tells Arthur that 'God hath gyvyn hem that grace at their grete prayer, bycause I ded batayle for them for their ryght, that they shulde bryng me hydder unto you'. The special quest that was set upon him because of the decapitated lady has allowed him not only to practise greater deeds of chivalry by serving ladies, but to indirectly participate in battle even after his death.[39] He is allowed to cross the boundary of life and death due to events set in motion by the corpse of the lady. However, this participation is ultimately futile, since Arthur is unable to fulfil the requirements Gawain sets. The slim chance of success offered by Gawain only adds to the tragedy of Arthur's defeat, since rather than being fated to fail, Arthur loses a battle he could conceivably have won.

The third decapitated lady also appears in the adventures set off by Arthur's wedding, and serves to condemn King Pellinore and his single-minded pursuit of his quest. While pursuing a lady (the equivalent of the white hart that Gawain has previously been sent after), Pellinore passes a damsel sitting by a well and holding a wounded knight in her arms: 'And whan she was ware of hym, she cryed on lowde, "Helpe me, knyght, for Jesuys sake!" But hynge Pellynore wode nat tarry, he was so egir in hys queste; and ever she cryed an hondred tymes after helpe.'[40] Although he notices her and her desperate situation, in spite of her cries he rides past. Pellinore's response mirrors the perception of ladies as a mere support for knightly deeds of valour who must submit to their role as foils for

---

[36] Malory, *Morte*, p. 108

[37] See discussion in Armstrong, *Gender*, p. 39.

[38] One possible exception that takes place shortly after this adventure (and which only serves to prove the rule) is Gawain's 'service' to Ettarde.

[39] Malory, *Morte*, pp. 1233–4.

[40] Malory, *Morte*, p. 114.

the heroes; though Pellinore was willing to pursue one lady as part of a quest, he ignored the other when helping her did not further his goals. The damsel, however, condemns him. 'What she saw he wolde nat abyde, she prayde unto God to sende hym as much nede of helpe as she had, and that he myght felle hit or he deyed.'[41] Then the knight, who is later revealed to be her lover, dies, and the lady kills herself with his sword. After Pellinore safely recovers the lady he had been pursuing, he returns the same way.

> And as they com by the welle thereas the wounded knyght was and the lady, there he founde the knyght and the lady etyn with lyons other with wylde bestis, all sabe the hede, wherefore he made grete sorow and wepte passynge sore, and seyde, 'Alas! hir lyff myght I have saved, but I was ferse in my queste that I wolde nat abyde.'[42]

At this point he is filled with grief and regret, realizing that he is to blame. Yet the expectations placed on a knight of Arthur's court and a member of the chivalric community make it difficult for him to choose: while aiding a lady is key to chivalry, so is fulfilling a quest, much more so when that quest involved rescuing a different lady. The rescued lady, now accompanying him, recommends that he have the knight's remains buried in a hermitage to be prayed for, then take the lady's head to court. At this point in the symbolic thread it has become clear that the burden of a lady's head is a sign of a particular kind of guilt – failure to behave as a true knight ought. When Pellinore arrives at court with the lady's head, he is informed by Merlin that the dead lady was his own daughter, Alyne. Merlin expands on Alyne's curse and tells Pellinore that 'he that ye sholde truste moste on of ony man on lyve, he shall leve you there ye shall be slayne', just as Alyne was left to die by her father, the one she should have trusted most, both as a kinsman and as a knight.[43] Although Pellinore's actual death is off-screen ten years later at the hands of Sir Gawain and his brothers, it is part of the breakdown of the chivalric community that these decapitated ladies foretell.

These decapitated ladies critique the chivalric community, while reshaping the chivalry of the knights who cause their deaths and who must engage with their corpses. The narrative punishes these knights for their misdeeds; however, these punishments are never at the expense of their fame or knighthood. Instead, the goal is to restore the position in the chivalric community that was lost when the knight's masculinity was compromised. However, for all these knights, this reshaping of

[41] Malory, *Morte*, p. 114.
[42] Malory, *Morte*, p. 118.
[43] Malory, *Morte*, p. 119. Whether or not the other specifics of Alyne's curse and Merlin's prediction are fulfilled is left to the reader's imagination.

their chivalry is ultimately futile. Gawain's warning does not prevent disaster, and Balin not only dies himself, but also kills his own brother. Pellinore is doomed and disappears altogether. While Martin Shichtman has particularly selected Malory's depiction of Gawain as an example of 'a well-intentioned failure, an unfortunate example of what is rather than what should be', due to his inability 'to fulfill the chivalric obligations imposed upon him by his peers, by himself, by the reader, and by God', he is not the only well-intentioned failure in this text who is crushed by the expectations of the chivalric community.[44] The encounters of these three knights with these decapitated ladies reveal the flaws of the community through the failures of individuals without providing an opportunity for correction.

Frequently, those who pass judgement on the knights, ordering them to bear their victims' corpses as part of their punishment, are the members of the 'inquest of ladies', living women (including Guenevere) who have taken a position of critiquing and sentencing knights who have failed in performing chivalry towards other ladies.[45] In so doing, these living ladies not only help to enforce the rules of the community as part of their function within the text, but also, by means of the corpses of their fellow ladies, subvert these knights' identities as members of the chivalric community by shaming them with the public display of their crimes. The remains bear witness against the knight's failure before the king and his court in order to subject the knight to an appropriate punishment. They participate in a narrative that both exposes the flaws in the chivalric community, especially with regard to the status of women, and attempts to correct those flaws in different ways, while remaining focused on the story of a single knight.

The influence of this contact with a decapitated lady extends beyond the official direct consequences, affecting the nature of the knight's chivalric identity and the course of his adventures afterwards. The weight of the corpse and the punishment associated with it have the power to both destroy and transform the knight, sometimes simultaneously, and subvert the knight's identity as a beacon of chivalry even while appearing to restore it through the knight's successful completion of the assigned punishment. Thus, the narrative must scramble to restore that masculinity through the appropriate adventure – hence the punishment-as-quest or challenge. Yet the effort is ultimately futile, and the last of the decapitated ladies directs the emasculated knight right out of the chivalric community and into a new, spiritual community, where he disappears from the narrative of courtesy and adventure into a hermitage.

[44] Shichtman, 'Gawain', p. 1.
[45] See Hodges, *Forging Chivalric Communities*, pp. 37–8 and 131.

The body of Pedivere's Wife is the climax of the series of decapitated ladies and the one who introduces the new alternative to the chivalric community to which the other bodies had belonged, moving the symbolic value of the decapitated ladies from the negative to the positive. She is also the one decapitated lady who appears after the Pentecostal Oath and the community's attempt to correct the flaws that had caused the deaths of the previous ladies. Significantly, the Pentecostal Oath makes no mention of God, although Malory's source texts were deeply religious, creating a deep chasm between the chivalric community bound by a secular oath and the spiritual community that rises up in response to it. Instead of merely criticizing the members of the chivalric community and its definitions and boundaries, the corpses of these ladies who have lost their lives under the community expectations reflected in the Oath set the stage for the creation of a new, spiritual community with new definitions and boundaries.

The decapitated corpse of Sir Pedivere's Wife builds on the readings of the previous decapitated ladies by revealing and critiquing the flaws of the community; however, rather than temporarily elevating Pedivere's knightly status through the punishment imposed upon him by the narrative and thereby reinforcing normative masculinity, she subverts chivalric masculinity and ends his career altogether, effecting a spiritual transformation of her husband. In fact, through its association with the pilgrimage to Rome, her corpse deepens the notion of decapitated-lady-as-punishing-burden and takes on the character of a hair shirt worn by penitents on pilgrimage. Through her, Pedivere is redefined, first as a pilgrim, then as a holy hermit, rewritten as powerless by the standards of the chivalric community.

This disturbing interlude in 'The Tale of Sir Lancelot' – that is, a tale about 'the nobelyst knyght of the worlde' who most closely fulfils the chivalric ideal – not only provides a snapshot of the failures inherent in that system but also calls for a similar spiritual transformation in the community at large, exemplified in the story of Lancelot himself.[46] The corpse's function as a penitential garment is similar to the actual hair shirt worn by Lancelot during his Grail quest. When Lancelot seeks a full vision of the Holy Grail, he quickly learns that in the spiritual realm of the Grail quest the rules are different, and chivalry as Lancelot understands it counts for less than nothing. Behaviours that had been previously accepted as part of his knightly persona, such as his love for Guenevere and desire for honour and worship above all else, are recoded as 'synne and wyckednes'.[47] He attempts to reinscribe himself in this new spiritual realm by wearing a penitential hair shirt against his skin for the remainder

[46] Malory, *Morte*, p. 1194.
[47] Malory, *Morte*, p. 896.

of the quest, but his transformation is incomplete and he is only given a partial, veiled vision before being sent home. When Lancelot returns from his pilgrimage, he seems to have also returned to the chivalric community, leaving the hair shirt behind. Yet the hair shirt's reminder of his failure has been internalized, and he knows that if he had been more spiritually minded and less focused on his own honour and love for the queen, he might had advanced farther.

However, the story of Lancelot's encounter with Sir Pedivere and his wife takes place long before the Grail quest, while Lancelot is still deeply enmeshed in the chivalric community and is, to all intents and purposes, the poster boy for the Pentecostal Oath, succeeding in almost everything he attempts. But, as with the other decapitated ladies, this is a story of failure: not only Pedivere's failure to behave as a proper knight, but also Lancelot's own failure to meet the expectations held by himself and the chivalric community. It is a minor failure compared to those that finally drive him first into a hair shirt and later into the priesthood, but for the exemplary Lancelot it is still deeply shaming. Significantly, it comes at the end of the Tale, after Lancelot encounters a string of hostile knights, many of whom have violated the rules of chivalry in various ways. Lancelot, the most chivalrous knight in the narrative, dominates all of these conflicts, often sending the surrendered knights on to King Arthur's court to be judged and restored to true knighthood. Pedivere's story is a striking anomaly, and his choice of rejecting chivalry and becoming a hermit is recorded immediately before all the characters from Lancelot's previous adventures arrive at the Round Table to tell stories of Lancelot's greatness. It undermines the celebratory tone of the text immediately following, and serves as a reminder that no knight can be perfect in every way.

The trouble begins when Lancelot tries to negotiate with a homicidally jealous knight who believes his wife has been committing adultery with her cousin, an accusation she denies emphatically. Lancelot swears to the lady that he will not allow her husband, Sir Pedivere, to slay her, and Pedivere agrees to cooperate with Lancelot. Still cautious, Lancelot has the lady ride on one side of him and her husband ride on the other. However, Pedivere distracts Lancelot with a fictive account of armed men riding behind them, breaking his word to Lancelot and causing Lancelot to break his own word to the lady: 'And so sir Launcelot turned hym and thought no treson; and therewith was the knyght and the lady on one syde, and syddeynly he swapped of the laydes hede.'[48] Lancelot, outraged, is about to kill Pedivere, but Pedivere begs for mercy and Lancelot, still determined that oaths should mean something even if his and Pedivere's

---

[48] Malory, *Morte*, p. 285.

had been broken mere seconds earlier, grants it based on the terms of the Pentecostal Oath, which requires him to give mercy to all who ask it.

It is uncertain which Lancelot considers more appalling, Pedivere murdering the lady or his doing so after deceiving Lancelot. Indeed, Lancelot's first words after realizing what had happened are 'Traytoure! Thou haste shamed me for evir!' His primary concern is with his own broken oath to the lady, not with her death; his frustration is then compounded by Pedivere's refusal to accept his challenge to combat. Pedivere has not only defied every expectation of knightly behaviour held by Lancelot and the community, but has also caused Lancelot to fail his own standards of chivalry. Lancelot is at a loss as to how to respond.[49] He finally orders Pedivere to 'take this lady and the hede, and bere [it] uppon the; and here shalt thou swere uppon my swerde to bere hit allwayes uppon thy bak and never to reste tyll thou com to my lady, Quene Gwenyver'.[50] The first sign placed upon the body by Lancelot, Pedivere's first judge, is evidence of failure, primarily Pedivere's, but also Lancelot's. Her body proves that not only can knights not be trusted to keep the oaths that are intended to maintain the community, but not even the most chivalrous knight, Sir Lancelot, can do so successfully. The system is flawed, and while Pedivere becomes the text's scapegoat who must bear the weight of its coming breakdown, Lancelot own failure is also inscribed on this corpse.

When Pedivere comes before the court, Guenevere reads the failure Lancelot has inscribed on the corpse, and her words are 'this is an horryble dede and a shamefull, and a grete rebuke unto Sir Launcelot',[51] leaving the exact nature of the 'dede' to which she refers ambiguously open-ended and corroborating Lancelot's fear of being shamed for having broken his word, however inadvertently. Later she refers to Pedivere's 'foule dedis', encompassing all of the chivalric failures that Pedivere has committed. Thus far, the story follows the same trajectory as that of the earlier decapitated ladies. However, upon Pedivere's appearance before Guenevere, the narrative shifts. She sends him to bear the corpse all the way to the pope in Rome, adding even greater significance to the weight of the corpse by associating it with a holy penitential pilgrimage to the centre of the Christian faith. Therefore the next sign, placed on the corpse by Guenevere, is a penitential call to repentance. Like Lancelot's hair shirt, the lady must be beside Pedivere at all times, not only a perpetual reminder of his sin and a punishing weight that he must bear, but now imbued with the seed of change. Penance, after all, is more than mere

[49] See discussion in Armstrong, *Gender*, pp. 107–8.
[50] Malory, *Morte*, p. 285.
[51] Malory, *Morte*, p. 286.

punishment – it is intended to purify the one who completes it and to remove not only the stain of their offences but also the inclination to do such deeds. Pedivere's physical pilgrimage to Rome mirrors his spiritual journey, from homicide to holiness and from the chivalric community of Arthur's court and the Forests of Adventure to the spiritual community of the Church.

Once he reaches Rome, the pope feels that the queen's penance has been adequate and removes the material weight of the lady from the knight. Significantly, in doing so the pope recognizes the corpse as an appropriate penitential garment capable of effecting real spiritual transformation. The lady is finally buried in Rome – a sacred space that recognizes both her innocence and the transformative role she plays – while Pedivere is sent back to the queen. The narrative gives no comment as to his reception back at court. Like the pope, Guenevere apparently feels that his penance is complete; whatever was supposed to be accomplished by his pilgrimage has been done, and he is free to choose his own direction again. Yet even after the lady is buried, the weight of her presence continues its hold. With each stop and each judge who encounters him and the corpse – Lancelot, Guenevere and lastly the pope – the body has taken on greater significance, until finally Pedivere internalizes that weight and carries it with him back to England, leaving the physical corpse in Rome. Instead of joining the Round Table as other defeated knights in 'The Tale of Sir Lancelot' do, he renounces chivalry altogether. He himself has inscribed the final sign on the now-absent corpse, making it a catalyst for transformation.

As a spiritual artefact, the body of Pedivere's Wife has the ability to force others also to define themselves in ways that defy the rules of the rest of the text, and when Pedivere takes on the weight of her body, she transitions his story from the dominant chivalric narrative to a spiritual narrative more closely aligned with the Grail quest. Instead of providing opportunities for chivalric adventure, then tactfully disappearing after this purpose has been accomplished like the other ladies, the corpse of Pedivere's lady is transformed by the text into a devotional aid, not unlike Lancelot's hair shirt, obeying Malory's rules governing religious objects in his text rather than those governing the female body. This is not because of something inherent in the body, but because of the significance that becomes attached to that body by the text. As Pedivere carries it from Lancelot to Guenevere to the pope, the body accrues meanings applied to it by the perpetrator and by his three judges, giving the body greater power than it had in life.[52] This body defies the ordinary rules of knight-

---

[52] P. Geary, *Furta Sacra: Thefts of Relics in the Central Middle Ages* (Princeton, NJ, 1991), p. 5.

hood and disrupts the expected course of chivalric adventure. Instead of functioning like a lady leading Pedivere on to greater deeds of valour, it functions as a penitential tool leading him out of knighthood altogether, and pointing out a new direction for Lancelot to follow. While Pedivere is neither the first, nor the last, knight in the text to break his oath and violate the laws of the community, he is the one made an example of by the text and used to preview a new direction for the community.

At this stage in the story, no one but Pedivere is able to feel the weight of the body. Lancelot goes back to the court to honour and celebration; it is still too early in his career as a knight for the crushing realization of his own failure that causes him to weep like a beaten child at the healing of Sir Urry. But the concluding lines of 'The Tale of Sir Lancelot', 'And so at that tyme Sir Lancelot had the grettyste name of ony knyght of the worlde, and moste he was honoured of hyghe and lowe', cannot completely erase the disquieting reminder of his failure and Pedivere's radical decision just a page earlier, and the phrase 'at that tyme' reminds the audience that this state is only temporary. Later the Grail quest and the penitential hair shirt will begin the process of shifting Lancelot's perspective from chivalric to spiritual, and the weight of his failure and penance will ultimately transform him, as surely as the weight of failure and penance signified by the corpse of Pedivere's Wife transforms Pedivere.

## Floating Ladies

After this suggestion of individual transformation, the dominant form of the symbolic female corpse changes shape from the decapitated lady to the floating lady, and broadens its significance from the individual to the community. Unlike the decapitated ladies who are carried along by a knight and primarily affect that one knight's position in the community, the floating ladies direct their own courses, showing a greater level of agency as well as greater disruptive power. The floating ladies have also both died from failures of the chivalric community, rather than from the failures of an individual knight – Percival's Sister, the first floating lady to appear in the text, loses her life to a custom of the castle, while Elayne, who appears after the knights return from the quest for the Grail, wastes away from the strictures of courtly love. Before their deaths, each directs that she be placed in a boat and sent to a location she pre-selects. These corpses have a transformative effect on the broader communities that they enter on their boats, either by confusing or recreating relationships.

The first of the two floating ladies, the corpse of Percival's Sister, disrupts the chivalric community whose rules have caused her death, but also builds on the spiritual alternative hinted at by Pedivere's Wife. As a floating lady, her influence is broader than that of Pedivere's Wife, but the appearance of the Wife earlier in the text has already established a precedent for reshaping knights into hermits.[53] The Sister joins Sir Percival, Sir Galahad and Sir Bors, the three successful members of 'The Tale of the Sankgraal', when they finally come together to complete their quest. Her presence even while living complicates the masculine community of the text, and she serves as an interpreter of the spiritual signs they encounter and provides the belt for Galahad's Sword of the Strange Belt by weaving it out of her own hair. When she allows herself to be bled to death to heal a lady suffering from leprosy, fulfilling a particularly grotesque custom of the castle,[54] her death can come as a shock to first-time readers, for she is one of the more complete and active female characters in the text. However, this is only the beginning of her reshaping of the community. Before her death she simply tells her companions to put her on a boat and 'lat me go as aventures woll lede me'. They do so, along with an explanatory letter. When the fellowship is temporarily divided and the three knights go their own ways, her little boat floats into Lancelot's quest, where for a time she accompanies him and later his son Galahad as well. In the end, her boat arrives in the city of Sarras, where the Grail is kept, just as the three knights are also arriving, and there they bury her, as she had previously requested. Galahad's and Percival's graves are later placed beside hers. She has not only remained a source of companionship for the other members of the party but has also become the heart of the tiny communities of both the living and the dead that form around her corpse, guiding the knights and the audience towards a new vision for community and masculinity.

Percival's Sister has been the subject of more scholarship than any of the other bodies discussed here, and with good reason – she is both fascinating as a character and significant to the success of the Grail quest. However, most criticism, of both Malory's *Morte* and his source, the French *Queste*, has focused on the first half of the Sister's story, ending with her death, and tends to fall into two camps – one perceiving the Sister's role as a sacrifice to a patriarchal, misogynist society and the other arguing for a proto-feminist model of (limited) female agency.[55]

---

[53] Both Percival's Sister and Pedivere's Wife are buried in holy ground – Sarras and Rome, respectively – their bodies permanently associated with and absorbed into the sacred.

[54] Balin had also travelled with a damsel who had to bleed for this custom of the castle; however, the ritual was not fatal in her case.

[55] On the one hand, the story as Malory received it from his source is essentially misogynistic, since as Ben Ramm argues, it requires the maiden to die and her identity to be cast out of the party and even out of her body in order to fulfil its goal, with her corpse instead functioning as the 'guarantor for the successful closure of the Grail

These readings are primarily concerned with the Sister's actions in life which ultimately lead to her death,[56] rather than her many appearances in the text after death and her crucial symbolic function as a corpse within the narrative.[57] While her actions in life are certainly significant, it is her body's function after death that participates in the broader transformation of the chivalric community. In fact, her body itself is transformed from mere corpse to relic, allowing it, like the hair-shirt-like corpse of Pedivere's Wife, to function as an object of spiritual development and a tool for transformation. The changes that Malory made from his French source show a consciousness of Percival's Sister as a sacred relic.[58] In his

mission'; B. Ramm, '"Por coi la pucele pleure": the Feminine Enigma of the Grail Quest', *Neophilologus* 87 (2003), 517–27 (p. 524). Martin Shichtman frames the Sister as a trafficked victim like all the other women in Malory's *Morte*, but as one for whom 'death provides the greatest opportunity to capitalize on her body', unlike the others, who are fortunate to be trafficked merely as wives instead of relics; M. Shichtman, 'Percival's Sister: Genealogy, Virginity, and Blood', *Arthuriana* 9 (1999), 11–20 (p. 12). This article also responds to many of the other criticisms discussed here, including those by Fries, Hoffman, Thornton and May, and Looper. Finally, Peggy McCracken interprets the Sister's attempted martyrdom as an ultimate failure, since, although the leprous lady is healed, she is not saved and she is ultimately killed in the storm of judgement shortly after the Sister's death; P. McCracken, *Curse of Eve, the Wound of the Hero: Blood, Gender, and Medieval Literature* (Philadelphia, 2003), pp. 8–9. Donald Hoffman, on the other hand, believes that while the Sister's role as interpreter is severely limited by the text, her sacrifice does accomplish a true salvific act, while providing an even clearer model of Christ for the readers than Galahad himself; D. L. Hoffman, 'Percival's Sister: Malory's "Rejected" Masculinities', *Arthuriana* 6.4 (1996), 72–84 (p. 73). Hoffman notes that the Sister's sacrifice also successfully destroys the custom of the castle in the same way that Galahad himself demolishes a number of long-standing adventures. Maureen Fries describes her as more of a female saint freely speaking wisdom and choosing death rather than a passively voiceless romance heroine, even though she 'sought to serve the patriarchy' by assisting the party of male knights and the patriarchal honour system; M. Fries, 'Gender and the Grail', *Arthuriana* 8 (1998), 67–79 (p. 76). Jennifer Looper sees Percival's Sister, even in the *Queste*, as problematizing the patriarchal model as part of a line of redemptive women stemming from Eve and continuing through Solomon's wife to the Sister herself; J. L. Looper, 'Gender, Genealogy, and the "Story of the Three Spindles" in the "Queste del Saint Graal"', *Arthuriana* 8 (1998), 49–66. And Ginger Thornton and Krista May would even go so far as to claim for the Sister a position of equal agency and authority within the quest as that of her brother and his male companions; G. Thornton and K. May, 'Malory as Feminist? The Role of Percival's Sister in the Grail Quest', in *Sir Thomas Malory: View and Reviews*, ed. T. D. Hanks (New York, 1992), pp. 43–53.

[56] Of the critics cited above, only Ramm and Shichtman even touch on her role after her death.

[57] Kenneth Hodges has an excellent summary of these and other perspectives on Percival's Sister and a measured reading of her character as both an agent and as a victim of the patriarchy (Hodges, *Forging Chivalric Communities*, p. 125).

[58] Another significant difference is the amount of authority added to the Sister's voice by Malory. For example, the Sister in the *Morte* is much more aggressive in embracing

source text, the Sister's body is preserved through embalming. 'Si firent au cors a la damoisele ce que ele avoit requis, et li osterent la bueille et tout ce que len devoit oster, puis l'embasmerent ausi richement com se ce fust li cors a l'empereor.'[59] ['Then they did for Perceval's sister what she had asked, removing her entrails and organs as necessary. They embalmed her body as lavishly as if she had been an emperor...']60 However, in Malory, these details are left out. Instead, it is simply noted that Sir Percival 'leyde hir in a barge, and coverde hit with blacke sylke'.[61] While in the *Queste*, her body is disembowelled and dismembered, mutilated and stuffed with foreign substances to prevent decay, in Malory her body is left whole, unaltered and untreated.[62]

Although another female body left alone in the wilderness and exposed to the elements, Pellinore's daughter, is 'etyn with lyons other with wylde bestis – all save the hede',[63] Percival's Sister remains incorrupt in spite of her journey and lack of protection from the environment. Holy corpses had the ability to withstand the decay of death, to retain their own identi-

her martyrdom to protect her companions and heal the leprous lady than she is in the *Queste*. In the *Queste*, she asks permission of the three knights, but in the *Morte* she simply announces her intentions, first to them and then to the members of the leprous lady's court. See Thornton and May, 'Malory as Feminist?'.

[59] 'Le Queste del Saint Graal', ed. Albert Pauphilet, *Les Classiques Français du Moyen Age* 33 (1949), 242.

[60] *The History of the Holy Grail* in *Lancelot-Grail: The Old French Arthurian Vulgate and Post-Vulgate in Translation*, ed. N. J. Lacy, trans. C. J. Chase, 5 vols. (New York, 1993), IV, p. 76.

[61] Malory, *Morte*, p. 1004.

[62] It must be noted that the embalming process described in the *Queste* does not necessarily mean the Sister was not perceived as holy in that text. Caroline Walker Bynum points out in *The Resurrection of the Body* that '[h]oly bodies were also embalmed because, as witnesses testified at one canonization proceeding, "God took such pleasure in" their bodies and their hearts'. However, this is still a significant contrast, as Malory allows an extra level of miraculousness to the Sister's death and integrity to her corpse, and thereby imbues her with an implied greater level of sanctity than she had possessed in the earlier version. Furthermore, this practice of opening and fragmenting the body, while common, was not uncontroversial, and during the late thirteenth century 'corpse tampering' was the object of many scholarly debates, especially as consensus built that 'what happened in and to the cadaver was an expression of person'. Thus this partition and fragmentation of the Sister's body in the *Queste*, while not necessarily unworthy treatment for a holy body, is still problematic, and Malory's deliberate choice to leave her body intact and preserved through miraculous means rather than human fragmentation becomes more significant. C. Walker Bynum, *The Resurrection of the Body in Western Christianity, 200–1336* (New York, 1995), p. 325. For more on medieval views of the fragmentation of corpses, also see Bynum's *Fragmentation and Redemption: Essays on Gender and the Human Body in Medieval Religion* (New York, 1992)).

[63] Malory, *Morte*, p. 118.

ties in spite of the passage of time and the abuses of the environment. When Lancelot later boards her boat, he finds not a mouldering corpse but 'a fayre bed, and therein lyynge a jantillwoman, dede', and moreover, while on this boat, he 'had the moste swettnes that ever he felte, and he was fulfilled with all thynge that he thought on other desyred'.[64] This incorruptibility, along with many of the other elements associated with the Sister – her perfect virginity and wisdom, the power of her blood and hair and the preservation of her body (miraculous or mundane) – frame her as a virgin martyr whose incorruptible remains are worthy of community veneration as relics rather than merely a victim of an unfortunate custom of the castle.

Although Lancelot and Galahad both spend months on board the barge with Percival's Sister, there is no indication that the corpse ever rots or shows any signs of becoming unpleasant at close quarters. Instead, her company is associated with sweetness and satisfaction of desire, both physical and spiritual, which are indications of the presence of sanctity. The presence of holy relics is where the heavenly and earthly touch, allowing those still living on earth a contact point with the divine. Relics draw the viewer's gaze not towards themselves but towards that future promise of glory, a powerful yet quiet act of self-effacement.[65]

Female saints and mystics, such as those Percival's Sister is patterned after, are often portrayed in their hagiographies and their own writings as embracing their physicality, which, in a patriarchal culture that perceived men as spiritual beings and women as merely bodies, becomes an opportunity for liberation and the experience of Christ's life-affirming suffering and death. As Gail Ashton notes, 'The body and, in particular, its fluids and emissions', such as the Sister's blood that filled the dish, 'becomes the site of this positive and celebratory reinscription and affirmation of human spirit.'[66] Ashton gives many examples of female saints who deliberately seek out the abject victims of leprosy, such as the leprous lady who is healed with the dish of blood, or re-enact the tortures of Christ's

---

[64] Malory, *Morte*, p. 1011.

[65] Saintly relics were also known to take a much more active role in the interest of their communities. As Patrick Geary explains, 'Saints were vital, powerful members of society and commanded reverence, honor, respect, and devotion. They were entitled to deference, service, and an enthusiastic cult. When people purposefully or accidentally failed to give them their due, either directly by acting improperly in their relics' presence or indirectly by infringing on their *honores* (their property, religious community, or devotees), they could retaliate with violence. They in turn owed, to their faithful, services that varied with the nature of the particular community.' P. J. Geary, *Living with the Dead in the Middle Ages* (Ithaca, NY, 1994), p. 120.

[66] G. Ashton, *The Generation of Identity in Late Medieval Hagiography: Speaking the Saint* (New York, 2000), p. 142.

Passion, rooting themselves in their female bodies while simultaneously sanctifying that physicality. The Sister falls firmly into this category, as a 'sacrificial victim opposing and diluting the male threat of violence', in this case the threat of the other knights at the leprous lady's castle, 'surrendering her body to Christ yet also making her own identity',[67] freely and deliberately choosing martyrdom as the climax of her own quest and transforming herself from living guide to holy relic. In so doing she sets herself against the violence instituted by the chivalric community in the form of the custom of the castle and establishes (yet again) the necessity of an alternative.

Another aspect of the Sister, unique to female saints and their embrace of their sacred physicality, is her body's association with life-giving sustenance.[68] At the same time that she provides guidance to the spiritually challenged Lancelot, while he is on her barge he is mystically fed by heavenly manna. She not only directs his attention towards the divine reality, but also feeds him divine food, a reflection of the traditionally feminine role of food preparation.[69] Female saints are frequently associated with food, both its lack and its provision. St Katherine's grave, for example, was said to flow with milk and oil, and many others were miraculously fed by angels during their trials or enabled to live on nothing but the sacrament.[70]

Her function as a saintly relic exists in tension with her function as a lady, which requires that she serve as a foil for knights to define themselves against. Martin Shichtman has argued that the text treats her, or more specifically her body, as merely a commodity to be exchanged to facilitate patriarchal bonding, and that while typically this is achieved by giving or taking a woman as a wife, because of her virginity she is of greater value as a set of relics. Shichtman concludes that 'Percival's sister is trafficked, sold, little more than an automobile brought by thieves

---

[67] Ashton, *Generation of Identity*, p. 145.
[68] The Sister's divine provision for Lancelot parallels her earlier action to provide life-giving blood to the leprous lady, the gift which ultimately cost her life. Women were frequently seen as inherently less spiritual than men, more sensual and fleshly and less capable of achieving true sanctity, and their association with the food of the Eucharist, the physical body of Christ, is often seen as a feminine response to this view of the female body, embracing their physicality by linking it to the physicality of Christ. For example, female mystics who were denied the Eucharist by male clerics would have visions of Christ himself sharing his body with them in the form of the Host, or even see themselves officiating at the Mass. See C. Walker Bynum, *Holy Feast, Holy Fast: The Religious Significance of Food to Medieval Women* (Los Angeles, 1987).
[69] While this is not a prominent association in Malory, for an inversion see the poisoning of Sir Patryse (Malory, *Morte*, p. 1049).
[70] Ashton, *Generation of Identity*, p. 142.

to a chop shop, worth more in her pieces than she was than she was as a whole.'[71] The text kills her off rather than allow her to see the Grail with living eyes as her male companions do, and her influence after death is primarily directed towards assisting these male companions in their quest, rather than achieving it herself. Yet like the other female corpses in the text, she gains the power of disruption after her death, and being 'trafficked' among the members of the chivalric community only allows that disruption to spread more widely. Even as she assists the party of knights in achieving their quest she also subverts their identities as knights, undermining the chivalric community that had required her to play the role of feminine foil and caused her death through its customs.[72]

As a relic she possesses greater significance and agency, not only than she had as a living woman, but even than the other female corpses of the text. As Ashton points out, a relic served as a '[mediator] between humanity and heaven' whom supplicants could ask to put in a good word for them to God, as well as 'affirm[ing] belief on behalf of the wider Christian community'[73] through miracles and other signs intended to encourage the living in their faith. Communities constructed themselves around relics to be as close as possible to these holy remains. In fact, space was so tight that as the graveyards outside church buildings filled up, older bones were translated into ossuaries within the church proper,[74] so that congregants had not only to pass through the community of corpses but worship surrounded by bones, a constant sign of the promise of the resurrection. It is no wonder that spiritual seekers like Lancelot and the saintly Galahad are drawn to her, as though by a magnet.

The relics themselves appear to feel the same attachment to these communities that have risen up around them. Medieval texts abound with stories of saints stepping in to defend the communities or individuals associated with their relics. A number of accounts describe wicked members of the nobility being thrown from their horses by a saint in order to punish their arrogance. The Church even had rituals for a religious community to incite the local relics into influencing a conflict affecting

---

[71] Shichtman, 'Percival's Sister', p. 19.

[72] The primary weakness in much of the criticism discussed earlier is that the critics are arguing from an anachronistically modern perspective on agency. The Sister completes the quest within the strictures of medieval culture, but within that context she has several means of unofficial female agency available to her, which she utilizes in order to reach her goals. Her primary means is through the role of a virgin saint, first as martyr and then as relic, and as a relic her power has particular resonance in the context of the creation of new communities.

[73] Ashton, *Generation of Identity*, p. 141.

[74] Bynum, *Resurrection*, p. 204.

the community or solving a local problem.[75] Percival's Sister's value, while living and as a corpse, is based on her guidance for the knights and her ability to direct their attention to God, rather than her hair, blood and corpse, which are signs of the higher reality to which this new community of knights aspires.

When the knights originally set out on the Grail quest, there is only one community paradigm available to them – the chivalric one. The problem, as discussed above with regard to Pedivere's Wife, is that the laws governing the chivalric community are inadequate and, in some cases, utterly opposed to the spiritual community centred around the Grail. This ignorance of and isolation from the spiritual community dooms most of them, including Sir Lancelot, to failure before they have even properly begun the quest. Only three completely succeed – Bors, Percival and the exemplary Galahad – and they do so only after having been brought together by Percival's Sister. While living, she is key to the formation of the community of Grail questers by bringing the last member, Sir Galahad, into company with Sir Bors and Sir Percival, and by providing direction during their journey. Other knights, enmeshed in the rules of the chivalric community and blind to the new vision of community before them, misunderstand the rules of the quest and fail to achieve their goals, but the Sister knows those rules so completely, so 'bone-deep' as it were, that she cannot merely get herself there, even after her death, but she can also direct others. As a corpse, she continues to expand the community by inviting Lancelot on to her barge. Although Lancelot's quest is ultimately a failure, at least by his standards, he has been transformed by his encounter with the spiritual community into which he is drawn.

Although the Grail questers part ways after the Sister's death, they are reunited in Sarras, the city of the Grail. Before her death, the Sister had prophesied that 'as sone as ye three com to the cité of Sarras, there to enchyeve the Holy Grayle, ye shall fynde me undir a towre

---

[75] Geary, *Living with the Dead*, chapter 5. Monks lacked the power of bishops to excommunicate or otherwise officially sanction those who had committed offences against the community, but they did control access to many sacred relics. Therefore, they could, and often did, 'mistreat cult objects and prevent popular access to them, thus disturbing the proper relationships between the human and supernatural orders, with consequences not only for the alleged opponent but for all of society dependent on these powers' (Geary, *Living with the Dead*, p. 96). The relationship between relics and community sometimes seems a bit dysfunctional in many of these stories, as a community accuses a saint of neglecting it and punishes the relics (which could range from humiliation on the floor to a beating by the local peasants) until the saint steps in and metes out some of his or her own punishment on the community's behalf.

aryved',[76] and her barge arrives just ahead of the three knights. "'Truly," seyde Sir Percivall, "in the name of God, well hath my syster holden us covenaunte!'"[77] This little spiritual community is so closely knit that two of the three knights are buried together with her.[78]

Sir Lancelot, on the other hand, goes home having had only a vision of the Grail and is left grieving and hungry for the spiritual community he tasted on the barge and in the castle of Carbonek, where he had a vision of a Grail which, for him, was the climax of his quest.[79] He goes back to Camelot dissatisfied with the status quo – the chivalric community and his place within it – but apparently with little power to change it.[80] Before the final transformation, the second floating lady, Elayne le Blanke, the Fayre Maydyn of Ascolat, must disrupt the patterns of the entire Round Table community, revealing the hidden rifts in the relationships among the members of that community. She signals the beginning of the end.

Elayne's first appearance is as a fairly ordinary baron's daughter who has, quite naturally, fallen in love with Lancelot while he stays with her family for a tournament. Like Percival's Sister, she is a maiden and unattached to any knight, but unlike Percival's Sister, she has no interest in maintaining this pure state and is desperate to become Lancelot's lady, either as his wife or lover. When he rejects her out of his love for Guenevere, she wastes away and dies. But first, she leaves her father and brother detailed instructions for the care of her corpse. She has them place her body on a boat with a letter telling her story, and sent down the river, and specifies that her body must be placed in the barge while still 'hote' and the letter wrapped in her hand until rigor mortis has set in so that it will not be lost. Her barge is steered by a silent servant who directs her to the location she has requested before her death. Elayne's goals as stated in her letter are simple – to publicize her grief, especially to the other women in this community who are under the same strictures as she is ('unto all ladyes I make my mone') and to be interred and prayed for by

---

[76] Malory, *Morte*, p. 1003.
[77] Malory, *Morte*, p. 1032.
[78] The third knight, Bors, returns to Camelot to tell the story of their adventures to the court and later continues to participate in the spiritual community alongside the chivalric by becoming a crusader in the Holy Land.
[79] Malory, *Morte*, pp. 1015–16.
[80] Hoffman, 'Masculinities', p. 79, posits an additional connection between Lancelot and the Sister in terms of repeated attempts at forming a truly Christ-like masculinity, as the Sister's character demonstrates the failures of previous iterations in otherwise flawless characters such as Galahad. Through contact with her, Lancelot eventually constructs a truly Christ-like, though still flawed, masculinity.

her beloved.[81] Elayne's carefully orchestrated postmortem performance is heavily dependent on the cooperation of the living. There is a striking contrast between this and Percival's Sister's almost careless send-off and self-directed journey.

Yet by reminding the readers of the relic-like body of Percival's Sister, Elayne condemns the community's fixation with chivalric love. These social expectations had both led her on in her romance with Lancelot while forbidding her from ever enjoying the fulfilment of the relationship. Lancelot's felt need to wear her sleeve during the tournament (a sign of love) as part of his disguise encouraged her to see their relationship as an example of chivalric love, even while Lancelot's noble loyalty to his true lady, Guenevere, prevented this. Elayne is trapped, and intends to show Lancelot and other ladies, potential victims, what this knightly behaviour had accomplished.

The appearance of Elayne's corpse in the narrative signals the downward spiral of the traditional chivalric narrative to the audience, as the classic knight–lady courtly love relationship, a key element of the community's structure and knightly self-definition, is revealed to be hazardous to all concerned. While Percival's Sister unites those who board her vessel both with each other and with the divine, Elayne's arrival in Camelot brings conflict, deepening the growing rift between Lancelot and Guenevere. Their relationship is key to the chivalric community as represented by their relationship as a knight and his lady. Since part of a knight's masculinity and knightliness is defined by his interactions with a lady, the relationship between the queen of the community and the best knight must be especially significant, and its breakdown especially traumatic for the community. Elayne's failed pursuit of the object of her desire is manifested in her corpse and issues a clear and specific warning to the court against this pillar of the chivalric community.[82] She spreads her own suffering throughout the community, forcing everyone to share in her pain.

When Lancelot leaves Guenevere after Elayne's appearance and his and Guenevere's subsequent quarrel, he suffers a major wound to both his dignity and his masculinity.[83] Later in the same book Guenevere is captured by Sir Mellyagaunt, a knight whose love for the queen has been thwarted for years by her relationship with Lancelot. Completely without malice, and while remaining utterly dedicated to the chivalric ideal,

---

[81] Malory, *Morte*, p. 1096.

[82] See Armstrong, *Gender*, pp. 26 and 174 on the role of heteronormatic desire in the fall of chivalric community.

[83] While sleeping next to a well, Lancelot is shot 'in the thycke of the buttok' by a lady hunter who mistakes him for her prey (Malory, *Morte*, p. 1105).

this relationship becomes the centre of the collapse. By the end of 'Sir Launcelot and Quene Gwenyvere' it has become clear even to the characters within the narrative that the chivalric community is fraying. When Lancelot's knightly virtue is proved by his miraculous healing of Sir Urry, 'Sir Launcelote wepte, as he had bene a chylde that had bene beatyn',[84] recognizing his own failures even in the face of triumph. The repeated encounters with the corpses of ladies – Pedivere's Wife, Percival's Sister and Elayne of Ascolat – have finally brought this reality home to him. Furthermore, the end of this narrative contains a warning that even after the recovery of the queen and the proof of Lancelot's virtue, all is not well: 'every nyght and day Sir Aggravayne, Sir Gawaynes brother, awayted Quene Gwenyver and Sir Launcelot to put hem bothe to a rebuke and a shame';[85] and this leads straight into the final story of the *Morte Darthur*: the Death of Arthur.

In this final chapter, though Lancelot continues to follow the rules of chivalry perfectly, his actions – undermining the unity of the Round Table through his relationship with Guenevere so that Arthur feels compelled to go to war against him and giving Gawain the wound that ultimately causes his death – are key elements in the community's collapse. It can no longer support itself when Mordred steps in. Ultimately, Arthur dies and Guenevere retreats to an abbey, refusing to participate in the chivalric community as an impetus for Lancelot's adventures. The chivalric community as Lancelot had known it no longer exists, and an alternative, as proposed by the ladies who were the victims of the original community, must be created. Lancelot becomes a priest and the head of a small spiritual community comprised of other former members of the Round Table, including Bors, the one surviving Grail quester. When he dies, the narrative suggests that he has become a saint, for when his friends find his body, they discover a smile on his face and 'the swettest savour aboute hym that ever they felte'.[86]

## Conclusion

The corpses of these ladies have built a symbolic pattern within the text. The simple presence of a lady's corpse indicates that there is something profoundly wrong with the narrative in which she is placed, and the repeated appearances of these striking images – a lady's decapitated corpse borne by a guilty knight and a lady's preserved corpse on a boat

---

[84] Malory, *Morte*, p. 1152.
[85] Malory, *Morte*, p. 1153.
[86] Malory, *Morte*, p. 1258.

– signal that this wrongness is endemic. The chivalric community has failed these ladies, and though the narrative attempts to use them for their original function – bringing honour to the knights who encounter them on adventure – their bodies bear witness against the knights and the community that depends on defining itself against the female body. Over the course of the narrative, one member of the chivalric community, Lancelot, internalizes their warnings, and finally embraces their alternative, becoming the heart of a new community where he and other members of the chivalric community can construct new identities, distinct, yet not entirely separate from, their former identities as knights of the Round Table.

# VI

# TRISTAN AND ISEULT AT THE CATHEDRAL OF SANTIAGO DE COMPOSTELA

## Joan Tasker Grimbert

Santiago de Compostela in north-western Spain is not a locale that we normally associate with the Tristan legend, and yet Tristan and Iseult make their appearance in the cathedral there twice during the Middle Ages, at two different times and in two different media. In the cathedral museum can be found a marble column – one of three salvaged from the original Romanesque façade – containing sculpted images that one prominent art historian, Serafín Moralejo, has identified as Tristan (and possibly Iseult). These images predate the earliest extant Old French poems and testify to a very early penetration of the legend into Galicia.[1] How and why these secular images came to be incorporated into the religious programme of the Romanesque façade of the cathedral is the subject of the first part of this essay.

At the beginning of the fifteenth century, the lovers make another appearance in the cathedral at Santiago, via the Icelandic *Saga af Tristram ok Ísodd* (*c.* 1400). In that text, once Tristram leaves Cornwall, he departs for his homeland (Spain), becomes king and marries Ísodd the Dark. After incurring a mortal wound in combat in 'Jakobsland' (Galicia), he dies and is eventually buried with Ísodd the Fair in 'the largest cathedral in the land'. The question of how and why Santiago de Compostela came to play such a significant role in the Icelandic version of the Tristan legend is explored in the second part of this essay.[2]

---

[1] The earliest poems (Béroul's *Roman de Tristran* and Thomas of Britain's *Roman de Tristran*), composed in Anglo-Norman, date from the last quarter of the twelfth century. For a survey of the legend from the twelfth century to the twentieth century, see *Tristan and Isolde: A Casebook*, ed. J. T. Grimbert (New York, 1995; repr. 2002), pp. xiii–cxviii, with a plot summary on pp. xviii–xx.

[2] My interest in this fascinating topic was sparked by a three-week course proposed by

## *Tristan and Iseult on the Romanesque Façade of the Cathedral*

The column containing the images from the Tristan legend is from the twelfth-century Romanesque façade (*c.* 1105–10) that once graced the north portal of the cathedral.[3] It depicts three scenes, the most evocative of which appears in the lower register. It shows a young man lying in a rudderless boat asleep or in a faint, grasping a notched sword in his right hand (Figures 1a, 1b). It was Serafín Moralejo who first proposed identifying the figure as Tristan.[4] As we recall, it is precisely because of the notched sword that the Irish princess Iseult, who has taken in and

the Consejería de Educación of the Embassy of Spain that took place in Santiago in July 2009. Taking as its theme various aspects of the pilgrimage route (history, art, music, food, literature and film), it was taught in part by José M. Andrade Cernadas and Therese Martin. I am profoundly grateful for their continuing interest, encouragement, numerous bibliographical suggestions and comments on earlier drafts. My heartfelt thanks go as well to Juan Miguel Zarandona, who organized a memorable 'Grail' excursion in July 2013 that took a group of us to many of the sites in northern Spain that are mentioned in this article (Estella, Sangüesa, San Millán de la Cogolla and San Juan de la Peña). Finally, I would like to thank Carol J. Chase, Marianne E. Kalinke and Alison Stones, for their sage counsel.

[3]   On the discovery of elements from the old north portal, see S. Moralejo, 'La primitiva fachada norte de la Catedral de Santiago', in *Patrimonio artístico de Galicia y otros estudios: homenaje al Prof. Dr. Serafín Moralejo Álvarez*, ed. A. Franco Mata, E. Romero-Pose and J. Williams, 3 vols. (Santiago, 2004), I, 21–46 (first publ. in *Compostellanum* 14 (1969), 623–88), and 'Saint-Jacques de Compostelle. Les portails retrouvés de la Cathédrale romane', in *Patrimonio artístico de Galicia*, I, 101–10 (first publ. in *Dossiers de l'Archéologie* 20 (1977), 87–103). See also M. Durliat, *La Sculpture romane de la route de Saint-Jacques: Conques à Compostelle* (Mont-de-Marsan, 1990), pp. 342–5.

[4]   For a complete description of the 'Tristan column', with excellent photographs of the images, see S. Moralejo, 'Fuste historiado con leyenda épica (Tristán?), Portada norte de la Catedral de Santiago, 1105–1110', in *Santiago, Camino de Europa. Culto y Cultura en la peregrinación a Compostela* (Santiago, 1993), pp. 382–4. Other articles by Moralejo relative to the column are 'Artes figurativas y artes literarias en la España Medieval: románico, romance y roman', in *Patrimonio artístico de Galicia*, II, 55-60 (first publ. in *Boletín de la Asociación Europea de Profesores de Español* 17, 32–33 (1985)); 'Artistas, patronos y público en el arte del Camino de Santiago', in *Patrimonio artístico de Galicia*, II, 21–36 (first publ. in *Compostellanum* 30 (1985), 395–430); 'Le origini del programma iconografico dei portali nel Romanico spagnolo', in *Patrimonio artístico de Galicia*, II, 121–35 (first publ. in *Wiligelmo e Lanfranco nell'Europa romanica, Atti del convegno, Modena 24-27 ott. 1985*, ed. R. Bussi (Modena, 1989), 35–51); and 'Column Shaft Decorated with Putti Gathering Grapes', item 92 in *The Art of Medieval Spain, a.d. 500–1200* (New York, 1993), pp. 212–13. Moralejo's thesis has been embraced by A. Stones, 'Arthurian Art since Loomis', in *Arthurus Rex, II*, Acta Conventus Lovianiensis 1987, ed. W. Van Hoeke, G. Tournoy and W. Verbecke (Leuven, 1991), pp. 21–78 (pp. 32–3); and M. Whitaker, *The Legends of King Arthur in Art* (Cambridge, 1990), pp. 92–3.

healed the man she believes to be a minstrel, realizes that not only is he a knight, but he is the very one who slew her uncle, the Irish champion Morholt.[5] Moralejo admits that the notch in the sword could possibly be due to simple deterioration, but we might well ask ourselves why the sculptor would have displayed the weapon so prominently if he had not intended to depict Tristan's notched sword.[6]

The aquatic environment is replicated in the scene on the middle register.[7] According to Moralejo, it depicts the wounded hero as swollen and sick and attended by a maiden, who, evidently endowed with miraculous curative powers, kneels solicitously before him. A spurt of venom issues from the mouth of a serpent. Moralejo plausibly relates this scene to the episode in which Iseult discovers Tristan in a faint from the poisonous flames emitted by the dragon which, we are told, let out a loud roar as the knight thrust his sword into its heart. In the scene depicted in the upper register of the column, a warrior with a coat of mail tries to defend his warhorse from the attack of birds of prey. Moralejo believes this image is reminiscent of the fact that in the legend the dragon attacks and destroys Tristan's horse, but he notes that here and elsewhere the sculptor allowed himself to transform and moralize the plot nucleus of the legend,

[5] Stephanie Cain Van d'Elden underscores the importance of the notched sword when she identifies as specific to the Tristan corpus the bath scene in which Iseult recognizes Tristan as her uncle's slayer; 'Specific and Generic Scenes in Verse *Tristan* Illustrations', in *Visuality and Materiality in the Story of Tristan and Isolde*, ed. J. Eming, A. M. Rasmussen and K. Starkey (Notre Dame, IN, 2012), pp. 269–98 (p. 272). But the notched sword is usually seen only in the bath scene. Martine Meuwese points out that we know of no other scene in medieval art that depicts Tristan lying in a boat holding an upright sword, much less one that is notched; 'Silent Witnesses: Testimonies of Tristan throughout Europe', in *'Li Premerains vers', Essays in Honor of Keith Busby*, ed. C. M. Jones and L. E. Whalen (Amsterdam, 2011), pp. 291–305 (p. 294).

[6] Meuwese, 'Silent Witnesses', who finds the Tristan identification problematic, in part because it lacks an inscription, believes that the notch is probably due to erosion and is thus unintentional (pp. 294–5). Like Stones, however, Whitaker, *King Arthur in Art*, asserts that the sword is 'unmistakably nicked' and that the figure is 'unmistakably' Tristan, although she sees him more generally as a Christ figure: 'Suffering and dying, he journeys according to God's will, finally reaching Ireland, which was the Celtic Otherworld in Welsh myths such as *The Spoils of Annwfn*. His prominent sword and shield recall St. Paul's allusion to spiritual arms [Ephesians 6. 15–17]' (pp. 90 and 92–3).

[7] It is this aquatic environment in part that led F. Prado-Vilar to propose that the artist meant to depict, not Tristan, but rather a 'Christ-like Ulysses' facing Scylla and the Sirens; the figure at the base of the column would be 'the sleeping hero sailing in the ship of salvation towards his celestial homeland – an image that performs a dual purpose, acting as a visual exegesis both in the context of the mythology of Ulysses, who was to arrive sleeping on the shores of Ithaca, and in that of the hagiography of Saint James, whose body was carried in a ship from the port of Jaffa to Galicia'; '*Nostos*: Ulysses, Compostela and the Ineluctable Modality of the Visible', in *Compostela and Europe: The Story of Diego Gelmírez* (Milan, 2010), pp. 260–9 (p. 267).

1a.   Santiago de Compostela, cathedral: Tristan figure on marble column formerly on north portal of Romanesque cathedral, currently preserved in Cathedral museum

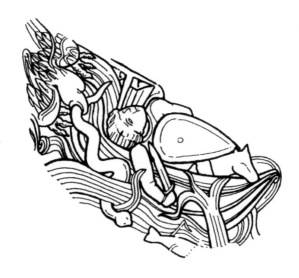

1b.   Drawing by Serafín Moralejo, *Santiago, Camino de Europa*, p. 382

1c.   Santiago de Compostela, cathedral: Tristan and Iseult on marble column
formerly on north portal of Romanesque cathedral, currently preserved in
Cathedral museum

incorporating various motifs from his repertory of models and his robust
imagination. The moralizing can be seen in the addition of various figures
that frame the three scenes – for example, an eagle pursuing a devil in the
first, the devil and sirens in the second. In any case, as Julia Walworth
notes, art historians long ago abandoned the attempt to link images with
specific texts, a trend that had dominated earlier art criticism. In a seminal
article published in 1975, Hella Frühmorgen-Voss stressed that pictorial
and textual works are really independent responses to the Tristan story,
adding that it is important to consider the type of work and function for
which it was made.[8]

The portal on which the Tristan figures once appeared is known as the
Puerta Francigena (or French Portal) because it was the endpoint of the
famous *via francigena*, the French pilgrimage route. We do not know
the exact details recounted in the oral tales that were circulating at the
beginning of the twelfth century and that may have been carried from

---

[8]   H. Frühmorgen-Voss, 'Tristan und Isolde in mittelalterlichen Bildzeugnissen', *Deutsche
Vierteljahrsschrift für Literaturwissenschaft und Geistesgeschichte* 47 (1973), 645–63;
J. Walworth, 'Tristan in Medieval Art', in *Tristan and Isolde: A Casebook*, ed. Grimbert,
pp. 255–99.

the British Isles and France by the numerous pilgrims who journeyed to Santiago. We can reasonably assume, however, that the devils, sirens and serpents – if they played a part in the stories the sculptor heard – were put to a religious use in a portal programme that was primarily focused on original sin. In an effort to explain why the sculptor depicted a popular secular hero on this portal, Moralejo recalls that in the early vernacular biblical play *Le Jeu d'Adam* (or *Ordo Representationis Ade*), the account of the drama of the Fall of man and the hope of his redemption is followed by a sermon reprimanding the spectator for being more interested in the exploits of Roland and Olivier than in the true epic of Christ's passion.[9] According to Moralejo, the sketch of the popular Tristan legend that appears on the Puerta Francigena with its moralizing gloss could possibly respond to a similar intention in contrast.

As if to admit that his analogy with the *Jeu d'Adam* is purely speculative, Moralejo concludes that in any case the motif of the navigation of a wounded hero in a rudderless boat could not have failed to be of interest, as *simile dissimile*, in a sanctuary that had welcomed the body of its patron saint transported by a similarly marvellous vehicle. The reference is, of course, to the legend according to which St James's martyred body was miraculously translated from Jerusalem to Galicia, in the space of six days, in a rudderless boat guided only by the hand of God. The *translatio* of his mortal remains is recounted in Book III of the compilation known as the *Codex Calixtinus* or the *Liber sancti jacobi*.[10]

But Moralejo's observation suggests to me another interpretation – the possibility that the sculptor did not mean for us to see Tristan as a secular figure *in contrast* to the religious figure of St James, but rather as a hero *quite similar* to the cathedral's patron saint whose aid was often invoked in the battle against the infidel. This theory gains credence when we note that Tristan is portrayed on the column as lying lifeless in the boat *not*

---

[9] Moralejo, 'Fuste historiado', 384. 'Plus volentiers orreit chanter / Come Rollant ala juster / E Oliver son compainnon, / Qu'il ne ferrait la passion / Que suffri Crist a grant hahan / Por le pecchié que fist Adam' (He would more willingly hear one sing of how Roland went off to joust with his companion Olivier than of how Christ suffered with great pain for the sin that Adam committed); *Le Mystère d'Adam (Ordo representactionis Ade)*, ed. P. Aebischer (Geneva, 1964), ll. 967–72 (my translation).

[10] The *Codex Calixtinus*, so-named because substantial parts of it were falsely claimed to be the work of Pope Calixtus II, is a five-part compilation of texts and music relating to the cult and shrine of St James and designed specifically to promote it. The earliest part of the work is dated to *c.* 1135. Although it is sometimes referred to as the *Liber sancti jacobi*, M. C. Díaz y Díaz reserves that designation for the hypothetical archetype, which he believes was in existence ten years earlier; 'El *Codex Calixtinus*: Volviendo sobre el Tema', in *The* Codex Calixtinus *and the Shrine of St. James*, ed. J. Williams and A. Stones (Tübingen, 1992), pp. 1–9; idem, 'El Liber sancti iacobi', in *Santiago. La Europa del peregrinaje*, ed. Robert Plötz et al. (Barcelona, 1993), pp. 39–55.

with his sword and harp, as the earliest extant versions of the legend would lead us to expect, but rather with his sword, shield and warhorse. In medieval art, as in a medieval literature, Tristan is presented variously as a lover, a musician and a warrior. At Santiago, he is clearly portrayed as a warrior, ready to do battle, ready to combat not just serpents and dragons in Ireland or the giant-like Morholt (another kind of unholy monster) in Cornwall, but all enemies of the Christian faith, especially in Spain, which St James was thought at one point to have evangelized and protected from its enemies.[11] Although the more aggressive figure of St James the crusader – and indeed Moor-slayer (*Santiago matamoros*) – did not actually emerge until some time after 1123 when Pope Calixtus II made it unambiguously clear that he considered the wars in Spain to be crusades, the pilgrims who flocked to St James's tomb well before the twelfth century certainly saw the saint as their protector.[12]

The carved images from the old Romanesque portal of the cathedral that Moralejo has identified as Tristan are like none other that we have seen so far of the Celtic hero in medieval art. The scene that appears to have been the best-known representation of Tristan was the Orchard Rendezvous, in which the lovers can be seen on either side of the pine tree that conceals the eavesdropping King Mark, casting a disapproving eye on the scene below.[13] This image owes its popularity, no doubt, to its compositional similarity to depictions of the Fall, where Adam and Eve stand on either side of the Tree of Knowledge in which the serpent lurks.[14] If we move from single scene images of the legend to narrative cycles, however, we see that medieval artists were very much drawn to the episodes of the legend in which Tristan is presented as a warrior

---

[11]  On the fascinating conflation (by artists) of the legends concerning St James's evangelization of Spain and the miraculous *translatio* (translation) of his remains from Jerusalem on a stone or in a stone boat, see S. Moralejo, 'Santiago y los caminos de su imaginería', in *Patrimonio artístico de Galicia*, II, 285–91 (first publ. in *Santiago, la Europa del peregrinaje*, ed. Plötz et al., pp. 75–89).

[12]  On the evolution of St James from evangelist to Moor-slayer, see F. Márquez Villanueva, *Santiago: trayectoria de un mito* (Barcelona, 2004), pp. 183–222; and K. E. van Liere, 'The Missionary and the Moorslayer: James the Apostle in Spanish Historiography from Isidore of Seville to Ambrosio de Morales', *Viator* 37 (2006), 519–43. My thanks to José Andrade and Therese Martin for suggesting these references.

[13]  Walworth, 'Tristan in Medieval Art', pp. 279–83.

[14]  Ibid., p. 280. See D. Fouquet, 'Die Baumgartenszene des *Tristan* in der mittlealterlichen Kunst und Literatur', *Zeitschrift für deutsche Philologie* 92 (1973), 360–70; and M. Curschmann, 'Images of Tristan', in *Gottfried von Strassburg and the Medieval Tristan Legend: Papers from an Anglo-American Symposium*, ed. A. Stevens and R. Wisbey (Cambridge, 1990), pp. 1–18 (pp. 7–17). See the stunning depiction of Adam and Eve on a capital in the Collegial of Saint-Pierre and Saint-Gaudens (Gascony) in Durliat, *Sculpture romane*, p. 299 fig. 305.

– the one in which he combats the giant-like Morholt to rid Cornwall of the odious obligation to pay tribute to Ireland, and the one in which he slays the dragon ravishing Ireland. This preference is particularly obvious in the three embroidered hangings from Kloster Wienhausen in Lower Saxony. Julia Walworth states that Norbert Ott, on examining the earliest of these hangings (c. 1300–10), concluded that of the twenty-two individual scenes shown, eight depict the fight with Morholt and six concern the combat with the dragon and the revelation of Tristan as the true dragon-slayer at the Irish court.[15] Walworth identifies as the main thematic message of these (and other) tapestries 'Tristan as a model knight, delivering his country from a feared oppressor'.[16] In the same way, the artist who carved the images at Santiago chose to allude precisely to those two episodes and to present Tristan primarily as a giant-slayer and a dragon-slayer fighting for a noble cause.

It should be noted that the Tristan figures identified by Moralejo are not mentioned in the description of the cathedral contained in 'The Pilgrim's Guide', Book V of the *Codex Calixtinus*. The guide's author is, understandably, much more interested in describing the religious figures. He does specify that there are six columns (some of marble and some of stone) at each of the two entrances to the north portal, but he then concentrates on describing the tympanum, which is primarily focused on original sin. He adds that 'around it, in truth, have been sculpted many images of saints, beasts, men, angels, women, flowers and other creatures' too numerous to describe or characterize.[17] It is not difficult to imagine how, given such a diversity of figures, Tristan and Iseult might easily have found a place.

Tristan's appearance on one of the marble columns of the original north portal of the cathedral seems even less surprising when we consider the number and variety of secular figures depicted on the façades of Romanesque churches, particularly in western Europe. At Santiago the scenes described by Moralejo recall Tristan's victories over the giant-like Morholt and the Irish dragon, and on other Romanesque buildings we see

---

[15] Walworth, 'Tristan in Medieval Art', p. 272; N. Ott, 'Tristan auf Runkelstein und die übrigen zyklischen Darstellungen des Tristanstoffes. Textrezeption oder medieninterne Eigengesetzlichkeit der Bildprogram', in *Runkelstein: Die Wandmalereien des Sommerhauses*, ed. W. Haug (Wiesbaden, 1982), pp. 194–239 (p. 206).

[16] Walworth, 'Tristan in Medieval Art', p. 275.

[17] 'Ibidem vero circum circa, multe immagines sanctorem, bestiarum, hominum, angelorum, feminanum, florum, ceterarumque creaturarum sculpuntur, quarum essenciam et qualitatem pre magnitudine sua narrare non possumus'; *The Pilgrim's Guide to Santiago de Compostela: Critical Edition*. II: *The Text: Annotated English Translation*, ed. P. Gerson, A. Shaver-Crandell, A. Stones and J. Krochalis, 2 vols. (London, 1998), pp. 72–3.

secular figures also fighting against unholy adversaries in the same way as their biblical counterparts, St James, St Michael and St George. In the pages that follow I examine a selection of these intrepid warriors, who – whether fictional, historical or a combination of both – have, like Tristan, attained mythical status.

## Slayers of Dragons, Serpents and Giants

### Sigurd the Dragon-slayer

Depictions of slayers of dragons, serpents and giants, both secular and bib-lical, can be found on the façades of many Romanesque churches along the pilgrimage routes in France, Italy and Spain. Several such figures appear on the spandrels and archivolts flanking the main (southern) portal of Santa Maria la Real de Sangüesa (Navarre).[18] It was William Anderson[19] who first identified the warrior figure in the top right-hand corner of the right spandrel as Sigurd the dragon-slayer (of the *Saga of the Völsungs*), killing the dragon Fafnir using an upward thrust of his sword, as he is instructed to do in the *Saga*. Depicted just below the dragon-slayer is a blacksmith working at his forge (Figure 2).[20] Struck by the juxtaposition of the two images, Anderson theorized that the blacksmith was Sigurd's foster-father, Regin, who forged the hero's sword Gram, for he noted the striking resemblance between this figure and the same representation on wood panels found in stave churches in Norway, especially the portal of Hylestad.[21] Ulrich Müller claimed in 1995 that this identification had been widely discussed and commonly accepted,[22] and some scholars actually

---

[18] Since there is some disagreement among scholars regarding the precise identity of a couple of these figures, I have tried to summarize the arguments put forward on both sides.

[19] W. Anderson, 'Internationalismen i konsten under 1100-talet', *Tidskrift för Konstvetenskap* 1 (1926), 33–4. The theory is sometimes attributed to A. K. Porter, who quickly signalled his agreement in his very influential book *Spanish Romanesque Sculpture* (repr. New York, 1969 [1928]).

[20] The story of Sigurd was extremely well known in Scandinavia during the early Middle Ages and became that of Siegfried in the thirteenth-century *Nibelungenlied*. See J. L. Byock, *The Saga of the Volsungs: the Norse Epic of Sigurd the Dragon Slayer* (London, 1999), which has an excellent introduction on the legend's very early origins and its spread throughout Europe. For the section of the *Saga* that recounts these par-ticular incidents, see pp. 63–6.

[21] The church, which dates from the late twelfth or early thirteenth century, was destroyed in the seventeenth century, but the intricate wood carvings from the doorway are pre-served in the Museum of Cultural History in Oslo.

[22] U. Müller, 'Nibelungen-Rezeption am Pilgerweg nach Santiago? Das Portal von "Santa Maria la Real" im nordspanischen Sangüesa', 3. in *Pöchlarner Heldenliedgespräch;*

2.   Sangüesa: Santa María le Real: right-hand spandrel of southern façade:
Sigurd the dragon-slayer and Regin the blacksmith

identified other images (on the left spandrel) that they said were also
inspired by the Sigurd saga, again relating them to analogous images
found all over Scandinavia.[23]

Anderson's theory has, however, been challenged. In a section of her
1997 dissertation, Beatrix Müller describes the theory (which she attributes to Kingsley Porter) and advances various arguments against it.[24] She
claims that the scenes that Porter (and others) have identified as being
inspired by the Sigurd saga are scattered over the two spandrels and are
not even by the same mason. The images on the left spandrel and the

*Die Rezeption des Nibelungenliedes*, ed. K. Zatloukal (Vienna, 1995), pp. 147–55. My
thanks to Stephanie Cain Van d'Elden for this reference.

23   See especially C. Milton Weber, 'La Portada de Santa María la Real de Sangüesa',
*Principe de Viana* 76–7 (1959), 139–86; and B. de la Serna, 'Las sagas nórdicas y
su posible vinculación con el arte escultório de Santa María la Real de Sangüesa',
*Principe de Viana* 144–5 (1976), 399–418.

24   B. Müller, 'Santa María la Real, Sangüesa (Navarra). Die Bauplastik Santa Marías
und die Skulptur Navarras und Aragóns im 12. Jahrhundert. Rezeptor, Katalysator,
Innovator?' (unpublished dissertation, Humboldt-Universität zu Berlin, 1997),
pp. 71–4 ('Eine Darstellung der nordischen Sigurdsage am Portal von Santa María?');
idem, 'La arquitectura plástica de Santa Maria la Real de Sangüesa', *Principe de Viana*
208 (1996), 247–82.

blacksmith image on the right one were carved by Leodegarius, whereas the 'Sigurd' image was added some fifteen to twenty years later by the workshop of the Master of San Juan de la Peña. Moreover, she finds unconvincing the comparison with the Hylestad carvings because those panels are intertwined. But Hylestad is not the only place in Scandinavia where Sigurd's story is depicted. According to Blanca de la Serna, there exist about forty examples of scenes from the saga, nine in medieval Sweden, one each in Russia, Denmark and northern England and twenty-eight in Norway and on the Isle of Man. Depicted on church portals and baptismal fonts, chests, furniture and Runic stones, they appear in all different arrangements. De la Serna herself is convinced that the images on the portal at Sangüesa are indeed scenes from the saga.

As a last counter-argument, Müller states that the motifs in question at Sangüesa are all widely disseminated within European Romanesque sculpture and are the usual Christian motifs of the fight between good and evil. The (well-known) fact that the dragon-slayer is a common motif in Romanesque sculpture, however, only makes Sigurd's presence on the spandrel more fitting. De la Serna theorizes that the master sculptors who knew of the legendary stories of pagan heroes so popular in Europe simply Christianized them.[25]

In their book on the iconography of this church, Alicia Ancho Villanueva and Clara Fernández-Ladreda Aguadé do not mention the Sigurd identification, no doubt because they do not subscribe to it.[26] They discuss the dragon-slayer simply in the context of the other figures on the two spandrels that show warriors combating dragons, serpents and other monsters and surmise that the figures all represent the battle between good and evil and vice and virtue. The only one of these warriors that they name (tentatively) is David, shown on horseback crushing Goliath, depicted as a gigantic figure lying under the horse's hooves, and indeed David is the biblical equivalent of secular dragon-slayers such as Sigurd and Tristan.[27]

The latest scholar to weigh in on this much-debated topic is José Luis García Lloret, author of a study on the workshop of San Juan de la Peña. Unlike Beatrix Müller, he does not seem troubled by the change in workshops at Sangüesa. He states that the workshop of San Juan de la Peña carried out and completed the iconographic programme of the first mason, Leodegarius. García Lloret notes that the dragon-slayer appears in other

---

[25] De la Serna, 'Sagas nórdicas', p. 417.
[26] A. Ancho Villanueva and C. Fernández-Ladreda Aguadé, *Portada de Santa Maria de Sangüesa. Imaginario románica en piedra* ([Pamplona], 2000), pp. 44–5. They are clearly aware of the 'Sigurd' identification, since they list in their bibliography Milton Weber, de la Serna and B. Müller.
[27] Ibid.

sites associated with this workshop – and in exactly the same posture. But because at Sangüesa the figure's placement just above that of the blacksmith appears 'premeditata' (premeditated), he believes it possible that the sculptor may indeed have had the Sigurd saga in mind, although he cautions that blacksmiths who aid heroes in Scandinavian and other northern sagas are fairly frequent.[28]

García Lloret's attitude towards the Sigurd identification is circumspect indeed – with good reason, no doubt. But if we cannot be sure that this Nordic hero did battle in Spain, there are plenty of other dragon-slayers (some secular but most biblical) on buildings in northern Spain, especially along the pilgrimage routes. Here they evoke the struggle against not only Satan but also the Moors.

## Moor-slayers: St James and St Isidore

In arguing that the artist who depicted the 'Santiago Tristan' as a warrior expected the pilgrims who entered the cathedral by the Puerta Francigena to make the connection with St James's combat for the Christian faith, we must consider briefly how the popular conception of this saint evolved over time from evangelizer to warrior-saint. Spanish Baroque painters (seventeenth and eighteenth centuries) were particularly enamoured with the concept of St James as a Moor-slayer, but, as mentioned above, this warlike image did not really emerge until the first third of the twelfth century. The sculpture of the saint on horseback with raised sword and standard that appears on the tympanum of a transept in the cathedral of Santiago has been thought by some to be the earliest depiction of *Santiago matamoros*. It is sometimes called the *timpano de Clavijo*, because many believe that it celebrates St James's miraculous intervention in the legendary Battle of Clavijo (834), which assured the triumph of Ramiro I of Asturias over the Moors. In gratitude for the apostle's divine aid, Ramiro I supposedly instituted the *voto de Santiago*, a tax on agricultural production that was to be paid to the saint's church. This battle never actually took place, however, and the so-called 'Diploma of Ramiro I' was forged by the canon Pedro Marcio shortly after 1150, but it reveals what the canon and his circle wanted people to believe about Santiago at that time.[29]

---

[28] J. L. García Lloret, *La escultura románica del Maestro de San Juan de la Peña* (Zaragoza, 2005), pp. 241–3. This scholar attributes the 'Sigurd' theory to Milton Weber; he does not mention the studies by B. Müller or Ancho Villanueva and Fernández-Ladreda.

[29] The charter also served very well the beneficiaries (archbishop, cathedral chapter, music chapel and Royal Hospital of Santiago), for they continued to collect the tax

The belief that St James had been responsible for the victory of the Asturian over the Moors in 834 did much to promote the saint as a Moor-slayer, but the image on the 'Clavijo tympanum' does not show him in that guise. He is simply *Santiago caballero*, and not 'a contemporary, militant Saint James, with the mangled bodies of Muslim soldiers beneath his horse's hooves', as one scholar claims.[30] On closer inspection it is clear that there is no one underfoot; rather, the only figures besides the horseman are on either side, and they are clearly in an attitude of prayer (Figure 3).[31]

When the image of *Santiago matamoros* did emerge in the mid-twelfth century, it quickly became the archetype of the warrior saint in Spain, but St Isidore was also portrayed in that way. In 1063 Ferdinand I, emperor of León-Castile, had Isidore's remains moved from their original resting place in Seville to the church that he had rededicated to the bishop of Seville, the basilica of San Isidoro in León. John Williams observes that this transla-tion 'effectively established the cult of Saint Isidore who was converted from the literary figure whose encyclopedic *Etymologiae* could be found in almost every monastic library in Europe into a healer, a miracle worker and eventually a warrior saint who assisted in the Reconquest of Spain'.[32] The many images of Isidore that appear in or on the basilica show him in his well-known guises as scholar and bishop, but there are several that show him as a warrior. Since *Isidoro matamoros* was created on the model of *Santiago matamoros*, these depictions are all late. The only medieval one is the famous *Pendón de Baeza* (end of thirteenth century/fourteenth century) where Isidore appears on horseback, wearing his bishop's vest-ments and mitre; he wields a sword in one hand and a Visigothic cross in the other.[33] The link with St James is assured by the emergence, from a cloud above, of the arm of St James holding a sword. The other images of *Isidoro matamoros* all date from the eighteenth century. Most can be seen on the painted vaults of the refectory. No doubt the most striking

even after the fraud was discovered at the end of the sixteenth century, until the tax was abolished in 1808. On the 'Diploma of Ramiro I', see F. López Alsina, *La Ciudad de Santiago de Compostela en la Alta Edad Media* (Santiago de Compostela, 1988), pp. 42-3. On the 'voto', see O. Rey Castelao, *El Voto de Santiago, claves de un conflicto* (Santiago de Compostela, 1993). For these references I am grateful to José Andrade.

30 See, for example, J. D. Dodds, 'Islam, Christianity, and the Problem of Religious Art', in *The Art of Medieval Spain, a.d. 500–1200*, pp. 27–37 (p. 36).

31 My thanks to Therese Martin for pointing this out to me and for sending me the image that appears here as fig. 3.

32 J. W. Williams, 'León and the Beginnings of the Spanish Romanesque', in *The Art of Medieval Spain, a.d. 500–1200*, pp. 167–73 (p. 168).

33 See the detailed description and discussion on dating in *Maravillas de la España medieval. Tesoro sagrado y monarquía*, ed. I. G. Bango Torviso ([Valladolid], 2001), item no. 16, 'Pendón de San Isidoro o Estandarte de Baeza'.

3. Santiago de Compostela, transept: *Santiago caballero on "timpano de Clavijo"*

and visible image appears as an eighteenth-century addition to the façade of the basilica; it depicts an equestrian figure dressed as a bishop riding roughshod over the enemy. All of these bellicose depictions of the church doctor recall the legend according to which Isidore appeared to Alfonso VII in a dream, promising to aid him in his battle against the Moors at Baeza in 1147. Entering the field mounted on a white charger, the good bishop ensured that the Christians would be victorious. The source of this legend is the *Miraculis Sancti Isidoro*, a defence of Isidore written by the historian Lucas de Tuy, canon of San León between 1221 and 1239, who simply copied the miracle of St James's intervention at Coimbra in 1064 and applied it to Alfonso VII in his siege of Baeza.[34]

Just as Isidore, the father of the Spanish Church before the conquest, is a potent symbol of pre-conquest Spain, the basilica of San Isidoro de

---

[34] E. Fernández González, 'La iconografía isidoriana en la Real Colegiata de Léon', in *Pensamiento medieval hispano: Homenaje a Horacio Santiago-Otero*, ed. J. M. Soto Rábanos, 2 vols. (Madrid, 1998), I, 141–81 (pp. 171–81). See also Márquez-Villanueva, *Santiago*, pp. 197–8.

León recalls the combat with Islam in both its history and its architecture. An earlier church was destroyed following the conquest of the area by Al-Mansur Ibn Abi Aamir (938–1002), and the main portal of the present sanctuary, the Puerta del Córdero (Portal of the Lamb), depicts a scene that is unusual for a tympanum. It is the sacrifice of Isaac, who was delivered on the basis of his father's faith: by Abraham's covenant with God, the people of Isaac's line were assured their ultimate victory. Because Isaac's half-brother Ishmael was considered the progenitor of the Arabs, the reconquest of Spain is recast here as a crusade.[35]

## Charlemagne and Roland

In this survey of secular warrior figures associated with the propagation of the Christian faith as slayers of giants, dragons or Moors, Charlemagne and Roland are crucial, since they are associated with the spread of Christianity and the crusade against Islam in Spain. They are particularly pertinent to our theory about the logic of placing an image of Tristan at Santiago because their legend became intertwined with that of St James as early as the twelfth century.[36] Although they were secular figures, they took on the aura of saints as their fame increased, owing in great part to the huge popularity of the *Historia Karoli Magni et Rotholandi*, which recounts Charlemagne's exploits in Spain. The *Pseudo-Turpin Chronicle*, as it is most often called because it purports to be the work of Turpin, archbishop of Rheims, was incorporated as Book IV into the *Codex Calixtinus* at the time the codex was put together in the twelfth century.[37] The *Chronicle* begins with St James's appeal to Charlemagne to come to Spain to liberate the saint's shrine from the Saracens. The emperor responds to the call and remains in Spain to combat the Moors in three battles where he owes his victory directly to St James's aid. At the end of the *Chronicle*, St James appears to Turpin, who dies shortly after Charlemagne, to assure him that although he and the emperor did not die in Spain, they deserved the same status as the martyrs alongside

---

[35] J. W. Williams, '*Generationes Abrahae*: Iconografía de la Reconquista en Léon', in *El tímpano románico. Imágenes, estructuras y audiencias*, ed. R. Sánchez Ameijeiras and J. L. Gabriel y Galán (Santiago de Compostela, 2003), pp. 155–80.

[36] On the links between the legends of Charlemagne and St James, see especially *El Pseudo-Turpin, lazo entre el culto jacobeo y el culto de Carlomagno*, ed. K. Herbers, Actas del VI Congreso Internacional de Estudios Jacobeos (Santiago de Compostela, 2003); and S. López Martínez-Morás, *Épica y Camino de Santiago: en torno al Pseudo-Turpin* (La Coruña, 2002). My thanks to José Andrade for these references.

[37] In 1619 it was removed from the *Codex* on the pretext that its author was not Calixtus II, but rather Archbishop Turpin. The motivation for this decision may have been the predominant role that a non-Spanish sovereign took in the Reconquista.

whom they had fought. This particular version of the *Chronicle* dates to 1135–40 and was clearly adapted to the needs of the *Codex Calixtinus*, which sought to attract pilgrims to Santiago,[38] but the earliest version of the work was probably composed in northern France between 1116 and 1145 (most likely around 1120–30).[39] Well before that, however, legends about Charlemagne and Roland were circulating orally. The earliest extant mention of Roncesvaux in a Spanish document is contained in the so-called *Nota Emilianense* inscribed on a margin of the Códice emilanense 39, which is currently housed in the Real Academia de la Historia.[40] Found originally in the monastery of San Millán de la Cogolla, this document, which has been dated to the third quarter of the eleventh century, represents an important Spanish intermediary between Einhard's *Vita Karoli Magni* (*Life of Charlemagne*, early ninth century) and the oldest extant (Oxford) version of the *Chanson de Roland* (early twelfth century) and shows that the French epic tradition was known in Spain at the time. As the legend of Charlemagne's and Roland's exploits spread orally throughout western Europe in the tenth and eleventh centuries, so too did the fame of St James, inciting more pilgrims to set out. 'The Pilgrim's Guide', Book V of the *Codex Calixtinus*, identifies Roncesvaux as a prominent site along the *camino francés*, as well as Blaye, which houses the relics of Roland, characterized here as a veritable martyr, gravely wounded and dying of thirst. The Guide also mentions Bordeaux, where Roland's companions, including Olivier, Ogier and Garin, are buried.

Charlemagne is the real protagonist of the *Pseudo-Turpin*, which differs considerably from the *Song of Roland*, in part because the emperor is an active and energetic military leader, unlike the hoary figure who – with the exception of the episode in which he confronts and defeats the emir Baligant – dominates the famous epic. Although Roland plays a secondary role, he does come to the fore in his combat against the giant Ferragut, champion of the Moors, sent to confront the Franks by the emir of Babylon with a huge army of Turks. Medieval illustrators portrayed episodes involving the colourful Ferragut with great relish, in part because,

---

[38] J. Subrenat, '*Laudatio Turpini*. Simples réflexions sur la *Chronique du pseudo-Turpin*', in *Le* Livre de Saint-Jacques *et la Tradition du* Pseudo-Turpin, *Sacralité et Littérature*, ed. J.-C. Vallecalle (Lyon, 2011), pp. 69–85.

[39] See the introduction to C. Meredith-Jones's critical edition, *Historia Karoli Magni et Rotholandi ou Chronique du Pseudo-Turpin* (Paris, 1936). For the sources on which the Pseudo-Turpin drew, see B. Gicquel, 'La genèse européenne du *Pseudo-Turpin* et l'évolution du mythe rolandien', in *Pèlerinages et croisades* (Paris, 1995), pp. 37–46.

[40] The Spanish philologist D. Alonso discovered the text in the margin of the Codex Emilianense and published it along with his study, *La primitiva épica francesa a la luz de una nota emilianense* (Madrid, 1954).

having insisted on fighting the Christian knights only in single combat, he would simply pick up his opponents and carry them off to his prison. He finally meets his match when confronted by Charlemagne's nephew and, since Roland is a giant-slayer like Tristan, it is worth noting that the young knight pleads with his uncle to allow him to confront Ferragut, just as the inexperienced Tristan begs his uncle Mark for the privilege of defending Cornwall against the threat of Morholt, the robust undefeated Irish champion who is said to have the strength of four men.

Roland eventually defeats the pagan giant by thrusting his sword (or the giant's own knife, depending on the version) into Ferragut's one vulnerable spot, which he has learned is his navel.[41] The scene describing the fatal blow, the most popular of the entire Roland iconography, is one that appears on an historiated capital of the building along the pilgrimage route known as the Palacio de los Reyes de Navarra in Estella San Miguel, which, as Therese Martin argues, was built in the 1160s.[42] There are actually three scenes from this episode depicted on different sides of this capital, which is located on the south façade of the palace.[43] The most prominent side (facing south) shows the climax of the duel, and an inscription on the abacus informs us in no uncertain terms of the identity of the two combatants and that of the artist, an unknown sculptor calling

[41] See the description of this episode and various images depicting it in D. D. R. Owen, *The Legend of Roland: a Pageant of the Middle Ages* (London, 1973), pp. 167–82.

[42] T. Martin, 'Sacred in Secular: Sculpture at the Romanesque Palaces of Estella and Huesca', in *Spanish Medieval Art, Recent Studies*, ed. C. Hourihane (Tempe, AZ, 2007), pp. 89–117.

[43] See Martin's detailed description of the three sides of this capital, 'Sacred in Secular', pp. 104–13. See also R. Lejeune and J. Stiennon, *La Légende de Roland dans l'Art du Moyen Age*, 2 vols., 2nd edn (Brussels, 1967), ch. X: 'Roland et Ferragut à Estella, Brioude, Tarragone et Salamanque', I, 92–6, II, plates 62–4. The identification of Roland and Ferragut at Estella is undisputed. The same cannot be said for Lejeune and Stiennon's assertion that the warriors on the frieze on the southern side of the western portal of the cathedral of St Pierre at Angoulême (1105–15) are Roland and Charlemagne battling Marsile and Turpin, respectively ('Le linteau d'Angoulême et la *Chanson de Roland*', I, 29–42; II, plates 15–18). A. Tcherikover believes that a secular interpretation (of the combats on this lintel) at Anglouême is 'generally plausible' but that a more specific one alluding to the *Chanson de Roland* 'seems somewhat strenuous'; *High Romanesque Sculpture in the Duchy of Aquitaine, c. 1090–1140* (Oxford, 1997), p. 151 n. 37. In 'La *Chanson de Roland* dans le décor des églises du XIIᵉ siècle', *Cahiers de civilisation médiévale* 40, 160 (1997), 337–72 (pp. 350–6), D. Kahn also criticizes the Lejeune/Stiennon interpretation but does believe that the images are from the *Roland* because of the presence of Charlemagne's *oriflamme* between the first and second image.

himself Martin of Logroño.[44] The first two moments of Roland's combat with Ferragut are depicted on the sides of the capital to the left and right of the climactic scene. On the left, Ferragut, carrying a round shield[45] and mounted on horseback, is heading into combat; on the right, the giant is depicted on foot wielding a battle axe against Roland, also on foot carrying an oblong shield (Figure 4). It is interesting that in this second 'preliminary' scene the mason slants the figure of Ferragut in a way that allows him to show his gigantic size; moreover, he gives free rein to his imagination in depicting his facial characteristics and hair, which make him appear frighteningly 'other', rather than truly Moorish, as is often the case in medieval epic. For the central scene recording the final moment of the combat, Ferragut and Roland appear to be of equal size, and they are both mounted nobly on horseback, although the Moor seems to be losing his balance as his lance breaks against the shield of his adversary, who thrusts his lance into the giant's navel (Figure 5). As Therese Martin observes, this depiction departs from the *Pseudo-Turpin*, where Roland is on foot when he thrusts his sword (or knife) into Ferragut's navel, since both of their horses have been slain. She further notes that whereas this dramatic moment is depicted in high relief on the capital, in low relief between the two horsemen appears 'Ferragut's decapitated body and head, teeth bared and eyes bulging, shown falling to the ground'.[46] According to the *Pseudo-Turpin*, Ferragut is said to have descended from Goliath, and this representation of his death in low relief recalls that of his ancestor, who was decapitated by David after being struck down by him.[47]

Martin goes on to examine another set of historiated capitals on the same façade, which she sees, along with the Roland/Ferragut capital, as integral elements of the palace's decorative programme. The second capital depicts sinners being dragged off to hell, 'represented by a boiling cauldron stoked by demons'.[48] The link between this capital and the depiction we see of the Last Judgement on so many Romanesque façades, including that of the church of San Miguel in Estella (see below), is clear.

---

[44] The inscription appears on two registers on the front of the abacus, but for lack of space the last three letters of 'Logronio' are placed on the right side of the capital:

| FERA | MARTINUS | ROLLAN |
|------|----------|--------|
| GUT | ME FECIT | DE LOGRO NIO |

[45] It is possible that this image is another Moor following Ferragut into battle, because the shield that he carries, though round, has a different design from the one on Ferragut's shield in the final scene.

[46] Martin, 'Sacred in Secular', p. 113.

[47] On this point, Martin cites M. Ruiz Maldonado, 'Algunas reflexiones sobre el Roldán y Ferragut de Estella (Navarra)', *Boletín del Seminario de Estudios de Arte y Arqueología* 50 (1984), 401–6 (p. 404).

[48] Martin, 'Sacred in Secular', p. 113.

4. Estella: Palacio de los reyes: capital with Ferragut and Roland combating on foot

5. Estella: Palacio de los reyes: capital with Ferragut and Roland combating on horseback

It underscores the idea that Roland's battle against the giant Ferragut is, like Sigurd's against the dragon and Tristan's against both the giant-like Morholt and the dragon, a variation on the representation of the combat of good vs. evil.

Since the *Pseudo-Turpin* was composed at a time when the *Chanson de Roland* was already quite popular, the author was obliged to include the battle of Roncesvaux, although he made a few significant changes, one of which is pertinent to our discussion: Roland actually kills King Marsile rather than simply severing his right arm as he does in the *Chanson*, and it is specified that when Marsile dies, his soul is carried down to hell, no doubt to establish a contrast with the fact, already stated in the *Chanson*, that Roland's soul is carried up to heaven by St Michael. This detail resonates with the depiction of warriors battling the enemy on the many Romanesque portals that feature the Last Judgement on their tympana. Indeed, on the lower left side of the north portal of San Miguel in Estella (1187–96), St Michael appears in his dual function: on the left he is trampling a serpent, and on the right he is weighing souls while a demon attempts to tamper with the balance so as to plunge the souls into hell, shown here, significantly, as the mouth of a monster (Figure 6). Similarly, at the cathedral of St-Lazarus in Autun, consecrated in 1130, the Last Judgement on the tympanum of the west portal depicts St Michael weighing souls while the devil tries to manipulate the balance in his favour.[49] On the west portal of the Saint-Foy abbey church at Conques (1140), sinners are being directed into the jaws of Hell, represented here as a huge dragon mouth. A similar scene is depicted on the tympanum of the south façade of Santa María la Real at Sangüesa: on the right are the damned entering the open mouth of the monster, which Villanueva and Fernández-Ladreda identify as the Leviathan, associated in the Old Testament with hell.[50]

---

[49] There is a literary counterpart to this image at the end of the *Pseudo-Turpin*. After receiving signs indicating that Charlemagne has died, Turpin sees a company of knights heading for Aix. One knight, 'blacker than a Moor', says they aim to get the emperor's soul and carry it off to hell. But on their way back, they report that St James intervened and put into the balance all the stones of churches that Charles had founded, which, with all the wood, ornaments and gold, weighed more than any evil he had done.

[50] Villanueva and Fernández-Ladreda, *Portada de Santa María de Sangüesa*, p. 20. According to J. Baschet, the iconographic motif of the 'gueule d'enfer' (jaws of Hell), seen as early as the ninth century in England, became generalized in the twelfth century. In France it soon became the obligatory way of representing hell; *Les Justices de l'au-delà. Les représentations de l'Enfer en France et en Italie (xiiᵉ–xvᵉ siècles)* (Rome, 1993), p. 279. My thanks to Carol Chase for this reference.

## King Arthur, San Geminiano, St George

Before concluding our discussion of profane figures depicted on Romanesque buildings, we should note that a very striking juxtaposition between secular and religious heroes combating giants/dragons/devils is be found on the side portals of the cathedral of Modena. The archivolt of the northern flank of the cathedral, the Porta della Pescheria, has long been known as the site of one of the earliest sculpted representations of Arthurian figures, the names of whom are clearly inscribed along the top edge of the arch. A distressed Guenevere is shown in the centre to the left of her abductor, the giant Mardoc. From the left approach three mounted knights with lances extended: an unidentified man, then Lancelot, then Arthur, who is met by the churl Burmaldus exiting the castle to confront them with his battle axe. On the right we see Carradoc leaving the fortress on horseback to meet the charge of three more mounted knights – Gauvain, Galeschn (?) and Kay.[51] Jeanne Fox-Friedman has noted how this famous narrative echoes the parallel one found on the lintel of the southern flank, the Porta dei Principi, where the cathedral's patron saint, Geminiano, is depicted coming to the rescue of another distressed woman, the Byzantine emperor's daughter, whom the devil has possessed in retribution for the saint's rejection of him.[52] Establishing a further parallel with the attempt to rescue Jerusalem during the First Crusade, Fox-Friedman evokes the eyewitness accounts of crusaders who claimed to have seen St George just prior to battle. This insight becomes more significant in our discussion of dragon-slayers when we recall the famous legend according to which St George rescued the daughter of the king of Silene, Libya from the dragon that was ravaging the town.

From this survey we can conclude that the number of warriors depicted as combating a monstrous enemy on the Romanesque façades of sanctuaries located along the pilgrimage routes to Santiago de Compostela offers real support for Moralejo's claim that the figures who appear on the column of the old Romanesque façade of the cathedral show Tristan – in scenes that recall his two most important military victories. In the image where he is grasping the notched sword and in the one where he has apparently fainted from the fumes of a dragon, we see reflected two important episodes in which Tristan triumphs over a monstrous adversary who threatens the land, and they are two combats that would have resonated with a medieval audience, accustomed to seeing figures such

[51] See R. S. Loomis and L. Loomis, *Arthurian Legends in Medieval Art* (New York, 1938), pp. 32–6 and figures 7 and 8.

[52] J. Fox-Friedman, 'Messianic Visions. Modena Cathedral and the Crusades', *RES: Anthropology and Aesthetics* 25 (Spring, 1994), 77–95.

6. Estella, Church of San Miguel, relief with St. Michael slaying the serpent and weighing souls on Judgment Day

as St Michael and St George battling demons. It makes sense, too, that stonemasons thought to use popular secular heroes such as Tristan, Sigurd and Roland to engage viewers while turning their attention to the very important subject – regularly presented on Romanesque façades – of the battle between good and evil, virtue and vice. In fact, Deborah Kahn, in her article on the depiction of the *Chanson de Roland* in twelfth-century churches, cites the use by preachers, in exempla and sermons, of references to secular heroes such as Charlemagne, Roland and Olivier for the courage they displayed in service to Christianity. These inspirational references were meant both to instruct and entertain the faithful.[53]

Recalling Moralejo's theory that the Tristan figures at Santiago were meant to remind pilgrims that they should be less interested in the exploits of popular heroes than in the epic of Christ's passion, we see here how

---

[53] Kahn, '*Chanson de Roland*', p. 372.

the Church recognized that such noble and courageous figures could be seen as embodying Christian virtues. Even popular sinners were put to use. As strange as it may seem at first, episodes from the *Roman de Renart* are also depicted on Romanesque church façades in France (on a tympanum of Saint-Ursin at Bourges, on a capital of St-Lazare at Autun), Germany and Italy, including on the lintel of the Porta della Pescheria (Modena) just below the Arthurian figures discussed above. Yet they too are *exempla* enlisted in the service of the combat between good and evil, vice and virtue, since they warn the faithful to beware of the wily fox, whose diabolically seductive traits were well known.[54] Because the earliest extant fables concerning Renart in Latin (Nitard's *Ysengrimus*) and French date from the mid and late twelfth century, respectively, the presence of these characters on Romanesque façades is further proof of the crucial role played by orality in the transmission of these popular legends.

## *The Transmission of Legends of Secular Heroes*

What were the routes by which these legends were transmitted? How did the stonemasons know about the secular heroes whose images they carved on the façades of Romanesque churches in western Europe? How did these legends arrive in Santiago, Sangüesa, Estella and Modena? We know that north-western Spain (along with Catalonia) was one of the two main portals by which the Tristan legend entered the Iberian Peninsula, largely – it has long been thought – through the influence of early French and Occitan oral and written works.[55] Moralejo surmises that it was the early French and British pilgrims who brought the Tristan legend to Santiago. He cites the reference made in the *Codex Calixtinus* to the huge diversity of nationalities represented among the pilgrims, all bringing their stories and songs;[56]

---

[54] See N. Le Luel, 'L'âne, le loup, la grue et le renard: à propos de la frise des fables du tympan Saint-Ursin de Bourges', *Reinardus: Yearbook of the International Reynard Society* 18 (2005), 53–68. The frieze is the only element left of the tympanum of this twelfth-century church, which was destroyed during the Revolution; it has been inserted into the wall around the gardens of the Prefecture.

[55] See, e.g., H. L. Sharrer, 'Spain and Portugal', in *Medieval Arthurian Literature: A Guide to Recent Research*, ed. N. J. Lacy (New York, 1996), pp. 401–49. More recently, J. Condé de Lindquist, 'Rethinking the Arthurian Legend Transmission in the Iberian Peninsula', *eHumanista* 7 (2006), 72–85, has examined four possible agents of transmission of the Arthurian legend, generally: the Vikings, the Plantagenets, the pilgrims to Santiago, and the Norman and Aragonese rulers of southern Italy before the Sicilian Vespers war (1282).

[56] Moralejo, 'Origini del programma iconografico', p. 132. For this famous passage, which is found in the *Veneranda Dies* sermon and clearly exaggerates the universal character of the pilgrims, see *Liber Sancti Jacobi 'Codex Calixtinus'*, ed. and trans. A.

and, as we have seen, 'The Pilgrim's Guide' identifies Roncesvaux and Blaye as two of the most important shrines along the French route. French scholars are familiar with Joseph Bédier's famous dictum 'Au commencement était la route' (At the beginning was the [pilgrimage] road), according to which the oldest extant version of the *Chanson de Roland* was composed by minstrels who accompanied the pilgrims on their trip from France to Spain, and although his theory about the composition of that particular work has been discredited, there is no doubt that pilgrims played a key role in the transmission of this and other popular legends, well before they were transcribed in the twelfth century.[57]

Brian Tate points out that sixth- and seventh-century Irish monks practised the pilgrimage as an important ascetic exercise. According to the *Anglo-Saxon Chronicle*, three Irishmen set out from Ireland to see King Alfred, choosing a rudderless boat because they desired, for the love of God, to live in permanent pilgrimage. The practice was considered one of the basic penitential categories because of its severity, and it can be said that these Irish monks began a tradition – that of the penitential pilgrimage – that anticipated those of the crusades. In 1095 when Pope Urban II launched the First Crusade, he declared that all crusaders would have complete remission of their sins.[58] Given the Anglo-Saxon enthusiasm for pilgrimages to European sanctuaries, there is no doubt that pilgrims began visiting Compostela shortly after the *inventio* (discovery) of St James's tomb in the early ninth century. The earliest pilgrims on record made the trip in the last quarter of the eleventh century. They were Normans living in England, a significant fact, for Norman pilgrims were the most likely to know the Tristan legend, since oral tales circulated in the British Isles and Brittany before the twelfth century, and the earliest extant Tristan poems are preserved in Anglo-Norman. Many of these pilgrims travelled by sea, which was faster and safer than by land. Since Galicia was one of the places where a boat could dock on its way to the Mediterranean, pilgrims who were heading for Jerusalem on crusade tended to make a stop at Compostela to visit St James's tomb, often proceeding on from there to

Moralejo, C. Torres and J. Feo (Pontevedra, 1992), pp. 198–201. For a critical reading of the passage, see J. M. Andrade, '¿Viajeros o peregrinos? Algunas notas críticas sobre la peregrinación a Santiago en la Edad Media', forthcoming in *Minius*.

[57] J. Bédier, *Les Légendes épiques: recherches sur la formation des chansons de geste*, 4 vols. (Paris, 1908–13). E. Mâle, who was much influenced by Bédier, devoted two chapters of his celebrated study (first published in 1922) to the enrichment of twelfth-century iconography along the pilgrimage routes in Italy and in France and Spain; *Religious Art in France. The Twelfth Century. A Study of the Origins of Medieval Iconography* (Princeton, NJ, 1978), pp. 246–315.

[58] B. Tate, 'Las Peregrinaciones marítimas medievales desde las Islas Británicas a Compostela', in *Santiago, Camino de Europa*, pp. 161–79 (pp. 161–2).

Rome. Santiago was to prosper in large part because of Galicia's strategic location along both the Mediterranean trade routes and the pilgrimage routes.[59]

The twelfth century witnessed the largest wave of both English and French pilgrims. The work of rebuilding the cathedral in the Romanesque style of the great pilgrimage churches of south-western France was initiated by Diego Peláez, bishop of Iria between 1070–71 and 1088. In 1094 the official see of Galicia was transferred from Iria to Santiago, and in 1100 Diego Gelmírez became the city's second bishop. In 1104 he obtained the privilege of wearing an archbishop's pallium on all major liturgical feasts, and in 1120 Pope Calixtus elevated his see to archiepiscopal rank.[60] It was then that Santiago expanded its influence, with Gelmírez playing a key role in attracting pilgrims to the city; it is he who is credited with promoting the compilation of the *Codex Calixtinus* with its pilgrim's guide, which highlights the French pilgrimage routes and was probably written or compiled by one or more Frenchmen.[61] The elaboration of the *Codex* took about forty years and, significantly, coincided more or less with Gelmírez's long episcopate.[62]

The Vikings are also credited with a possible role in the legend's spread to Spain. They raided the Iberian Peninsula in 844, 858–61, 966–71 and 1008–38. They even dreamed of establishing a second Normandy in Galicia from which they might easily reach North Africa and the other Mediterranean lands.[63] Initially, they came mostly as raiders and pillagers, but since they were among the first Scandinavians to convert to Christianity, they soon began coming for religious reasons.[64] From the

---

[59] D. Lomax, 'Los peregrinos ingleses a Santiago', in *Santiago. La Europa del peregrinaje*, ed. Plötz et al., pp. 373–83 (pp. 373–4). See also C. M. Storrs, *Jacobean Pilgrims from England from the Early Twelfth Century to the Late Fifteenth Century* (Santiago de Compostela, 1994).

[60] On this protean figure, see the fascinating study by R. A. Fletcher, *St. James's Catapult. The Life and Times of Diego Gelmírez of Santiago de Compostela* (Oxford, 1984). The *Historia Compostellana* was written under Gelmírez's supervision to extol his many achievements. See the edition by E. Falque Rey (Turnholt, 1988) and her Spanish translation, *Historia Compostelana* (Madrid, 1994).

[61] For the probable authors or compilers of the twelve extant manuscripts of the Guide, see A. Stones and J. Krochalis, 'Qui a lu le *Guide du pèlerin* de Saint-Jacques?', in *Pèlerinages et croisades*, pp. 11–36.

[62] Although many assume that Gelmírez ushered in the golden age of pilgrimages, the documentation is too limited to justify defining this period as such. See Andrade, '¿Viajeros o peregrinos?'

[63] V. Almazán, *Gallaecia scandinavica: introducción ó estudio das relacións galaicoescandinavas durante a Idade Media* (Vigo, 1986), p. 21.

[64] C. Krötzl, 'Del Mar báltico a Santiago de Compostela. Peregrinajes et influencias culturales', in *Santiago. La Europa del peregrinaje*, ed. Plötz et al., pp. 385–91.

ninth to the eleventh century, these enterprising Northmen, given their widespread presence in England, Scotland, Ireland and Normandy, could well have been familiar with the oral versions of the Arthurian legends, including the Tristan legend, and could have brought their tales to Spain.[65] It is even more probable that they conveyed their knowledge of the Scandinavian sagas, thus accounting for the possible presence of Sigurd on the façade of Santa María la Real de Sangüesa. Although most of the sagas were not written down until the thirteenth century, they had circulated orally much earlier, and the *Saga of the Völsungs* was particularly well known.

## The Cathedral of Santiago in the Icelandic Saga af Tristram ok Ísodd

Just as pilgrims from France and the British Isles were no doubt primarily responsible for the materialization of the Tristan images on the northern Romanesque portal of the cathedral of Santiago, it may well be the countless pilgrims, returning to Scandinavia from Galicia, who account for the appearance of Santiago in a large number of Scandinavian sagas. The names of Santiago or Galicia feature in no fewer than sixteen sagas. Three sagas dedicate substantial parts to St James, including the *Karlamagnús saga*, whose ten branches are compiled from a number of different sources, including the *Pseudo-Turpin*, the *Chanson d'Apremont*, the *Pèlerinage de Charlemagne*, the *Chanson de Roland* and the *Moniage Guillaume*. Four of the Scandinavian sagas devote just a few chapters to St James, and nine make only sporadic mention of him or of Galicia.[66]

The Icelandic *Saga af Tristram ok Ísodd* (c. 1400)[67] falls into the last category, but the appearance of Santiago de Compostela is very striking indeed, and this work is the only one of the Tristan tales of northern Europe in which Spain, Galicia and Santiago play a significant role. In most versions of the legend, Tristan spends his exile in Brittany or the British Isles, and, although in the work on which the Icelandic *Saga* appears to be based – the Old Norse adaptation of Thomas of Britain's poem – Spain is one of the countries he visits before settling in Brittany,

---

[65] Condé de Lindquist, 'Rethinking the Arthurian Legend Transmission', 74–7.

[66] Almazán, *Gallaecia scandinavica*, pp. 270–1. The bulk of E. F. Halvorsen's *The Norse Version of the Chanson de Roland* (Copenhagen, 1959) is a comparative study of Branche VIII of the *Karlamagnús saga* with the Oxford version of the *Chanson de Roland*.

[67] *Saga af Tristram ok Ísodd*, ed. P. Jorgensen and trans. J. Hill, in *Norse Romance*, ed. M. E. Kalinke. *I. The Tristan Legend* (Cambridge, 1999), pp. 241–92.

he does not remain there. In the Icelandic *Saga*, however, the two main poles of attraction for Tristram are actually Spain and England.

Tristram is born in Spain of King Kalegras and Blenziblý, who share a passion that prefigures their son's own with Ísodd, including the couple's death within days of each other and their burial side-by-side in a stone coffin. Tristram spends his first nine years in Spain before an invading king captures him and sells him to pirates, who, failing to ransom him as they had hoped, eventually abandon him on a reef off the coast of England. From there he swims to land and presents himself at the court of his uncle, King Mórodd (as Mark is called), where he is joyfully welcomed into the royal household. He continues his knightly training and soon becomes the king's champion. When King Engres of Ireland invades England, Tristram meets him in combat and slays him. Nevertheless, he is severely wounded when a piece of Engres's sword lodges in his head. The narrator notes that it seemed likely that the piece would not come out 'nema guð allsvaldandi sendi honum þann lækni, er beztr er í allri veröldunni' (266) (unless Almighty God sent him the best physician in the world) (267). That physician turns out to be Engres's daughter, Ísodd, after Tristram arrives in Ireland. He needs the princess's skills a second time during this stay when he defeats a dragon that is ravishing the land and becomes infected by the poison from the segment of the beast's tongue that he has cut off and preserved in his pouch. Although this feat wins him the king's daughter, he proposes to offer her to his uncle, despite her objections and those of her mother, Queen Flúrent.[68] Flúrent prepares a special drinking horn for use by Ísodd and Mórodd on their wedding night, and although it is not specified that it contains a love potion, when the two young people consume its contents they fall madly in love and delay their return to England by three months.

Tristram and Ísodd's time in the English court follows roughly the same pattern as in the French and German versions, with the king refusing to believe that they have betrayed him until, returning from church one day, he catches them together in his bed. Following a seven-day exile in the forest, after which Mórodd, convinced of their innocence, invites the lovers to return to court, Tristram attempts to end his affair: while leading the English army against that of the invading heathen King Fúlsus, he promises to give up his dalliance with Ísodd if God grants him the victory. When Tristram hears the heathens musing that their opponent is the devil, considering how much harm he is doing them, he replies that he is doing it

---

[68] The original 'bride quest' episode, conflated here with Tristram's first visit to Ireland, is considerably altered. After being offered Ísodd's hand, Tristram returns to England to propose that his uncle marry the princess. When Mórodd readily agrees, Tristram goes back to Ireland to fetch her.

'allt fyrir frúinnar sakir' (282) (all for the sake of the lady) (283). In view
of his vow to give up Ísodd, the lady in question may well be the Virgin
rather than his lover, as most scholars have assumed. Geraldine Barnes
notes that 'Tristram's pledge to God before the battle with Fúlsus and his
victories over aggressively heathen opponents – Fúlsus, for example, is
condemned by the narrator as *heiðinn sem hundr* (280) (heathen as a dog)
(281), his forces invoke Mahomet, and his soul goes to hell – endow him
with some Crusader qualities'.[69]

It is shortly afterwards that Spain again becomes the theatre for
Tristram's exploits. He returns to his homeland where King Benðsus has
seized power along with two earls and raised an army against Tristram,
who nevertheless defeats them and is awarded both the land and the earls'
sister, Ísodd the Dark. According to the narrator, it is said that Tristram
only gradually gives up thinking about Ísodd the Fair, and his wife senses
that she is not in full possession of his love. Nevertheless, the couple
apparently consummate their union, for after three years Tristram's wife
produces a son, Kalegras. Tristram is greatly esteemed in Spain, and
eventually answers an appeal for help from Tristram the Stranger, causing
him to travel west with his namesake to 'Jakobsland' (Galicia). As Barnes
notes, two of the seven brothers against whom the hero is engaged to fight
have names (Ayad and Dormadat) that lead one to believe that he and his
companion are combating Saracens.[70] Thus, Tristram, already a giant- and
dragon-slayer as he appears in the earliest extant versions of the legend,
is transformed in this episode into a genuine Moor-slayer. Tristram comes
out of this combat mortally wounded and, as in Thomas's poem, he sends
for his lover and dies of despair when his wife informs him, untruthfully,
that the ship he is awaiting has black 'awnings' (the sign in this saga that
his beloved is not on board). Arriving too late to heal her lover, Ísodd the
Fair dies of grief. The Icelandic *Saga* follows the lead of the early French
and German poems, where the lovers are interred either in the same coffin
or in separate ones, sometimes on opposite sides of a church; however,
here they are buried in what could only be the cathedral of Santiago de
Compostela:

Síðan váru þau flutt ok grafin at þeiri höfuðkirkju, er mest var í landinu. Ok
stóðu menn mjök daprir yfir þeira grefti, fyrir hörmuligt líflát, er þau biðu.
En hann var greftr fyrir norðan en hún fyrir sunnan. Þá rann sinn lundr
upp af leiði hvárs þeira með hinum fegrsta ávexti, ok þar til óxu viðirnir at
þeir mættuz yfir kirkjuburst. Þá vöfðuz limar\<nar\> saman, ok svá hátt óxu

[69] G. Barnes, 'The Tristan Legend', in *The Arthur of the North. The Arthurian Legend in the Norse and Rus' Realms*, ed. M. E. Kalinke (Cardiff, 2011), pp. 61–76 (p. 72).
[70] Ibid.

viðirnir í lopt upp, at varla hafa menn sét hærri tré. Ok standa þar þessir viðir enn, til marks at Tristram fífldi ekki Ísodd hina fögru fyrir illsku sakir við Mórodd kóng, frænda sinn, heldr fyrir þat at sjálfr guð hafði þeim skipat saman af sinni samvizku. En fyrir þá sök þá Tristram ekki Ísodd hina fögru af Mórodd kóngi, at hann unni honum hins bezta raðs, ok mátti hann þó fyrir engan mun við sköpunum vinna.

(Afterwards they were carried out and buried in the cathedral, which was the greatest in the land, and men stood very sadly over their tombs because of the tragic death they had suffered. He was buried on the north side and she on the south. Then a tree with the most beautiful fruit sprang up from each of their graves and the branches grew until they met above the roof of the church. Their limbs entwined and the branches grew so high that men have scarcely seen higher trees, and these trees are still standing there as a sign that Tristram did not beguile Ísodd the Fair out of malice towards his kinsman Mórodd but rather because God Himself in His wisdom had destined them for each other. And the reason why Tristram did not accept Ísodd the Fair from King Mórodd was because he wanted him to have the best match, and yet he was by no means able to withstand the fates.)[71]

We may well wonder how it is possible for this famous pair of adulterous lovers to end up buried in such a prestigious symbol of Christianity as the cathedral of Santiago. It may be partly because Tristram does appear to be something of a crusader, but the answer may also lie in the progressive Christianization of the Tristan legend in Scandinavia. According to the prologue of *Tristrams saga ok Ísondar*, in 1226 King Hákon Hákonarson of Norway (r. 1217–63) commissioned a cleric, Brother Robert, to compose a version in Old Norse of Thomas of Britain's *Roman de Tristran*.[72] By proposing the translation of French courtly literary works, King Hákon wished to refine the taste and mores of the Norwegian court where ecclesiastics set the tone. It was members of this circle who had been trained in France who undertook these 'translations', which included adaptations of some of Chrétien de Troyes's romances.[73]

---

[71] *Saga af Tristram ok Ísodd*, ed. Jorgensen, pp. 288–9.

[72] Because this prologue appears only in the two seventeenth-century manuscripts in which the romance is preserved, but not in the earlier fifteenth-century fragment of the work, some scholars believe that it was added later, but S. Tómasson, 'Hvenær var Tristrams sögu snúið?', *Gripla* 2 (1977), 47–78, has offered convincing evidence of a thirteenth-century dating for the work as a whole.

[73] J. Kjær, '*Tristrams saga ok Ísöndar* – une version christianisée de la branche dite courtoise du "Tristan"', in *Courtly Literature: Culture and Context*, ed. K. Busby and E. Kooper (Amsterdam, 1990), pp. 367–77. For a concise discussion of King Hákon's crucial role in importing Arthurian romance into Norway, see M. E. Kalinke, 'The

Moreover, Hákon, whose status as king was eventually confirmed by the papal legate, was, in the view of many, an ideal, even 'saintly' king. Shortly after his death, his son commissioned a royal biography/saint's life known as *Hákonar saga Hákonarsona*. Adam Oberlin calls it 'the first depiction of a Norwegian king according to continental modes of *rex iustus* and divine selection', explaining that this saga presents the picture of a king who was both Christian and courtly: 'Ordained by God and crowned in the presence of a papal legate, as well as a lover of the popular literature of his day, Hákon shows a fondness for falconry and other court pastimes, enjoyment in the pageantry of well-outfitted processions, graciousness in the face of uncivil enemies, and a constant reliance on God's mercy.'[74]

Under these circumstances, it is hardly surprising that the Norwegian redactor chose to tone down the theme of adultery and to present King Mark as the representative of God – wise, merciful and worthy.[75] He also has Tristram's parents marry in a legal, Church-sanctioned ceremony rather than eloping. When Tristram and Isönd are living in the forest in exile, they do not worry about finding sustenance, so confident are they that God will grant them nourishment enough. The Christian cast given to this version appears very clearly in the pious ending that the Norse adapter appends to Thomas's poem. Indeed, whereas the most shocking element of the Old French poems is the way the lovers engage in their adulterous passion without apparent remorse, in the Norwegian saga, Isönd, before dying, prays to God for forgiveness. She reminds him that he saved all mankind, including Maria Magdalena, and begs him to be merciful and forgive sinners like her. Although Tristram's jealous wife has them buried on separate sides of the church in order to keep them apart, trees spring up from the two graves and intertwine above the gable of the church. The author adds: 'Ok má því sjá, hversu mikil ást þeira á

---

Introduction of Arthurian Literature in Scandinavia', in *The Arthur of the North*, ed. Kalinke, pp. 5–21 (pp. 9–13).

[74] A. Oberlin, '"Translating" Tristan: *Hákonarsaga* and the Possibilities of *Translatio*', *Tristania* 25 (2009), 49–68 (pp. 54–5). Oberlin goes on to demonstrate the possible influence exercised by the Tristram saga on *Hákonarsaga*. In his 'Vita Sancti, Vita Regis: The Saintly King in *Hákonar saga Hákonarsonar*', *Neophilologus* 95 (2011), 313–28, Oberlin endeavours to show the pervasive influence of hagiographical themes and argues that 'the saga's portrayal of the king as a saintly figure serves to compare him to the greatest Christian kings of the preceding centuries, even if only within the memorialization of the text itself and not in later memory' (p. 313).

[75] Kjær, '*Tristrams saga ok Ísöndar*', pp. 371–2. As Kalinke, 'Introduction of Arthurian Literature in Scandinavia', p. 12, notes, since the Arthurian romances and courtly lays that were translated in Hákon's court had as their focus a strong king, they clearly had a didactic function.

milli verit hefir' (222) (By this we can see how great the love between them had been) (223).[76]

As we saw in our earlier discussion of the Icelandic saga, the author took the pious ending of the Norwegian saga and further embellished it, not only by choosing the cathedral of Santiago as the lovers' final resting place and by stating that God had actually destined them for each other, but also by explicitly putting a positive interpretation on Tristram's relationship with his uncle, which is unusually complex. Indeed, earlier in the Icelandic saga, the king, upon meeting his bride-to-be, actually suggests that his nephew and she would be better matched, given her age, adding: 'en ek ann þér allvel konunnar ok ríkisins' (276) (and I freely grant you the lady and the kingdom) (277). The hero courteously demurs, however, telling him he does not want to be king while his uncle is able to reign, and, as we have seen, the author explains at the end of the poem that Tristram wanted his uncle to have the best match. The youth's apparent lack of interest in Ísodd has fuelled speculation that this work is actually a satire,[77] but Tristram's attitude also makes the lovers seem less guilty and more worthy of being buried in the cathedral of Santiago.[78] Another surprising change wrought by the author of the Icelandic *Tristram* is the mention that King Mórodd eventually leaves on pilgrimage to the Holy Lands, where he ends up living out his life as a holy hermit in Jerusalem. It is also to Tristram's credit that, given his progeny (Kalegras Tristramsson is a model king), he is celebrated at the end of the saga as a dynastic founder.[79]

---

[76] *Tristrams saga ok Ísöndar*, ed. and trans. P. Jorgensen, in *Norse Romance. I. The Tristan Legend*, ed. Kalinke, pp. 23–226.

[77] See P. Schach, 'The *Saga af Tristram ok Ísodd*: Summary or Satire?', *Modern Language Quarterly* 21 (1960), 336–52; idem, 'Tristrams *Saga ok Ýsoddar* as burlesque', *Scandinavian Studies* 59 (1987), 86–100.

[78] Although homosocial bonds can be seen in French Arthurian traditions, M. E. Kalinke argues that the way in which the Icelandic author has reworked the romantic triangle to put more emphasis on the homosocial bond between Tristram and his uncle is an indication of acculturation – adaptation of the legend to Icelandic literary traditions; 'Female Desire and the Quest in the Icelandic Legend of Tristram and Ísodd', in *The Grail, the Quest, and the World of Arthur*, ed. N. J. Lacy (Cambridge, 2008), pp. 76–91. Kalinke acknowledges her debt to her doctoral student, K. Lurkhur, who attributes this emphasis to the influence specifically of the family sagas or *Íslendingasögur*. See Lurkhur's article, 'Tristan in the Old Icelandic Tradition', *Tristania* 25 (2009), 69–94.

[79] Barnes, 'The Tristan Legend', p. 73. The Christianization of the legend in the north is also underscored in the haunting Icelandic ballad, *Tristrams Kvæði* (The Poem of Tristram), which was influenced by the Old Norse saga and was probably in circulation by the time the Icelandic saga was composed. It describes the lovers' very Christian burial, attended by priests with candles, hymns and bells. The bodies are carried into the church, placed in a holy cell and lowered into stone sepulchres from which spring

The prominent role that Spain plays in the Icelandic saga is quite surprising. One possible explanation is that King Hákon, who sought closer relations with Alfonso X el sabio (a candidate for becoming the Holy Roman Emperor), arranged a marriage between his daughter Kristín and infante Felipe (Alfonso's brother). In *Hákonar saga*, composed *c.* 1260, the Icelandic biographer Sturla Þórðarson describes Kristin's journey to Spain and her reception at the royal courts both of King Jaime of Aragon and Alfonso of Castile.[80] Given the large role played by Iceland in preserving Norwegian literature, it is not surprising that there were many Icelanders present at the court of a man like Hákon, who sought to present the image of a powerful monarch celebrated for his promotion of European culture and his connections with other powerful leaders.

## Conclusion

In this essay, we have seen the startling appearance of Tristan on the Romanesque façade of the cathedral of Santiago de Compostela, and we have noted the cathedral's unexpected presence in the Icelandic *Tristram* saga. These conjunctions of the Tristan legend and the cathedral can be explained by the remarkably close contacts that existed between northwestern Spain and the rest of northern Europe throughout the Middle Ages, owing in large part to the numerous pilgrims who travelled by sea or land from as far away as Finland to pray at the shrine of St James. The Apostle was much revered from the earliest times in the seafaring communities of Ireland and Brittany, which felt a great affinity for Galicia ('little Gaul').[81] The kings of León-Castile, the only ones granted the title of emperor, in recognition of their links to the Visigothic realm, maintained exceptionally close ties with France, particularly with the abbots of Cluny.[82] The Romanesque art of northern Spain owes a tremendous debt

---

two trees that are joined in the middle of the church. See *Tristrams Kvædi*, ed. and trans. Robert Cook, in *Norse Romance. I. The Tristan Legend*, ed. Kalinke, pp. 227–39. It is preserved in four versions in seventeenth- and eighteenth-century manuscripts.

[80] Kalinke, 'The Introduction of the Arthurian Legend in Scandinavia', p. 14. My thanks to Marianne Kalinke for suggesting this explanation for Spain's prominent role in the Icelandic saga.

[81] D. Péricard-Méa, 'La Prédication de Saint-Jacques en Irlande et en Bretagne', in *Pèlerinages et croisades*, pp. 67–82.

[82] As S. Moralejo notes, Ferdinand's son, Alfonso VI, 'chose the Leonese abbey of Sahagún for his family pantheon and made it the head of a broad monastic empire reformed along French lines. In 1080 the Cluniac monk Bernard d'Auch (later archbishop of Toledo) was put in charge of Sahagún itself, which became the Saint-Denis and Cluny of the kingdoms of León and Castile'; 'On the Road: the Camino de

to French models, especially those provided by Sainte-Foy in Conques and Saint-Sernin in Toulouse, which were on the French pilgrimage route.[83] The architects of the cathedral at Santiago (whose names, Bernard and Robert, indicate that they were French) drew on stylistic features of the great pilgrimage churches of western France in Tours, Limoges and Toulouse, as well as the abbey church of Cluny.

One of the clearest proofs of the bonds forged between France and Spain in Compostela can be found in the celebrated Charlemagne window at Chartres cathedral. Dated between 1210 and 1220 and based on events recounted in the *Pseudo-Turpin*, it is an excellent illustration of the intertwining of the legends of Charlemagne and St James found in the *Codex Calixtinus*, depicting the emperor principally as an energetic Christian crusader and builder of churches. The lower register concerns Charlemagne's campaign in the Orient in response to Constantine's call to combat the Saracens in Constantinople. The second and third registers are devoted to the emperor's campaign in Spain: in the right-hand panel of the second register, St James appears to Charlemagne in a dream, asking him to liberate his tomb from the Moors; in the left-hand panel, the emperor gazes at the Milky Way, which St James has assured him will serve as a guide. In the central panel, Charlemagne is shown setting out for Spain, praying and taking a city in Spain. The window also includes panels depicting Charlemagne's victory over the pagan king Aigolant and others before leaving Spain. The central panel of the next register celebrates Roland: he is shown trying to break his sword and sounding the olifant as the body of the giant Ferragut lies in two pieces at his feet. This description follows that of Mary Jane Schenck, who plausibly establishes the dominance of Charlemagne over Roland by assigning more panels to the emperor than had previous scholars and contends that the window is based on a vernacular version of the *Pseudo-Turpin*. The intertwining of the Carolingian and Jacobean legends at Chartres is further highlighted by the existence of a window devoted to St James that is very similar to the Charlemagne window, which, however, is given pride of place.[84]

In view of the extraordinary ties between France and Spain outlined in this article, it is curious that neither of the Spanish prose versions

Santiago', in *The Art of Medieval Spain, a.d. 500–1200*, pp. 174–83 (p. 179). See also M. Defourneaux, *Les Français en Espagne aux XIᵉ et XIIᵉ siècles* (Paris, 1949).

[83] See Durliat, *Sculpture romane*, pp. 15–41, where he summarizes the influence that he studies in more detail in the second part.

[84] M. J. Schenck, 'Taking a Second Look: Roland in the Charlemagne Window at Chartres', *Olifant* 25, 1–2 (2006), 371–85; idem, 'The Charlemagne Window at Chartres: Visual Chronicle of a Royal Life', *Word and Image: A Journal of Verbal/Visual Enquiry* 28, 2 (2012), 135–60. See also *The Old French Johannes Translation of the Pseudo-Turpin Chronicle*, ed. R. N. Walpole (Berkeley, CA, 1978).

of the legend of Tristan and Iseult, which date from the late fourteenth to sixteenth centuries, transplants the legend to Spain nor – unlike the Icelandic *Tristram* saga – gives Spain a larger role. These works, which both derive ultimately from the same non-extant version of the thirteenth-century French Prose *Tristan* that spawned the Italian *Tristan*s, retain for the most part the same place-names as in the French work.[85] Even in the part of the *Corónica nuevamente emendata y añadida del buen cavallero don Tristán de Leonís y del rei don Tristán de Leonís el joven su hijo 1534* (Newly Revised and Expanded Chronicle of the Great Knight Tristan de Leonis and of his Son, King Tristan of Leonis the Younger 1534) that tells the story of the lovers' offspring, Tristán and Yseo, the son accedes to the thrones of Cornwall and Leonís. However, he does marry the infanta María and arranges his sister's marriage with his brother-in-law, King Juan of Spain,[86] details that suggest an attempt at long last to appropriate the legend and plant it firmly in Spanish soil.

---

[85] See J. T. Grimbert, 'The "Matter of Britain" on the Continent and the Legend of Tristan and Iseult in France, Italy, and Spain', in *A Companion to Arthurian Literature*, ed. H. Fulton (Oxford, 2009), pp. 145–59 (pp. 154–7).

[86] *Tristán de Leonís y el rey don Tristán el joven, su hijo, 1534*, ed. M. L. Cuesta Torre (México, 1997). It is curious that the Icelandic *Tristram* also includes a genealogy that extends the hero's story two generations into both the past and the future. After Tristram's death, King Mórodd sends to Spain for his grand-nephew, Kalegras Tristramsson, and hands the English throne over to him. Kalegras later marries the daughter of the emperor of Saxland by whom he has two sons and a daughter. But of Spain nothing more is said.

# VII

# TREVELYAN TRIPTYCH: A FAMILY AND THE ARTHURIAN LEGEND

## Roger Simpson

Direct lineal descent from King Arthur has been claimed by and for sundry English monarchs, Henry VII, Elizabeth I and Charles I among them. More recently the egregious Arthur Pendragon has declared himself a re-embodiment of that king, while Laurel Phelan, a Canadian, reportedly learns through regressive therapy that she is a reincarnation of Queen Guinevere.[1] Less aspirational perhaps than all of these, but still exceptional, is the Trevelyan family's claim of descent from a knight of Arthur's Round Table.

From comparatively modest beginnings in Cornwall, the Trevelyans rose to prominence through a series of advantageous marriages which gave them the major estates of Nettlecombe in Somerset and Wallington in Northumbria. For two centuries their menfolk, distinctively intellectual, radical and somewhat puritanical, were largely benevolent landlords at home and yet played leading roles as public administrators, politicians, historians and natural scientists, while their wives brought into the family a complementary artistic prowess revealed in collections, enlightened patronage and personal skill in the fine and applied arts. This article will trace how three members of this remarkable family took up the Arthurian legend and made significant and very individual contributions to its recreation and reinterpretation through widely different media in the twentieth century.[2]

---

[1] See A. Pendragon and C. J. Stone, *The Trials of Arthur: The Life and Times of a Modern-Day King* (London, 2003); and L. Phelan, *Guinevere; The True Story of One Woman's Quest for her Past Life Identity and the Healing of her Immortal Soul* (New York, 1996).

[2] I have been greatly helped by staff in Birkbeck College Library, British Library

## Mary, Lady Trevelyan (1882–1966)

Mary, more usually known as 'Molly', was born Mary Bell into a family of wealthy ironmasters who were important patrons of the Arts and Crafts movement. Her grandfather, Sir Isaac Lowthian Bell, and two of his children had all commissioned Philip Webb to design their new houses, and William Morris to supply decorations therein. Her father, Sir Hugh Bell, had by a previous marriage another daughter, Gertrude, who would become a leading Arabic scholar and explorer, while his second wife, Florence, the mother of Molly, wrote novels and plays.

Many women of the family also displayed very considerable needle-work skills. Among the commissions Isaac Lowthian Bell gave Morris was one for a series of five panels based on the theme of Chaucer's *The Romaunt of the Rose*, for which Edward Burne-Jones supplied the composition and figure drawings. These embroideries were then worked in silk, wool and gold thread on a linen ground by Lady Margaret Bell and her daughters Florence and Ada Phoebe, exercising great skill and patience over a period of eight years. The result was highly admired by Morris.[3] One of Burne-Jones's original designs for these panels would later hang inspirationally in Molly's parlour at Wallington.

When in 1904 Molly married Charles Philips Trevelyan (1881–1958) they spent their honeymoon 'walking a hundred miles in Cornwall' before returning to live in a comparatively small house at Cambo, close to Wallington itself.[4] It was here that she formulated an ambitious scheme that probably derived from her honeymoon excursion: to create a large embroidery depicting the Trevelyan family's legendary connection with King Arthur (Figure 1).

This family legend probably entered the literary record in the early seventeenth century, when the topographical historians Richard Carew and William Camden described the submersion of the terrain between Land's End and the Scilly Isles, a disaster from which a man called Trevelyan (there are various spellings of the name) contrived to escape on horseback. His feat became part of Cornish folklore, and was allegedly the source of the Trevelyan family crest, which showed a horse rising from the sea. However, though the sunken land was commonly identified with the lost Lyonesse I can find no early account of this heroic survivor's connection

Manuscripts, the National Trust, Senate House Library, Trinity College Library; and by Lord St Levan, Professor Michael Dower, Steve Dixon and Linda Gowans.

3   L. Parry, *William Morris Textiles* (London, 1983), p. 18; and *William Morris*, ed. L. Parry (London, 1996), pp. 240–1.

4   L. Trevelyan, *A Very British Family: The Trevelyans and Their World* (London, 2006), p. 117.

1   Needlework panel by Mary, Lady Trevelyan at Wallington

with Arthur, nor of a Trevelyan sitting at the Round Table. Admittedly Arthur's court has long been linked with the Jack the Giant Killer legend of St Michael's Mount, and just after 1800 there was a minor poetic flurry of Arthurian association which sought to locate the sleeping king within the Mount. Both Sir Hardinge Giffard and a certain J. H., for example, evoked 'the deep cell, / Where Arthur's giant warriors dwell' entranced in 'charmed slumber'.[5] But a novel reinterpretation of the story is indicated by Lady Molly's title for her work: *From St Michael's Mount the Knights of King Arthur's Court strive for a wager to swim ashore. Sir Trevelyan alone wins to shore.* In other words she idiosyncratically drops the traditional association with a fabled seismic disaster in Lyonesse, replacing it by a later social incident, a feat carried out for a boastful wager. In doing so she may have seriously weakened the impact of the ancient story by reducing a myth once resonant with potential social and personal disaster to the trivial level of a sporting competition.

Lady Molly's project was nonetheless on a grand scale. In the knowledge that her husband was the heir of Wallington, she planned her

---

[5]   J. H., 'Lines', *European Magazine* 62 (1812), 450; [Ambrose] H[ardinge] Giffard, 'St Michael's Mount', in *Verses* (Colombo, [1822]), pp. 29–31.

embroidery to occupy a fitting space one day in the Wallington drawing room, and estimated that her work would take thirty years to complete. To formulate her design she did not choose a household name but generously exercised her patronage with considerable acumen in selecting the youthful John Edgar Platt, a prize-winning student at the Royal College of Art, London, and an artist who would later achieve some eminence as a colour woodcut printmaker.[6] He presumably drew up a design in 1909 according to her wishes. It presents a bold heraldic statement of the house's owners, the family's lineage and her own branch within it. At the four corners appear the crests of previous owners, the Fenwicks and Blacketts, complemented by those of the Trevelyans and the Bells. Under a tree sits an owl, the crest of the Calverleys, marriage with whom brought the house into Trevelyan possession, while centrally the embroidery promotes the origin myth of the Trevelyans and embodies it in the form of Charles Trevelyan, a knight in shining armour rising from the waves.

To create an Arthurian fabric was not unprecedented. Fabrics depicting the Arthurian legend have had a long history stemming from medieval times, and they figured frequently in the nineteenth-century revival of handmade artefacts. Not only was the legend a lifelong concern for William Morris and Edward Burne-Jones from their early creations for Red House to the magnificent Holy Grail series at Stanmore Hall, but there was also a major series of Arthurian tapestries designed by Herbert Bone for the Royal Windsor Tapestry Manufactory, and the subject matter was commonly found among aesthetic circles promoted by the *Studio* magazine.

Unlike previous Arthurian fabrics, however, this design presented a very specific location: Mount's Bay against the background of St Michael's Mount crowned by a medieval fortress. And what makes Lady Molly's work additionally distinctive is that her design gradually evolved during the twenty-three years she devoted to it, continually incorporating fresh public and private incidents that could not have been predicted within the original plan. These include major national and political developments, with which her husband was closely concerned, for it is his career that is celebrated in this portrayal of the legendary hero, Sir Trevelyan. Along the bottom border, for example, her starting date of this section is marked in black: 'May 1917 at War'. The eventual armistice is recorded by placing a line of gold on one of the waves from which the horse rises in the Trevelyan shield. The Peace Treaty of 1919 is symbolized by the white mark on the red collar of the horse – had the treaty been more satisfactory (in the Trevelyan opinion) a gold mark would

---

[6] In my description of Molly's embroidery I draw heavily upon detailed information sent me by the National Trust.

have been chosen. Sir Charles's appointment as president of the Board of Education in Ramsay MacDonald's cabinet is denoted by the initials JRM, worked with the 1924 date, on the red scroll around the tree. His resignation in 1931 is shown by a band in his green and white election colours being worked on the tip of the scroll bearing Lady Trevelyan's name. The red flag on the small boat records the 1931 election, when Sir Charles retired from Parliament. Besides these allusions to public affairs, Molly also incorporated data about her family life. For example, the birth of Marjorie, her fourth child, is shown by the child's initials within the knight's helmet, and the birth of Geoffrey, her youngest child, by the initials GWT on the front fold of the saddle-cloth. Later the birth in 1931 of her first grandchild, Susan Dower, is marked on one of the small fish in the bottom border.

Molly began with the top border on 6 July 1910 by using a small frame held on the knee, and used the same technique much later with the bottom border. An attractive watercolour portrait by Phyllis Bicknell shows Molly at work in 1921, when the main body of the work was being done on a large standing frame.[7] In order to achieve a grand scale for her embroidery she made it in three separate sections, which were later sewn together and then embroidered over the joins. The two borders were also sewn on. With the knight's face she faced serious difficulty, so she asked her aunt, Florence Johnson, a skilled embroideress, to work the face for her. This was done on a separate frame then sewn down on top of the original face, the helmet rim forming the join between the two pieces. Another problem lay in obtaining uniform wools throughout the process. Sadly the English wools that had to be used for the left-hand lower border during the First World War were inferior to the French wools used elsewhere in the embroidery and have faded.

A family memoir gives us a glimpse of the slow progress of the embroidery's completion. One of Molly's daughters, Katharine, recalls that every day as she came down before breakfast, her mother would already be sitting at her great piece of needlework, and would then allow Katharine 'to pull the needle through from underneath, as she stabbed it from above'.[8] For a later relative, Laura Trevelyan, it seemed that as Charles's political career stalled, he withdrew from his wife, who 'sought comfort in her thirty-year task' and 'was unable to hide her unhappiness from Charles'.[9] From one point of view, of course, he obtained remarkable success – serving as a Liberal MP from 1899 to 1918, then as a

[7] The portrait is reproduced in R. Trevelyan, *Wallington, Northumberland*, rev. edn (London, 2004), p. 12.
[8] K. Trevelyan, *Fool in Love* (London, 1962), p. 27.
[9] Trevelyan, *A Very British Family*, p. 119.

Labour MP from 1922 to 1931, and twice enjoying cabinet office at the Board of Education – and yet he nonetheless appears to have failed to fulfil his own highest ambitions, and suffered accordingly.

In Charles's own description of Wallington, he highlights the armorial symbolism of the embroidery, its function in uniting the needlework traditions of the Blacketts and the Bells.[10] Curiously, he does not mention the Arthurian aspect of the work, and although he is said to have spent evenings in his closing years reading aloud 'the Border Ballads he loved so well' while Molly stitched at other embroideries, he may have disliked the fabled elements of the family story.[11] Unwittingly perhaps the embroidery panel reveals much of his nature. As the only person represented, he cuts rather a cold and very lonely figure. In actuality, despite his many admirably philanthropic qualities, he seems to have been quite a difficult person to get on with, while his combination of pacifist aspirations with an admiration for Stalin's 1930s Russia suggests great naivety, if not dangerous folly. Did he feel increasingly uncomfortable at being continually confronted by this embroidered image of his faded youthful aspirations? And is there perhaps a lurking irony in that this knight has turned his back on the great household he came from, for in real life Charles was preoccupied with severing future generations of his family from the ownership of Wallington. Though ensuring that he would live there himself until his death, the property would at that point be handed over to the National Trust.

## Robert Calverley Trevelyan (1872–1951)

Robert Calverley Trevelyan was a younger brother of Sir Charles, and thus brother-in-law to Molly. In contrast to both his father and Charles he never sought public office, choosing instead to devote his life to creative and scholarly pursuits. His copious publications, however, never received widespread praise or even attention, and as a younger son he did not enjoy great affluence until the death of his mother in 1928. However, he enjoyed a comfortable, gentlemanly, enlightened existence at his Surrey home, The Shiffolds, and retained a wide circle of accomplished friends.

In comparison with Molly's close involvement with the family's Arthurian origins, Robert seems to have displayed no interest in the matter. In childhood his early reading was closely shaped by his father,

[10] Sir C. Trevelyan, *Wallington: Its History and Treasures*, 8th edn (privately printed, 1953), p. 27.

[11] A. J. A. Morris, *C. P. Trevelyan, 1870–1958: Portrait of a Radical* (Belfast, 1977), p. 193.

George Otto Trevelyan, who nurtured in his son a deep love for Greek and Latin literature, a cultural orientation that would never change throughout a long writing career.[12] Consummately bookish, he is appropriately depicted as a reader in the portrait by Aubrey Waterfield that now hangs at Wallington. After his death, close friends reassembled his considerable and choice library of over five thousand volumes and presented it to Birkbeck College, London, as a memorial. The catalogue of this allows us to glimpse what he read and when he bought it.[13] His range is impressive. He read in Greek, Latin, French, German, Spanish, Dutch (his wife was from Holland) and Italian. He not only read, but he translated copiously, from Greek, Latin and Italian. He owned books about the Middle East, India and the Far East. He also read widely in art, philosophy, religion, psychology, natural history and astronomy. His main concern was, of course, with creative literature, particularly poetry, and his main topics were drawn from the classical world. Like Matthew Arnold his unadorned style avoids colourful imagery, takes its subject from the mythical past and is intensely concerned with the age-old human problems: freedom, violence, justice, kindness and death.

Among his many works he twice attempted a quasi-Arthurian drama. Here we might also note that from around 1890 to 1910 he was reading quite widely among medieval writers. Besides the to-be-expected Malory, Geoffrey of Monmouth, *Mabinogion* and Marie de France, he acquired many of Jessie M. Weston's translations of more uncommon Arthurian romances. And significantly he was, like his Trevelyan and Bell forebears and contemporaries, deeply interested in German culture. He was, for example, well read in Wolfram von Eschenbach's *Parzival*, for he owned not only Weston's translation (1894) but also Alphonse Grandmont's French translation (1892) and, perhaps most importantly, Karl Bartsch's three-volume edition of *Parzival* and *Titurel* in the original German (1875–77).[14]

Though a Grail theme frequently provided the subject for late nineteenth-century English literature, its handling at that time stemmed very largely from English sources, namely Malory's *Le Morte Darthur*, especially as filtered through Tennyson's 'Sir Galahad' and *Idylls of the King*. All such works focused on the angelically immaculate and superhumanly strong Galahad as hero, and this residual tradition was not easily altered by new fire from France or Germany. When therefore Robert chose instead to follow Wolfram and adopt the humanly imperfect Parsifal as titular hero

---

[12] See R. C. Trevelyan, *Windfalls: Notes and Essays*, 2nd edn (London, 1948), p. 143.

[13] The librarian of Birkbeck kindly loaned me a copy of the catalogue.

[14] Alphonse Grandmont appears in a group photograph taken in Sicily in 1899 (Trinity College, Cambridge, Robert Calverley Trevelyan Collection MS JOT/41).

of a blank-verse drama it was a considerable departure from precedent. *The Birth of Parsival* (1905), however, endows Wolfram's story with a new plot which, omitting Amfortas as a Grail lord, allows Titurel to pass on this sacred office directly to his son, Frimutel.[15] But the ungrateful Frimutel has a brief affair with Herzeloide, the daughter of a friendly king he has just rescued from pagan attack, and by this indulgence he breaks his father's strict taboo on having sex unsanctioned by the Grail. Consequently the Grail – which is all-knowing – sends Kundry to curse him with dethronement, madness and woe. In response Frimutel rejects his Grail kingship, insanely kills Herzeloide's sleeping brothers and runs wild into the forest. He is, of course, unaware that the now pregnant Herzeloide has fled the court in order to protect her baby, Parsival, by raising him secretly. But when the infant is discovered, she has to confess her motherhood to save the child from death. As punishment she and her son are banished to the forest. Here she meets the mentally recovered Frimutel, and the plot hinges on a debate between the parents, that is, between head (the rationalist Frimutel who refuses to accept priestly authority) and heart (Herzeloide's love and compassion). Since stalemate ensues, Herzeloide departs with Kundry to bring up Parsival in peace and holiness until he can fitly succeed to the Grail lordship. The drama closes inconclusively with Frimutel vowing defiance. Thus not only has Robert declined to treat his family's own Arthurian legend, but he has chosen a hero who emphatically rejects the constraints of family tradition.

A very favourable review in the *Athenaeum*, probably written by Gordon Bottomley, a close friend, seems to have inside information about Robert's plan to write a trilogy, in the second part of which Frimutel would be killed by his son, and in the third of which Parsival would reign as king and return to the sacred East with the Grail.[16] Throughout this first play Robert shows little interest in, or sympathy with, formal religion, plays down the Grail lords' theological differences with paganism and condemns the 'superstition' of cruel Christian priests who wish to burn the Parsival babe as 'a witch's brat'. The author's own allegedly 'disputatious' character,[17] however, proves an advantage occasionally by prodding his characters into either a searching ideological debate (Parsival and Herzeloide on reason versus guilt) or a display of forensic virtuosity (Herzeloide's pleading with the priest for her son's life). Indeed the play's dedication to B.A.W.R., that is, Bertrand Russell, probably signals Robert's radical and rationalist intent. Russell, a close friend at

[15] R. C. Trevelyan, *The Birth of Parsival* (London, 1905).
[16] *Athenæum*, 20 May 1905, 620.
[17] E. Samuel, *Bernard Berenson: The Making of a Connoisseur* (Cambridge, MA, 1979), p. 319.

Cambridge and beyond, had recently published *A Free Man's Worship* (1903), and though he, like Robert, would have been appalled by the violence committed by Frimutel, he would have enthusiastically endorsed Robert's advocacy of nature, maternal love, freedom, reason and truth in their struggle against such concepts as monarchy, priestcraft, family tradition and restraint on sexual intercourse.

The play was quite widely reviewed – Robert employed an agency to send him press cuttings, and twenty-two of these are preserved in the Trinity College archives. Only two are hostile: the *Liverpool Courier*, for whom the 'Grail myth ranks among the most lugubrious of the mediaeval monkish nightmares of early Christendom', and *The Times*, which thought the work 'vague' and 'flat'. Most others found the intention admirable and the verse well crafted, but agreed with *The Times* that Robert's play was fundamentally undramatic and lacked human warmth. He was later urged by Bottomley to write a sequel, but did not do so.[18] Yet the story was evidently much in his mind, and in 1912 he published 'Paraphrased from Wolfram von Eschenbach', which is certainly full of human warmth, and his choice of a particularly tender passage from his source probably reflects a personal tragedy of his own: his acute grief over the early death of his first child, Paul, in 1909, and his understandable concern for his second child, Julian, born in the following year.[19] The translation runs to fifty-eight unrhymed lines, usually of fifteen syllables, about the pregnant Herzeloide's lament for her dead husband, Gahmuret. This is the scene where she uncovers her breast and presses out a few drops of milk:

> Though baptism I had ne'er received, yet well instead thereof
> Wouldst thou have served me. Now for teardrops shalt thou
>     serve me oft,
> Whene'er in public or in secret I lament my lord. (ll. 26–8)

And after the birth of Parsival, when she sighs that his masculine gender will necessarily involve him in warfare, this maternal breast imagery returns:

> Oft to herself these pious words she said:
> 'The most sublime of queens once gave her breast to him who
>     endured
> A cruel death, nailed to the cross to prove his love for man.' (ll.
>     51–3)

---

[18] Letter from GB to RCT, 17 August 1908 in Gordon Bottomley Papers BL Add MS 88957.

[19] R. C. Trevelyan, 'Paraphrased from Wolfram von Eschenbach', in *The Bride of Dionysus: A Music Drama, and Other Poems* (London, 1912), pp. 68–9.

As for continuing with his planned *Parsival* trilogy, by 1908 Robert had come to acknowledge its faults and to conclude that he was 'more at home in Greek subjects than mediaeval'.[20] Bottomley's intriguing solution was to continue the *Parsival* along the lines of a Stuart masque, an idea curiously in chime with Robert's poetic development at that moment for he had just completed a libretto for a proposed opera by Donald Tovey.[21] In due course an unlikely association between a classical subject and musical drama would determine the development of a very new Parsival that Robert would soon create. The catalyst was the imminent expiry of the copyright of Richard Wagner's *Parsifal*.

The influence of Wagnerian opera in the late nineteenth century was immense in both depth and breadth, and among Wagnerian operas *Parsifal* was a special case. His final work in this genre, its performance was largely limited to Bayreuth for thirty years. This restriction, and the opera's consequent difficulty of access, seems to have enhanced its particular appeal. Being officially classed as a *sacred festival* music drama meant that the journey to see its performance in Bayreuth from 1882 onwards was frequently described as a 'pilgrimage'. Among the numerous 'pilgrims' who made the expensive trip was a very large contingent from England and America, and these left many detailed accounts of their experience.[22] Besides making a deep impression on its Bayreuth audience, the wider influence of Wagnerian opera on contemporary and later musicians was profound, for he set the agenda for a generation. In England there was a steady flow of publications about his *Parsifal* – texts, scores, translations, retellings, illustrated forms, children's versions, commentaries and so on, but this flow ran in a very confined channel and did not spill over appreciably into new creative art and literature, as it had done on the Continent.

Nonetheless the expiry of the *Parsifal* copyright on 31 December 1913 swiftly prompted European opera houses to mount their own productions, and the early New Year saw it produced in Berlin, Paris, Barcelona, Brussels, Rome, Milan and Bologna, while London followed suit on 2 February 1914. Amid this furore of reverent anticipation, Robert determined to write an irreverent celebration in the form of *The New Parsifal*.[23] To do so he rejected the stately slow-moving style he had used in *The Birth*

---

[20] Letter from RCT to Thomas Sturge Moore, 7 August 1908. Senate House Library, London, Thomas Sturge Moore Papers MS 978.
[21] Letter from RCT to GB, 31 August 1908. BL Add MS 88957.
[22] Among the visitors was Gertrude Bell, who was shown the stage one morning by the Grand Duke of Hesse, allowed to sit in the orchestra and ring the Parsifal bells. Letter to her mother, 16 August 1899, in *The Letters of Gertrude Bell*, ed. Lady Bell (1927), I, p. 16.
[23] R. C. Trevelyan, *The New Parsifal: An Operatic Fable* (London, 1914).

*of Parsival* and continued instead with a racier Aristophanic mode that he had recently used in *Sisyphus: An Operatic Fable* (1908). Antedating Robert's irreverent treatment of Wagner there had been a few other sceptical precursors among English poets. The decadent Arthur Symons, for example, had lamented the pure fool's rejection of the sweet joys of sexual encounters with women, and a comparably erotic ethic is reflected in verse by two non-decadents: Francis Money Coutts's 'Bayreuth: An Antithesis' and Arthur Bell's 'Frimutelle and the Grail'.[24] But Robert's work is far longer and more complex. In many ways he wrote as an insider, as he owned Jessie Weston's edition of *The Legends of the Wagner Dramas* and a translation of Nietzsche's *The Case of Wagner*, and although his library catalogue does not list anything by Wagner himself, he liked the music, attended the London performance of *Parsifal*[25] and had previously gone to Bayreuth – I do not know when because a key letter is undated, but he owned an 1895 copy of Baedeker's *Southern Germany*, which suggests that he made a trip there shortly after.[26] What is more he dedicated the work to his close friend Bernard Berenson, a lifelong admirer of Wagnerian opera. Thus I suspect that for both Berenson and Robert the satire was good-natured.

Undoubtedly Wagner would not have seen the funny side himself. In a brightly inventive induction Robert imagines his play being examined by the state censors. In a hurry to stop for lunch they are anxious to give the play a cursory approval – it's only 'the merest literary twaddle'[27] – but are delayed by the Ghost of Wagner, who wants it banned as 'it's one long blasphemous outrage / On the holiness of the Wagnerian Grail, and the sacred gospel of Bayreuth'.[28] But Wagner is too easily offended by the polite ignorance of the censors and departs in a huff, leaving them to sanction the play and move on to the more serious business of lunch.

In the action that follows Robert drastically reshapes the conventional Grail story. His knights have tired of their 'chaste and holy religion' and have allowed Klingsor to become Lord of the Grail.[29] Thus empowered

---

[24] A. Symons, 'Parsifal', in *Images of Good and Evil* (London, 1899); F. B. Money Coutts, 'Bayreuth: An Antithesis', in *Musa Verticordia* (London, 1905); and A. F. Bell, 'Frimutelle of the Grail', in *The Dear Land of the Heart* (Hove, 1913).

[25] A letter from GB to RCT on 25 February 1914 (BL Add MS 88957) indicates that both poets thought Ernest Newman's recent hostile criticism of Wagner 'offensive and vulgar'.

[26] Undated letter from Goldsworthy Lowes Dickinson to RGT. Trinity College, Cambridge, MS RCT 2:50.

[27] Trevelyan, *The New Parsifal*, p. 2.

[28] Trevelyan, *The New Parsifal*, p. 4.

[29] Trevelyan, *The New Parsifal*, p. 4.

he decides to remove it from Montsalvat and sail off with the knights and Flower Maidens to the island of Circe. There he replaces the customary dove with the Arabian phoenix to de-Christianize the Grail, turning it into a Dionysiac emblem with Circe as its high priestess. Suddenly there arrives the new Parsifal, in the guise of an entirely family-free, modern philistine aviator named Percival Smith. Like his prototype, this Percival is a sportsman and so promptly shoots the phoenix. Immediately attracted to him, Circe begs for an elopement but his plane is just a single-seater so he has to leave her behind.

A year later he returns as promised, inspired to do so by the enchanted drink Circe had given him. This has made him love Beauty, and so he has come back to get the Grail by whatever means. He brings along in his steam-yacht a comparative mythologist (perhaps based on Sir James Frazer), a literary journalist and a futurist poet. To eliminate these threats to his lordship, Klingsor sets them an aesthetic test. They have to distinguish between a true and a false Grail by judging the value of five pieces of verse by well-known poets (they are based on Longfellow, Tennyson, Kipling, Yeats and Masefield). Only Percival passes this test by disliking them all, but Klingsor then cheats by seizing the true Grail and trying to fly up to an aesthetic heaven. However, his levitation is curtailed by the phoenix (now happily recovered), who condemns Klingsor's sterile view of culture. Percival, as quiz champion, is then offered the Grail but modestly refuses it. Egoistical Wagner, though, steals the Grail himself, and disappears with Circe into a subterranean Venusberg while Klingsor ascends into a sterilized heaven. Percival then sails back home with the disillusioned knights and Flower Maidens, and his scholarly companions who still believe their false Grails are true. However, Percival has made the right choice in rejecting the unwholesome Brahminism of religious and aesthetic Graildom. And we are left to reflect that the common-or-garden workaday world is far preferable.

What should we conclude? I think Robert's sympathies are mixed, but his judgements spoken through the mouth of the phoenix are astute. On one hand Venusberg shelters many of Robert's cultural heroes – Orpheus, Dionysus and Aeschylus – and he would surely have approved of a hellenized resort free of sacerdotalism. Again Klingsor's cultural dedication is applauded, but he is finally reproved for the unwholesome Brahminism of his aesthetic: 'Better hadst thou lived out more tolerably thy span / In charity with thy still submerged, less cultured brother man'.[30] So, paradoxically, Percival, the blithe candid philistine, is the real hero, celebrated by the phoenix as one of

[30] Trevelyan, *The New Parsifal*, p. 68.

                    those free
        Unconscious souls, in whom, yea though they know it not,
        My spirit dwells and moves and works, unheeded or forgot,
        A secret kindling power, a serene influence,
        Quickening to loveliness and life the pastures of each sense.[31]

Despite its setting in mythical time the play is determinedly modern in application, burlesquing a range of contemporary intellectual opinions and boldly adopting an ultra-modern hero, the aviator. Robert interestingly reveals a command of the appropriate technical terms: Percival flies a Blériot monoplane and knows the advantage of having a Gnome engine. In choosing an aviator for a quasi-Arthurian role, Robert may have been influenced by current newspaper reports of the daring exploits of the pilot Lancelot Gibbs and even of the German airship class named *Parseval*. What is, however, surprising is that Robert represents his aviator purely as a sportsman, for the potential military application of aircraft was by that date very widely canvassed in newspapers, magazines, boys' adventure stories by Herbert Strang and the pioneering science fiction of H. G. Wells. As Robert, like his brother Charles, was strongly opposed to any form of militarism, not to recognize this new threat reveals a remarkable myopia on his part.

Contemporary critical reception of the work was understandably polarized. Of the ten reviews preserved in the Trinity College archives, three were extraordinarily hostile, accusing the author of 'bad language, rude remarks', 'a senseless lack of reverence' and of being a philistine himself, while four highly appreciated the satire. *The Times*, however, judiciously noted the paradox that Robert's comedy lacked a suitable audience, for those who understood the allusions would probably dislike them. The play has never, to my knowledge, been performed. Moreover, not only did Robert lack an audience, he lacked a publisher, for he had to print his book privately.

Undeterred, he returned to further aspects of the subject and the genre two years later in *The Pterodamozels*, a sequel but with a very different purpose and tone.[32] Percival Smith and his aeroplane make their reappearance but the Grail is not named, and the whole can be viewed as a quasi-Arthurian work only at a very distant allegorical remove. Essentially this is an anti-war tract dedicated to Robert's elder brother, Charles, who had resigned his cabinet post in protest at Britain's declaration of war in 1914. Robert supported his brother's stance, and though too old to be enlisted himself, he would later shelter the young pacifist poet John Rodker when

---

[31] Trevelyan, *The New Parsifal*, p. 69.
[32] R. C. Trevelyan, *The Pterodamozels: An Operatic Fable* (London, [1916]).

he tried to evade arrest in 1917. The plot of this new operatic fable presents a Prometheus so sickened by mankind's folly in fighting the Great War that he resolves to replace human beings with a new creation: pterodamozels, virginal flying women. When one of these beings is, unfortunately, wounded by a British cruiser she is rescued – in a remarkable reversal of the Parsifal story – by the aviator Percival Smith, who has fled the war along with two other conscientious objectors. Prometheus's misanthropic plan is, however, confounded by the pterodamozels' wish to marry men, and by Percival's argument that man is not essentially corrupt – only his leaders are. Accordingly, when the pterodamozels kidnap the senior politicians, financiers and editors, international peace breaks out and a worldwide federation of free republics is instituted with Percival as president. At this news Prometheus sinks to Venusberg, causing an earthly flood, and, despite the pterodamozels' wish to let the former leaders drown, the humanitarian Percival insists on their rescue. Such a dramatically limp finale, alas, fatally weakens the play's credibility, and although Robert insists that humour is a crucial human virtue the verse lacks that very quality. It marked the end of Robert's engagement with the Arthurian world. Thereafter he would revert to classical subjects, which were probably much closer to his deeper interests.

## Sir George Trevelyan (1906–96)

On the death of Sir Charles in 1958, George as his eldest son succeeded to the baronetcy, but not to the house and estate.[33] By that time, however, George's career path had already diverged markedly from that of previous heirs to Wallington. The novel pattern had been set in infancy when Charles sent him not to Harrow, where he, his father and two brothers had been pupils, but to Sidcot, a Quaker boarding school in Somerset, the ostensible reason being that as Charles was opposed to Britain's involvement in the Great War he wished George to receive a pacifist education. Family orthodoxy was re-established, however, at university level because George proceeded, like his forebears, to Trinity College, Cambridge. Thereafter heterodoxy took over. George immersed himself in the Alexander technique (a new method of head–neck–back integration), trained as a master craftsman in furniture design and taught craft, literature and history at Gordonstoun (a new public school with a pro-

---

[33] Information about George's life has been drawn from obituaries in the *Daily Telegraph*, 9 February 1996 and *The Times*, 17 February 1996; F. Farrer, *Sir George Trevelyan and the New Spiritual Awakening* (Edinburgh, 2002); and P. Dawkins, 'Sir George Trevelyan 1906–1996' in the online archive www.sirgeorgetrevelyan.org.uk.

nounced emphasis on outdoor pursuits). Moreover, unlike many previous Trevelyan heirs, George had not sought a wealthy bride. Consequently it is possible that by this stage Charles had formed the opinion that his son was too unreliable to prove a safe custodian of Wallington, and decided that the house and its collections, which Charles was determined to preserve, would be more secure under the aegis of the National Trust. A preliminary process to effect this change was set in motion by Charles in the late 1930s. George, nevertheless, was reportedly saddened by his loss of the ancestral home. Fortunately he found a substitute of sorts because in 1947 he was appointed warden of the newly formed Shropshire Adult College, which was housed in Attingham Park, a mansion that had recently been donated to the National Trust by a penurious aristocrat. Although the state rooms were reserved for tours by visitors, the college was permitted to occupy some seventy rooms on the other three floors, and herein George resided for the next twenty-four years. Thereafter he was tirelessly active in setting up trusts and foundations that would spread his message to the world.

Unlike Robert, George was, according to his biographer, Frances Farrer, deeply influenced by the family story of Sir Trevillian, as its link with the court of King Arthur 'was greatly to his taste'.[34] Indeed Farrer even allows herself to be carried away into a description of Sir Trevillian as 'a Knight of the legendary Holy Grail'. Moreover this family-bred fantasy was strongly underpinned by the Arthurian theories promoted by Rudolf Steiner. To these George was indirectly inducted in 1942 by his sister Kitty's suggestion that he attend a lecture on Steiner given by a former Steinerian pupil, Dr Walter Johannes Stein. The occasion seems to have been a significant turning point in George's mental development, with profound repercussions. In a quasi-Pauline moment of conversion he rejected his inherited agnostic rationalist background in favour of Steiner's Anthroposophical movement, which asserted that humans and animals have, in addition to their physical body, three non-material bodies: the etheric, the astral and the ego. George would later pursue this holistic approach into ever-broadening concerns with education, medicine, agriculture, conservation, architecture and international affairs, not excluding the more exotic areas of reincarnation, lost Atlantis, ley lines and healing crystals.

Among Steiner's key areas of interest was the Arthurian legend, and the influence of his very idiosyncratic interpretation of this is evident in George Trevelyan's own treatment of the subject. Steiner expounded his general theory in *Cosmic Christianity and the Impulse of Michael* (1924),

---

[34] Farrer, *Sir George Trevelyan*, pp. 60–1.

a work that was quoted approvingly by Edward Matchett in *Twelve Seats at the Round Table* (1976), a book of which Trevelyan was co-author.[35] According to Steiner, seven archangels individually administer the cosmic intelligence in cycles of about 300 to 400 years each. Of these angels, Michael represents the Sun, and an earlier cycle of his had included the heroes Alexander and Arthur. Our own understanding of Arthur's real significance is to be gained, however, not from historical documents but through *vision*, by standing on the actual site of Tintagel Castle (Steiner has no doubt this was the 'citadel' where King Arthur's Round Table stood) and gazing over the sea 'with the eyes of the spirit': 'There, in a comparatively short time, one can perceive a wonderful interplay between the light and the air, but also between the elemental spirits living in earth and air...'[36] What is more, if we look back 'with occult sight',[37] we can see that those who lived on 'Arthur's Mount' had chosen this spot because of the natural forces displayed there, and that the knights received through their 'etheric bodies' the Christ impulse streaming away from the Sun. To take hold of these spirit forces required a special group of men, that is, Arthur as the Sun and twelve knightly zodiacal companions each possessing a particular cosmic influence. Hence they drew strength from the Sun to empower them on 'mighty expeditions' through Europe to 'battle with the wild demonic powers of old'. This Sun-spirit was the Christ as he was in pre-Christian times. Steiner defines this novel concept as 'pagan Christianity' or 'Arthur Christianity', and it was from Britain that such influences were diffused throughout the world.

Counterbalancing this 'stream' (the term favoured by Steiner) is the Grail stream bearing the real Christ, for at Golgotha Christ died to the Sun and came down to earth. Consequently this complementary stream largely derives not from Britain and the North but from the South, that is, Palestine, via Greece, Italy and Spain, and it flows not through nature (wind and wave) but through blood (the hearts of men). A meeting of the two streams (of the pre-Christian Christ and the real Christ) occurred in what Steiner considers a key year, AD 869 (Steiner supplies a diagram), when the Ecumenical Council formally adopted the view that man consisted of body and soul – a dichotomy – rather than the trichotomy of body, soul and *spirit*. Our own age, however, which began around 1870, is once again a Michael cycle, and thus another period when spiritual culture is spread widely abroad. Once more we are confronted, Steiner

---

[35] R. Steiner, *Cosmic Christianity and the Impulse of Michael*, trans. D. S. Osmond, 3rd edn (London, 1953); Sir G. Trevelyan and E. Matchett, *Twelve Seats at the Round Table* (St Helier, Jersey, 1976).

[36] Steiner, *Cosmic Christianity*, p. 37.

[37] Steiner, *Cosmic Christianity*, p. 76.

believes, with the problem of how Michael himself, not a human being like Parsifal, can find the path leading from his Arthurian knights, who strive to ensure his cosmic sovereignty, to the Grail knights who seek to lead him into the hearts of men.

Such very unorthodox theories would continue to shape George Trevelyan's outlook. In *Twelve Seats of the Round Table*, for instance, the authors' preface develops the suggestion that Arthur's Round Table might have been 'a place of learning and initiation' at which the knights experienced 'twelve conditions of being', each of which gave to them 'different strengths and sensitivities'.[38] A series of appropriate meditations and self-development exercises is supplied in the book's succeeding chapters. Leo, we are told, is ruled by the Sun, and 'advanced souls' under this sign are 'noble and courageous', 'the peaks of true chivalry'; displaying 'the warrior urge to save humanity', they are 'a royal Arthurian type'.[39] The book is illustrated with reproductions of the large zodiac mosaic which had recently been created by Attingham students inspired by George's concepts. In similar developments of these theories, George lectured at Attingham on 'The Quest of the Grail' and ran a course on 'the Arthurian stream of ancient wisdom' and its links with eastern Sufism. The inspiration here would have stemmed from Wolfram's *Parzival*, with George stressing the links between the western Christian Parsifal and his eastern pagan half-brother Fierefiz. When he later set up the Wrekin Trust he taught a course that connected Parsifal both with the Arthurian knights and the archangel Michael. A pilgrimage followed to St Michael's Mount, relating this site to both the cosmic Christ and the coming of Arthur: 'All is one community' was George's keyword.[40]

One senses that the family legend was also being re-enacted here, suffusing his life with a chivalric aura. The charismatic George, we learn, 'held himself like a knight'.[41] His Attingham secretary, Ruth Nesfield-Cookson, called her memoir 'a tribute to a Knight from his Squire'.[42] Another recollection, by Caroline Myss, a fellow teacher in the Findhorn Community, describes the day she was driven by George to 'where Camelot had been'.[43] She remembered what he was wearing on that occasion, and though she 'can't quite recall where this was' she knew that the experience was 'a rare moment'. On New Year's Eve at Attingham in

[38] Trevelyan and Matchett, *Twelve Seats*, p. 7.
[39] Trevelyan and Matchett, *Twelve Seats*, p. 42.
[40] Farrer, *Sir George Trevelyan*, pp. 136, 139 and 143.
[41] Farrer, *Sir George Trevelyan*, p. 115.
[42] R. Nesfield-Cookson, 'Memories of Sir George Trevelyan – a tribute to a Knight from his Squire (1960–1975)', in the online archive www.sirgeorgetrevelyan.org.uk.
[43] Farrer, *Sir George Trevelyan*, p. 198.

1970 George and his class dined as King Arthur, his queen and court – George, of course, taking the role of King Arthur.[44] But George's familial awareness was also profoundly transmuted by the Goethean concept of *wahlverwandschaffen*, later endorsed by Stein, namely that one's family is created not necessarily from one's blood relations but from the rest of the world. The knight from Lyonesse was thus to be universalized into a broader community as George steadily devoted his life to wider philanthropic ends.

## *Conclusion*

Of the three family members discussed above, Robert has, despite publishing so many books – often through Leonard and Virginia Woolf's prestigious Hogarth Press – and being a friend of such Bloomsbury Group luminaries as Bertrand Russell, Roger Fry, Goldsworthy Lowes Dickinson and E. M. Forster, probably left the weakest trace. Certainly his friendships rather than his close family gave rise to many verse epistles which number among his best work, yet in biographies of his acquaintance he is presented merely as a shadowy figure in the background, his own literary efforts separate from the main concerns of his circle. He suffers therefore from belonging to no major movement. Intellectually he had close friends in two other poets, Gordon Bottomley and Thomas Sturge Moore, with whom he conducted a voluminous correspondence, and shared a desire to reject much of High Victorian taste while remaining distinct from the Modernism of Pound and Eliot. Such an approach has effectively debarred Robert from critical or commercial attention since his death. Unhappily, too, the London Blitz destroyed the publisher's stock of his *Collected Poems*, and this collection has never been reprinted. Probably the sole book of his that sold widely, and is still often found second-hand, is *From the Chinese*, an anthology he made of translations by other writers, which appeared at the end of the Second World War when pro-Chinese sympathies were running high in the west.[45] Sadly even the one visible memorial to him – his library of some five thousand volumes, which was donated by his friends to Birkbeck College as a specially named memorial collection – no longer exists as a discrete entity. However, perhaps there are a few signs that the critical ice has recently started to melt: an abridged form of Tovey's *The Bride of Dionysus*, for which Robert wrote the libretto, has now become

---

[44] Farrer, *Sir George Trevelyan*, p. 104.
[45] *From the Chinese*, ed. R. C. Trevelyan (Oxford, 1945).

available on CD,[46] and even his Arthurian works have received some attention by being summarized by Alan Lupack in *The Oxford Guide to Arthurian Literature and Legend*, while Donald E. Stanford has provided a sympathetic scholarly account of his entire *oeuvre* in *A Critical Study of the Works of Four British Writers*.[47]

If Robert's studious life was largely confined to his domestic household and circle of close friends, George's career was determinedly different. Though he wrote on a broad range of topics, and contributed forewords to books by his associates, he was not – nor did he claim to be – an original thinker. But he moved in much wider social circles than Robert, where he excelled as an orator and an inspirer. Through his teaching, his organization of conferences and the setting up of trusts he was essentially a missionary with the zeal to effect change in virtually every aspect of the world. He has thus established quite a reputation as an important guru of the modern New Age movement, and public knowledge of his views persists through a substantial website, while the Wrekin Trust he estab-lished still functions on a minor scale. His comparative celebrity slips, of course, under the radar of Academe, which very rarely takes note of New Age approaches. Nonetheless, while such approaches need not compel our belief, they should be addressed, because much of the modern inter-est in the Arthurian legends springs from such sources and these show no signs of decline. For example, Walter Stein's *The Ninth Century: World History in the Light of the Holy Grail* has recently been reprinted with an introduction by John Matthews, which claims it to be 'one of the most valuable and original works on the Grail yet to appear in any language'.[48]

Molly's role was markedly different from that of her son or brother-in-law, who both pursued their tangential ways, in being more firmly associ-ated with the life of her relatives, both through her continual support for her husband's political career and the creation of her great embroidery as a family icon. It may seem paradoxical that the rationalist Trevelyan family should have fostered such a fanciful legend – and indeed Molly's other brother-in-law, the historian George Macaulay Trevelyan, had scant interest or belief in either the historical or the mythical King Arthur[49]

---

[46] D. Tovey, *Excerpts from 'The Bride of Abydos'*, Belfast Philharmonic Choir and Ulster Orchestra, conducted by George Vass. Dutton Digital. CDLX 7241 (2009).

[47] *The Oxford Guide to Arthurian Literature and Legend*, ed. A. Lupack (Oxford, 2005); and D. E. Stanford, *A Critical Study of the Works of Four British Writers: Margaret Louisa Woods, Mary Coleridge, Sir Henry Newbolt and R. C. Trevelyan*, ed. R. W. Crump (Lewiston, NY, and Lampeter, 2006).

[48] W. Stein, *The Ninth Century: World History in the Light of the Holy Grail*, trans. I. Groves, rev. J. M. Wood, with an introduction by J. Matthews (London, 2009 [1988]).

[49] See G. M. Trevelyan, *History of England*, new edn (London, 1937 [1926]), pp. 33 and 36–7.

– but as Wallington now belongs to the National Trust and is open to the public, the embroidery, a dominant feature in one of the main rooms, is seen by thousands of visitors every year and is reproduced in colour in the guidebook. Paradoxically, too, Molly's creativity, which was, in comparison with that of Robert and George, quite self-effacing in motive, has resulted in her achievement becoming probably the most durable, for the embroidery's reputation is spreading, and its image appropriately appears in the modern guidebook to another great house, St Michael's Mount in Cornwall, which is now also in the care of the National Trust.[50] Moreover, as images of National Trust artefacts have recently become available online, global access to the embroidery is assured. Whether or not there really was a strong family tradition of an Arthurian provenance for Sir Trevelyan before Molly stitched him into the story, her artefact has succeeded in giving the tale continuing strength. Promoted too by George's biographer and the associated website, the tale is now commonly found among internet accounts of the Trevelyan family while in more traditional print forms a new American genealogical study of the worldwide Trevillian family claims to begin with 'Sir Trevillian, a knight in King Arthur's court';[51] and the material has been developed by Craig Weatherhill into his trilogy of fantasy novels set in Lyonesse.[52] The family's complex involvement with the Matter of Britain has taken strong root.

---

[50] J. St Aubyn, Lord St Levan, *St. Michael's Mount: The Illustrated Historical Guide* (London, 2004), p. 5. This image had not appeared in the 1978 edition.

[51] R. Trevillian, *The Rearview Mirror* (Bloomington, IN, 2001).

[52] C. Weatherhill, *The Lyonesse Stone/Seat of Storms/The Tinners' Way* (Padstow, 1991, 1995 and 2010).

# VIII

# *KAAMELOTT*: A NEW FRENCH ARTHURIAN TRADITION

## *Tara Foster*

First broadcast in 2005, the extremely popular French television series *Kaamelott* takes on the Arthur of the medieval French tradition and casts a humorous new light on the monarch and his court. The series ran for six seasons on France's television channel M6, ending on a cliffhanger in October 2009. The spelling 'Kaamelott' takes its inspiration from the spelling 'Kamaalot' found in some manuscripts of the thirteenth-century French Prose *Lancelot–Grail* cycle, and whether by accident or design, the back-to-back 'A's in the title prominently feature the initials of Alexandre Astier, *Kaamelott*'s creator, writer, director, editor, composer and principal actor. In the early seasons of the series we find none of the highly stylized medievalism of Eric Rohmer's *Perceval le Gallois*, nor the grim and bloody realism of Robert Bresson's *Lancelot du Lac*, two memorable cinematic adaptations of the medieval French literary canon. Rather, the series has more in common with *Monty Python and the Holy Grail*, for we are treated to a parade of human failings that flies in the face of the Round Table's reputation for perfection. Charged with the divine mission of finding the Holy Grail, Arthur finds himself impeded at every turn by the shortcomings of the knights in his entourage, parodies of the literary figures. This essay will focus on some of the ways in which Astier, in the early seasons of the series in particular, plays with and challenges the French literary tradition, ultimately inventing for his televised text an authority equal to that of any tradition that has preceded it.[1]

The humour of the series is multifaceted and ever present, albeit much subdued in the fifth and sixth seasons, when the tone darkens to reflect the disintegration of Arthur's court and the format moves from episodes of approximately three and a half minutes each to seven and then around

---

[1] I would like to thank Professor Norris J. Lacy for his helpful comments and suggestions on this essay.

fifty minutes each. The mini-episodes of the early seasons, though, are irrepressibly funny. In her analysis of the British television series *The Blackadder*, set in the fictional fifteenth-century reign of Richard IV and starring Rowan Atkinson, Katherine Lewis notes that 'much of the humor in Blackadder [*sic*] relies on intricately plotted farce and wordplay, in concert with Atkinson's famed "rubber face" qualities',[2] and we might make a similar observation about *Kaamelott*'s early seasons. Centred on dialogue, these episodes revel in both the comedic physical mannerisms of and verbal exchanges between the characters. Astier has chosen to set the series in the Roman Britain of the fifth century rather than in the High or Late Middle Ages, and he says that as he writes the scripts, he is conscious that 'les événements doivent aussi bien fonctionner avec la famille Pendragon qu'avec Romulus Augustule, l'empereur de 11 ans qui règne à l'époque d'Arthur' (the events must work as well with the Pendragon family as with Romulus Augustulus, the eleven-year-old emperor who reigns in Arthur's time).[3] As he imagines potential dialogues between the last Roman emperor and the *dux bellorum* installed in Britain by the Empire, however, Astier deliberately uses 'un langage qui est le nôtre, avec un souci de proximité entre le spectateur et les personnages' (a language that is our own, in the interests of creating a proximity between the spectator and the characters).[4] Unlike many Arthurian films that adopt a 'pseudo-medieval language' that 'ranges from the archaic to the elevated to the genuinely literary',[5] *Kaamelott*'s court uses a decidedly twenty-first-century form of speech that is heavily laced with slang and profanity. As Judith Shoaf points out, the 'low-key vernacular ... is both contemporary and (usually) appropriate to the situation ... There are plenty of fart jokes and vulgarities, too.'[6]

The linguistic aspect of the series, then, constitutes an important aspect of its humour, as does its exploitation of the possibilities inherent in situation comedy. Although many audience members might know the cast of

---

[2] K. J. Lewis, '"Accident, My Codlings": Sitcom, Cinema and the Re-writing of History in *The Blackadder*', in *Mass Market Medieval: Essays on the Middle Ages in Popular Culture*, ed. D. W. Marshall (Jefferson, NC, 2007), pp. 113–25 (p. 117).

[3] E. Pincas, 'Entretien avec Alexandre Astier', *Forum de l'Acteur Alexandre Astier* (25 December 2006). http://www.alexandre-astier.com/t88-Historia-Mensuel-Arthur-et-sa-légende.htm. All translations in this essay from modern or Old French to English are my own.

[4] Pincas, 'Entretien'.

[5] R. H. Osberg and M. E. Crow, 'Language Then and Language Now in Arthurian Film', in *King Arthur on Film: New Essays on Arthurian Cinema*, ed. K. J. Harty (Jefferson, NC, 1999), pp. 39–66 (p. 43).

[6] J. Shoaf, '*Kaamelott*: A Semi-heroic Epic', *The Heroic Age* 13 (2010), §5, http://www.heroicage.org/issues/13/forumc.php

Arthurian characters only by reputation, that reputation is so well established that seeing them blunder along and hearing them curse or use
terms such as 'tatati tatata' (yadda yadda yadda) and 'chevaliérisation' (a
made-up word that we might translate as 'knightification') are inherently
funny. For those viewers who are familiar with the various literary (and
cinematic) incarnations of Arthur and his knights, the parodic treatment
of the legendary characters holds even more resonance. As Andrew Elliott
puts it, 'If tradition insists that Arthur's knights are brave, noble, and pure,
then the logical subversion of tradition is its direct reversal, which would
seek to emphasize their cowardice, their rashness, or else to undermine
its gravitas in order ultimately to render Camelot "a silly place".'[7] Bohort,
one of the three elite of *La Queste del Saint Graal*, is a cowardly fop who
claims that guarding the interior storeroom of blankets during an attack
on the castle is a most worthy deed. Karadoc, the hero of Robert Biket's
*Lai du cor* who also features prominently in the First Continuation of
Chrétien de Troyes's *Roman du Graal*, is a dim-witted glutton who sleeps
with a stock of sausages and other meat products in his bed. He has no
particular interest in searching for the Holy Grail until news reaches the
castle that the Grail might in fact be a horn of plenty, at which point he
can't pack his bags and begin the quest fast enough. Gauvain, praised in
a great many texts of the medieval French Arthuriad, styles himself 'le
Chevalier au Pancréas' (the Knight of the Pancreas) and is defeated by
a large splinter while on a mission with his uncle. Despite his reputation as Britain's greatest enchanter, even Merlin cannot escape a gleeful
skewering. With accomplishments such as vanquishing the Winchester
Weasel, drafting a potion for ingrown toenails and writing the treatise
'Le Druidisme expliquée aux personnes âgées' (Druidism Explained to
the Elderly) to his name, we understand why Merlin initially refuses to
face the magician who controls the wolves of Caledonia, slew the Snow
Dragon and invented the Potion of Unlimited Power. Unimpressed with
the cowering Druid, Arthur asks Merlin, 'C'est vrai ce qu'on dit, que
vous êtes le fils d'un Démon et d'une pucelle?' (Is it true what they say,
that you are the son of a demon and a virgin?),[8] referring to the legend as
found in the work of Robert de Boron and other medieval writers. When

---

[7]   A. B. R. Elliott, 'The Charm of the (Re)making: Problems of Arthurian Television
    Serialization', *Arthuriana* 21.4 (2011), 53–67 (p. 60).
[8]   A. Astier, *Kaamelott: Livre I, première partie* (Paris, 2008), p. 107. Transcriptions
    of the first season's dialogue are taken from this text and from A. Astier, *Kaamelott:
    Livre I, deuxième partie* (Paris, 2008); readers should note that there are occasional
    discrepancies between the printed dialogues and the dialogue produced by the actors as
    the episodes were filmed. Passages will be cited by season, episode and page number.

Merlin confirms his parentage, Arthur replies, 'Vous avez plus pris de la pucelle' (You take more after the virgin) (I.15, 107).

In 'Le Rebelle', an episode near the end of season 2, Lancelot has presided over a meeting of the Round Table in Arthur's absence and has worked himself into a lather over what he perceives as Arthur's shortcomings, ending the meeting by shouting, 'Le Roi, je l'emmerde!' (Screw the king!).[9] When Arthur returns and asks for an explanation, Lancelot gets caught up in his frustration again and tells the king to go screw himself. Lancelot is duly banished from court as a kind of time out, but he returns with his frustration unabated and his resentment smouldering just beneath the surface. The interaction between Arthur and Lancelot here contrasts sharply with Lancelot's attitude towards the king in the thirteenth-century prose romance *La Mort le roi Artu*. In the medieval text, Lancelot has taken Arthur's place in bed and accepts his exile after returning the queen to her husband; he regrets losing his place at the king's side and refuses to show the least sign of hostility towards Arthur. Even when the king besieges Lancelot at Joyeuse Garde and attacks him with the intent to kill, the narrator says that 'quant Lancelot le vit venir, il ne s'apareille pas de lui deffendre, fors de soi couvrir, car trop amoit le roi de grant amour' (when Lancelot sees him coming, he does not equip himself for defence except to cover himself, for he loved the king with too great a love).[10] Hector must strike Arthur down in Lancelot's stead, but Lancelot definitively rejects his cousin's suggestion that Lancelot kill Arthur now while he has the chance; Lancelot's love for Arthur thus saves the king's life. In Astier's series, Lancelot has taken the king's place by occupying his throne during the meeting and by throwing several knights in jail, both acts which suggest that he would like to take Arthur's place with the queen as well. He believes that he would make a better king than Arthur and lashes out: 'Eh ben faites des efforts pour arrêter de vous comporter comme un connard! J'en ai plein le cul de seconder un merdeux de dix ans qui est même pas foutu de trouver un Graal ou de faire un môme à sa femme! Alors oui, je m'assois sur votre trône parce que je fais la moitié de votre boulot!' (Well then make an effort to stop acting like an asshole! I've had it up to here with helping a little snot-nose who can't even bloody well find a Grail or give his wife a kid! So yes, I sit on your throne because I do half

---

9   A. Astier, *Kaamelott: Livre II, deuxième partie* (Paris, 2008), p. 212. Transcriptions of the second season's dialogue are taken from this text and from A. Astier, *Kaamelott: Livre II, première partie* (Paris, 2008); readers should note that there are occasional discrepancies between the printed dialogues and the dialogue produced by the actors as the episodes were filmed. Passages will be cited by season, episode and page number.

10  *La Mort le Roi Artu*, ed. J. Frappier, 3rd edn, Textes Littéraires Français 58 (Geneva, 1964), p. 152.

your work!) (II.85, 215). The anger here emanates from Lancelot and is directed at Arthur rather than vice-versa. Although he sends Lancelot away to cool his heels, the king is ultimately looking for a reconciliation with his best knight. He does not succeed, for upon Lancelot's return, Arthur remarks: 'Il me déteste encore plus qu'avant' (He hates me even more than before) (II.85, 216). Indeed, where love inspires the literary knight to save his king despite their dispute, hatred drives *Kaamelott*'s Lancelot to resolve their differences by attempting to assassinate Arthur in the final episode of the fifth season.[11]

This reversal of roles is part of what Valérie Florentin points to as 'le décalage entre ce qui est relaté et l'idée populaire que chacun a de la légende et des hauts faits d'armes des chevaliers de la Table Ronde' (the gap between what is related and the popular idea that each [specta-tor] has about the legend and about the great feats of arms of the knights of the Round Table).[12] That popular idea is born of the treatment of the legend in literature, and if the gap is filled with the spectators' laughter, it is because Astier's humorous play on the literary tradition relies in large part on audience awareness and recognition of that tradition. In some cases, Astier turns an episode or a theme from the literature on its head. The episode 'L'Ambition', for example, calls into question the reputation of Camelot as the place to which everyone gravitates, for people from all ranks announce that they are going to leave the court for greener pastures. The chief farmer, the guards, Père Blaise and even Lancelot have better opportunities elsewhere and are anxious to take advantage before it's too late: the farmer will act as an agricultural consultant in Caledonia, the guards have taken an internship to become officers, and Lancelot will return on a part-time basis to his role as knight errant rather than con-tinue in his humdrum role as full-time minister at Camelot. Blaise, who is Arthur's scribe in the series rather than Merlin's, has a shot at becoming pope and explains his eagerness to abandon the quest for the Holy Grail: 'Ouais, la quête du Graal, c'est sympa mais on ne parle pas de la même chose, là … Pape! Je vous parle de devenir Pape!' (Yeah, the quest for the Grail is nice and all but we're not talking about the same thing here … Pope! I'm talking about becoming pope!) (II.74, 151). In another upend-ing of the literary status quo, Lancelot, who was raised by the Lady of

---

[11] Lancelot does not follow through with his plan, principally because Arthur has already attempted suicide, and the knight finds the king bleeding to death in his bath. It seems that Lancelot has not yet been entirely consumed by his hatred, however, for the final seconds of the episode provide a glimpse of what can only be Lancelot trying to heal Arthur's slit wrist.

[12] V. Florentin, 'Les anachronismes comme procédé d'humour verbal: Une étude de la série télévisée française *Kaamelott*', Voyages in Translation Studies, Concordia University, 27 March 2009.

189

the Lake in the Prose *Lancelot*, cannot see and has never interacted with the Lady in the television series; in the early seasons of the series, she is visible and audible to Arthur alone.[13]

More often than a complete reversal, however, Astier presents his audience with an alternative version or explanation of events and figures encountered in the literature. Thus Yvain, who in the series is Arthur's brother-in-law, has begun styling himself 'le Chevalier au Lion' not because of any of his adventures as in Chrétien de Troyes's romance, but because he thinks that 'ça fait hyper classe' (it sounds ultra classy) (II.62, 81). In another twist on Chrétien's work, Guenièvre is abducted not by Méléagant but by a fictional band of Pictish warriors. In fact, the queen has simply gone surreptitiously to the tavern as instructed by her mother, a Pictish queen invented by Astier, so that the two women can extort the ransom money from Arthur and Guenièvre's father Léodagan and divide it between them as a counter to having no say in their respective arranged marriages. Unlike what we see in Chrétien's romance and the *Lancelot–Grail* cycle, Guenièvre and Lancelot's adulterous relationship remains unconsummated in the television series: deeply committed to the ideals of courtly love that exalt the lady above her humble suitor, Lancelot has vowed not to sully his love for the queen by sleeping with other women. In a nod to Marie de France's *Lanval*, which features the spurned queen accusing the companionless knight of preferring 'vaslez ... bien afaitiez' (attractive young men) to women,[14] we learn that Lancelot's lack of female companionship has not been interpreted as fidelity, as Guenièvre gently implies: 'Ben ... on vous voit jamais avec une femme ... C'est vrai qu'on raconte des choses – pas mal de choses, même – mais pas que vous êtes fidèle' (Well ... you're never seen with a woman ... It's true that people say things – lots of things, even – but not that you're faithful) (I.37, 238). Because of his ideals, then, Lancelot has never experienced what the troubadours termed 'le soreplus' and remains entirely ignorant of the mechanics of sex. When Guenièvre, who is also still a virgin and nearly as ignorant sexually as Lancelot, finally joins the knight in bed, she is more than a little dismayed at her discovery. She has never succeeded in convincing her husband to sleep with her despite many attempts, although he does regularly sleep with a cohort of official mistresses. The queen pleads with Lancelot to ask some of his men what to do, but Lancelot refuses, fearing the taunts that he would

---

[13] In Season 5, we learn that the Lady of the Lake was, in fact, present during Lancelot's early childhood, but she was told to abandon her post as his tutor in favour of the young Arthur. During the first four seasons, Lancelot has no memory of this period of his childhood.

[14] Marie de France, *Lais*, ed. K. Warnke (Halle, 1925; rpt. Paris, 1990), p. 148.

have to face if they found out that he is a 'grosse pucelle'; disclosure of his virginal state would certainly not be 'bon pour [son] autorité' (good for his authority) (IV.34). Perhaps Astier was inspired by a passage from Sir Thomas Malory's *Morte Darthur*, in which the narrator tells us that 'as the Freynshhe booke seyth, the quene and sir Launcelot were togydirs. And whether they were abed other at other maner of disportis, me lyste nat thereof make no mencion, for love that tyme was nat as love ys nowadays.'[15] Malory's coyness will serve Astier well: as we shall see, the theme of texts glossing over what really happened will resurface repeatedly in the early seasons of *Kaamelott*.

Astier also exploits the alternative versions of the legend presented within the literary canon to great effect, such as in the episode 'En forme de Graal' (Grail-Shaped). During this particularly noteworthy meeting of the Round Table, Bohort announces to his cohorts the staggering news that it is 'tout à fait possible que le Graal ne soit ni un vase, ni une coupe mais … un récipient!" (altogether possible that the Grail is neither a vessel nor a cup, but … a container!) (I.18, 124). Karadoc infers from Bohort's hand gesture that the Grail must be a kind of salad bowl, and an exasperated Arthur exclaims that whether it's a vessel, a salad bowl or a dessert service, it makes no difference as they have no leads. Perceval joins in the discussion at this point, revealing to the company that he was informed a year before by a bizarre and smelly man in Wales that the Grail is an incandescent stone, doubtless a reference to Wolfram von Eschenbach's *Parzival*. When a now indignant Arthur asks why he has not shared this crucial news before, Perceval admits that it is because he does not know what 'incandescent' means. He suggests that perhaps it means 'able to contain liquid' in response to Léodagan's request for an explanation as to how a stone can be used to collect blood. Later, we see an informal conversation between Karadoc and Perceval in the tavern, during which Karadoc asks what Perceval would have used if he were Joseph of Arimathea. Without hesitation, Perceval replies that an anchovy jar would best serve the purpose, because he could easily capture a half-gallon of blood and then close up the jar without having to worry about it spilling all over his bag. Perceval's affirmation concludes the episode: 'Si Joseph d'Arimathie a pas été trop con, vous pouvez être sûr que le Graal, c'est un bocal à anchois' (If Joseph of Arimathea wasn't too much of a dumbass, you can be sure that the Grail is an anchovy jar) (II.18, 128).

The confusion over what the Grail is and what it looks like reflects the confusion in the literary sources. Roberta Davidson notes that

---

[15] Sir Thomas Malory, *Works*, ed. E. Vinaver, 2nd edn (Oxford, 1971), p. 676.

Traditionally, the history of both the representation and identification of the Grail was far less iconic than our contemporary perception of it. Its association with a holy cup does not occur until the late twelfth or early thirteenth century, in Robert de Boron's verse romance, *Joseph d'Arimathie*, or *Le Roman de l'Estoire du Graal*. Previous versions of the Grail or Grail-like objects included a serving platter (*Perceval*), a cauldron that brought the dead back to life (*Branwen, Daughter of Llyr*), and one that would only cook food for the brave (*Spoils of Annwn*).[16]

Astier is clearly aware of the unfixed nature of the Grail, and he returns to its multiplicity in the third season, when we discover that even the gods who have commanded Arthur to undertake the Grail quest do not know what the object is. Their messenger, the Lady of the Lake, reminds Arthur that although there is a good chance that it is a vessel, it could be an incandescent stone, and there is also the possibility that it is a horn of plenty; given the lack of any authoritative information, Arthur should be looking for all three. A disconsolate Père Blaise wails that he will have to change all of his illustrations in the manuscripts, and Léodagan reiterates that they should just give up on this ridiculous quest. As Lancelot succinctly remarks in 'En forme de Graal', 'Le problème, c'est qu'il y en a pas un qui dit la même chose' (The problem is that not a single person says the same thing) (I.18, 126). To this observation Perceval adds a complaint about the object's nomenclature: 'Pourquoi forcément un mot compliqué qui veut rien dire? Ils l'auraient appelé "la Coupe" ou "le Vase", on serait fixé!' (Why did they have to use a complicated word that doesn't mean anything? If they had called it 'the Vessel' or 'the Cup', we would know!) (I.18, 127). By underscoring the range of literary possibilities for the Grail, Astier reminds us that although 'the audience assumes it knows what the Grail looks like',[17] we in fact do not, nor can we turn to any one text for a definitive answer.

That Perceval has thrown the knights into such confusion with his new information about the Grail is fitting, for confusion surrounds his character's every move. He does not understand maps, directions or military tactics; he has serious gaps in his vocabulary, leaving him at a loss in any number of conversations; and like his namesake in Chrétien de Troyes's *Conte du Graal*, he does not even know his own name. In the medieval romance, the narrator tells us that 'cil qui son non ne savoit / Devine et dit que il avoit / Percevaus li Gualois a non, / Ne ne set s'il dit voir o non, / Mais il dit voir, et si no sot' (he who did not know his name is inspired and says that he was named Perceval the Welshman;

---

[16] R. Davidson, 'Now You Don't See It, Now You Do: Recognizing the Grail *as* the Grail', *Studies in Medievalism* 18 (2009), 188–202 (pp. 188–9).

[17] Davidson, 'Now You Don't See It', p. 188.

he doesn't know if he speaks truly or not, but he did speak truly and yet did not know it).[18] Astier's Perceval is a much-exaggerated version of the naive bumpkin who comes to court in Chrétien's work, but the Perceval of *Kaamelott* displays far more linguistic incompetence than naivety. He has unwittingly gained a stellar reputation because he has been calling himself not 'Perceval le Gallois' (Perceval the Welshman), but 'Provençal le Gaulois' (Provençal the Gaul), unable to distinguish between the words. Confused and confusing rumours of the marvellous prowess of a knight known variously as 'Provençal' or 'le Chevalier de Provence' or 'le Chevalier gaulois' have made their way to Arthur's court, much to the annoyance of Lancelot, who claims that such a knight does not exist. When the company realizes that the knight in question is in fact Perceval, Lancelot feels justified in having disbelieved the rumours since Perceval's prowess is nearly non-existent. Arthur remains baffled about how this buffoon can have made such a name for himself; Père Blaise even has a record of the name in his chronicle. Léodagan says somewhat pityingly, 'C'est quand même pas de chance pour lui: les rares fois où il arrive à faire quelque chose de ses dix doigts, il se goure quand on lui demande son nom!' (It's unlucky for him: on the rare occasions when he actually manages to do something on his own, he screws up when he's asked his name!) (I.4, 43). The final words in the episode come from a slightly miffed Perceval: 'N'empêche que je suis une légende!' (Nonetheless, I'm a legend!) (I.4, 44).

Questions about the reliability of the legends circulating about the knights of the Round Table (whether the figures exist; whether the events occurred as recounted or, indeed, at all; whether these stories can be trusted) surface frequently in *Kaamelott*, particularly in the first season. In addition to the episodes about Perceval and Provençal and about the nature of the Grail, we also occasionally find members of Arthur's entourage deliberately spreading false rumours. In one instance, we see Père Blaise giving a guided tour of the castle to a group of tourists. As the visitors enter the throne room, he introduces Arthur to them as Lancelot's squire and announces that they will next visit King Arthur's tomb in the lower level. Blaise later explains that the empty treasury has prompted this complete falsehood: 'Si je dis aux gens que vous êtes mort – dans des conditions héroïques, hein, attention! "brandissant Excalibur, dans un dernier souffle de vie…" […] Du coup, c'est plus des touristes qui viennent visiter la cabane, c'est des croyants qui viennent en pèlerinage' (If I tell people that you died – in heroic conditions, mind you! 'brandishing Excalibur, with his dying breath…' […] Then it's no longer tourists

---

[18] Chrétien de Troyes, *Le Conte du Graal*, ed. C. Méla (Paris, 1990), p. 260.

who come visit the place, it's believers making a pilgrimage) (I.69, 118). Pilgrims are more desirable than tourists because pilgrims part much more readily with their money. This episode, entitled 'La Mort le roy Artu', naturally calls to mind the prose romance of the same name, but it also evokes Gerald of Wales's account of the miraculous finding of Arthur and Guenevere's tomb by the monks of Glastonbury and suggests a venal motive for the discovery that was made after fire had devastated the abbey, a period when its coffers, like Arthur's, were in dire need of refilling.[19] The episode further underlines the powerful attraction of the legend of King Arthur, for the second tour group includes Perceval. Although he is a permanent resident of the court, he tells the king that he has joined the tour to see the tomb because 'ça doit avoir de la gueule!' (it must look totally sweet!) (I.69, 120). In a concession to the scandalized Arthur, Blaise leads the third group to see the tomb of Queen Guenièvre instead, and his parting shot takes aim at modern-day Arthurian pilgrims and tourists: 'Nous vous rappelons que des répliques d'Excalibur vous seront proposées à l'issue de cette visite' (We remind you that replicas of Excalibur are available as you make your way out) (I.69, 120). Those who have visited sites associated with Arthur will no doubt recognize this familiar sales pitch.[20]

We might expect more reverence for the truth from Père Blaise, the court's official scribe, since he is ostensibly responsible for accurately recording events, but we see in 'Enluminures' (Illuminations) that other considerations again take precedence over the truth. In this episode, an incoherent story recounted by Perceval puts Blaise's skills to the test, and his temper endangers the transcription of the quest: Blaise flies into a rage over the corrections required by the constantly changing tale and threatens to leave the record as it is rather than ruin another page of parchment. His fury prompts the following discussion of his activities and their purpose:

> Père Blaise: Non mais je crois qu'on s'est mal compris, là …
> Vous avez une idée du temps qu'il me faut pour tracer une lettre avec ces putains de plumes?
> Léodagan: Personne vous demande de tout écrire, aussi!
> Arthur: Ah si! Pardon, c'est moi qui demande!
> Calogrenant: On se demande bien pourquoi!

[19] See J. S. Brewer, ed., *Giraldi Cambrensis Opera, scilicet, Speculum Ecclesiae*, Rolls Series 21, vol. 4 (London, 1873; rpt. 1964), pp. 47–51; and G. F. Warner, ed., *Giraldi Cambrensis Opera, Vol. VIII, De Principis Instructione Liber*, Rolls Series 21, vol. 8. (London, 1891; rpt. 1964), pp. 126–9.

[20] See, for example, J. Noble, 'Tintagel: The Best of English Twinkie', in *King Arthur in Popular Culture*, ed. E. S. Sklar and D. L. Hoffman (Jefferson, NC, 2002), pp. 36–43.

> Père Blaise: Pour vous faire entrer dans la Légende! Parce que
> je vous rappelle qu'entre vos chevaux morts et vos chevaux
> malades, moi, je dois faire une légende! ...
> Galessin: Qu'est-ce qu'on en a à foutre, de vos bouquins? ...
> Père Blaise: Ah mais si tout le monde s'en fout, je vais pas
> insister pour me faire des crampes aux doigts!
> Arthur: Non mais si! C'est pas une option! Vous notez tout,
> c'est comme ça et pas autrement!

> (Father Blaise: No, I think there's been a misunderstanding here
> ... Do you have any idea how long it takes me to form a
> letter with these fucking quills?
> Léodagan: No one's asking you to write everything down, too!
> Arthur: Oh yes they are! Excuse me, *I*'m the one asking!
> Calogrenant: We really wonder why!
> Father Blaise: To put you into the Legend! Let me remind you
> that between your dead horses and your sick horses, *I* have to
> make a legend! ...
> Galessin: What the hell do we care about your books? ...
> Father Blaise: Oh, well if no one gives a damn, I'm not going to
> keep at it so that my fingers cramp up!
> Arthur: Oh yes you are! It's not a choice! You write everything
> down, and that's all there is to it!) (I.51, 16)

This conversation obviously draws on literary passages found in works
such as *La Mort le roi Artu*, in which we see Arthur order his clerks to
record the knights' accounts of their activities: 'Lors fist li rois metre
en escrit toutes les aventures que li compaignon de la queste del Saint
Graal avoient racontees en sa court' (then the king had put into writing
all the adventures that the companions of the quest for the Holy Grail
had recounted in his court).[21] *Kaamelott* undermines the claims to truth
made in the medieval texts, however, for despite Arthur's insistence that
Father Blaise write everything down, two of the adventures that Arthur
hears in the first season of the series do not make their way into the
chronicles. Père Blaise feels compelled to censor the account given by
Gauvain and Yvain in 'Le Prodige du fakir' (The Marvel of the Fakir),
in which they meet a small group of travelling Hindus and mistake their
street performance for an attack. The fakir in particular frightens the two
knights since he appears to be threatening them with his genitals. After
hearing the description of the spectacle, the scribe tells Arthur that even
emphasizing the exoticism of the encounter will not be enough to excuse
including it. He reluctantly states, 'Ben non, je suis désolé, je peux pas
faire une légende avec un vieux qui enroule sa bite sur un bâton' (Well

---

[21]  *La Mort le Roi Artu*, 1–2.

no, I'm sorry, I can't make a legend with an old man who coils his dick around a stick) (I.60, 70); Arthur approves the omission.

Another quest fails to be included in the legend not because its content is too risqué but because it is absurdly pedestrian, and the episode suggests that this kind of anti-adventure happens all too often. 'La Quête des deux renards' (The Quest of the Two Foxes) features Karadoc and Perceval enthusiastically narrating the quest that kept them away from Camelot for three weeks. Having already revealed that they did not enter into combat, bring back any treasure or find any magical objects, they launch into a description of the weather on the day they left the court and how hungry they felt upon arriving at the Two Foxes tavern. Evidently accustomed to the pair's sub-par adventures, Blaise mutters, 'Je sens que ça va *encore* être épique' (I sense that it's going to be epic *again* [emphasis mine]) and suggests that they cut straight to the action since he can come up with 'une jolie intro' (a nice intro) later (I.96, 272, 273). When it transpires that the knights accomplished nothing more than recovering from a bad case of food poisoning at the tavern, however, Blaise admits defeat as Arthur and Léodagan look on, nonplussed. Perceval and Karadoc remain with Blaise after the meeting 'pour tenter de formuler leur histoire de la plus romanesque façon' (to try to formulate their story in the most sensational way) (I.96, 274), but the fact that the two knights never once drew their swords and in fact forgot them at the tavern causes Blaise to put down his quill and abandon any further attempt at salvaging something for the annals. Even his (seemingly quite prodigious) embellishment skills cannot compensate for a total lack of action. Given the underperforming nature of so many of the knights of *Kaamelott*, we can safely assume that the official chronicle omits a fair number of failed quests.

Père Blaise's remark to Calogrenant in 'Enluminures' and his initial response to the tale in 'La Quête des deux renards' clearly indicate that in order to create a legend worthy of the name, the scribe is fully prepared to make alterations, even very substantial ones, to the knights' testimony. He apparently manages to craft an acceptable entry for the legend in most cases, and we learn that his tendency to improve upon the accounts is not limited to aggrandizing adventures that do not meet the minimum criteria for the legend or to expunging undesirable details from otherwise acceptable quests; it surfaces even when the veracity of his source and the quality of the content are not in question. In 'Les Fesses de Guenièvre' (Guenevere's Buttocks), Blaise tells Arthur and Perceval that the records of two quests need to be completed that day before being illuminated: one in which Perceval mistook a phial of liquid manure for a truth serum (an enhancement of decidedly marginal content) and another undertaken by Perceval and Arthur together (a modification of a successful quest). The written version of the latter will surely include Arthur's acquisition of the

Shield of Airain by climbing down into the Pit of Doom and will surely not include a panicked Perceval who lets go of the rope that Arthur was holding. In the updated text read out to the king for his approval, Blaise lists 'Guenièvre-à-la-blanche-fesse' (Guenevere of the White Buttock) among those who salute Arthur upon his victorious return to court, a curious detail that Arthur certainly did not include in his telling, given that he has never slept with the queen or seen her naked and therefore does not know whether she has white buttocks or not.[22] When questioned by a sputtering Arthur, Blaise points out, '[I]l faut pas prendre ça au pied de la lettre. "Guenièvre-à-la-blanche-fesse", ça veut pas forcément dire que votre femme a les fesses blanches. [...] Ça s'appelle une licence poétique. [...] [Ç]a veut pas forcément dire ce qu'il y a marqué' (You mustn't take it literally. 'Guenevere of the White Buttock', that doesn't necessarily mean that your wife has white buttocks. [...] It's called poetic licence. [...] It doesn't necessarily mean what it says) (I.72, 136). Perceval replies, 'C'est pour ça que je pane rien aux livres, moi! Ça veut pas dire ce qu'il y a marqué!' (That's why I don't get anything when it comes to books. They don't mean what they say!) (I.72, 136).

Perhaps the best example of the suspect nature of books is in the episode 'Le Serpent géant' (The Giant Serpent), in which Arthur receives a report from several of the knights with Père Blaise in attendance to make a record of the narratives. We again see that Blaise cannot faithfully record the testimony of the knights for a variety of reasons after he reads the conclusion of the quest just recounted off screen by Perceval and Karadoc: 'Moi, à la limite, je peux le tourner comme ça (*se relisant*): "Embarqués sur frêle esquif, Perceval et Karadoc estoquèrent le Serpent Géant du Lac de l'Ombre et revinrent glorieux festoyer aux villages alentour"' (I could potentially phrase it this way (*rereading what he wrote*): 'Aboard a frail vessel, Perceval and Karadoc struck down the Giant Serpent of Shadow Lake and returned, glorious, to feast in the surrounding villages') (I.54, 31). Although both knights are quite pleased with the phrasing, Perceval points out that they were not aboard a frail vessel, and during the ensuing questions from the king and the scribe, the whole quest unravels. The pair did indeed set out to conquer the giant serpent, but upon catching an aquatic creature (an eel) along the shore of the lake and giving it to the grateful villagers (who were suffering from an infestation of eels), they assumed that they had completed their task. Not until the exasperated Arthur explains that the giant serpent was certainly in the centre of the lake rather than at the shoreline do the

---

[22] The moniker recalls Yseult aux Blanches Mains (Isolde of the White Hands) from the *Roman de Tristan*, an appropriate connection since both marriages were based on expediency and remained unconsummated.

knights begin to understand that their three-month-long mission was an utter failure. The scene closes with Blaise wondering what to do with the legend. Next, Perceval and Karadoc warn Bohort of Arthur's displeasure, to which he cheerily replies, 'Moi, je viens avec des combats contre les Démons, une romance impossible, la trahison d'un frère et même un Dragon! [...] Sensations garanties!' (I'm coming with combats against the Demons, an impossible romance, the betrayal of a brother and even a Dragon! [...] Guaranteed thrills!) (I.54, 35). *La Queste del Saint Graal* tells us that 'li rois fist avant venir les clers qui metoient en escrit les aventures aus chevaliers de laienz. Et quant Boorz ot contees les aventures del Seint Graal telles come il les avoit veues, si furent mises en escrit' (the king had the clerks who put into writing the adventures of the knights there come forward. And when Bohort had recounted the adventures of the Holy Grail such as he had seen them, they were put into writing.)[23] *Kaamelott* tells us something quite different. Again we hear the conclusion of Blaise's rendition of Bohort's story: '...alors que le grand Dragon Rouge abandonnait son trésor aux mains du héros et que la pupille de son œil pourpre lançait des éclairs de rage tout autour de lui' (...as the great Red Dragon gave up his treasure to the hero and the pupil of his crimson eye flashed furiously all around him) (I.54, 35). Bohort is also quite pleased with the narrative, but his story falls apart even more spectacularly than that of Perceval and Karadoc. When Bohort comments that deep blue would make a good choice for the dragon's eye, Père Blaise asks, 'Non mais après on peut toujours tricher mais, en vrai, il était comment?' (Well we can always cheat afterwards, but, really, what did it look like?) (I.54, 36). Bohort's response indicates that the adventures were not at all 'such as he had seen them', but entirely as he had invented them: 'Comment "en vrai"? Mais ... attendez, il faut que ce soit vrai, tout ce qu'on dit, là?' (What do you mean 'really'? But ... wait, everything we say has to be true?) (I.54, 36).

Thus Astier reminds us repeatedly that we cannot put our faith in the literary texts, 'the immaterial and shifting stories and legends through which the Arthurian past has traditionally been transmitted',[24] for they are as fictional as Bohort's adventure with the Red Dragon. Bert Olton states that television shows 'which include Arthur, Merlin or any of the other characters from the Round Table are often of questionable merit. Even more often, they make clear departures from the accepted tradi-

---

[23] *La Queste del Saint Graal*, ed. A. Pauphilet, 2nd edn, Classiques Français du Moyen Age 33 (Paris, 1984), p. 279.
[24] M. J. Seaman and J. Green, 'Sacrificing Fiction and the Quest for the Real King Arthur', in *Cultural Studies of the Modern Middle Ages*, ed. E. A. Joy, M. J. Seaman, K. K. Bell and M. K. Ramsey (New York, 2007), pp. 135–54 (p. 140).

tions handed down in the literature which culminates with Malory.'[25] His comment suggests a correlation between the shows' 'questionable merit' and their departures from the literary canon, but Astier clearly invites us to view these texts as unreliable sources, imaginative works of various individuals writing with various agendas at various points in time. Astier has stated that he relies on historical sources more than literary ones such as Chrétien's *Perceval* or *Le Chevalier de la Charrette*, in which the author declares that 'matiere et san li done et livre / la contesse, et il s'antremet / de panser, que gueres n'i met / fors sa painne et s'antancïon' (the countess gives and furnishes him with the matter and the meaning, and he applies his thoughts, for he adds only his labour and his industriousness).[26] Since, as Astier puts it, 'le travail de cet auteur médiéval répond à une commande officielle de Marie de Champagne' (this medieval author's work is in response to an official command from Marie de Champagne), he finds it far less intriguing than what he calls the 'messy' period when Roman civilization is confronted with a spectrum of barbarian cultures and Roman paganism crosses paths with Druidism and a fledgling Christianity.[27] By privileging the scanty historical material over the copious literary material, Astier frees himself from the constraints of following another author's vision of Arthur. He allows himself to explore what Jerome de Groot calls 'the spaces between knowledges', since 'it is the very insubstantiality of the past that allows [historical novelists] to introduce their version of events'.[28] As the creative genius behind the show, Astier is very much an author whom we might compare to a historical novelist, in either the modern or the medieval sense. He has in fact called each of the six seasons of the series a 'livre' (book); the individual discs are labelled 'Tome 1', 'Tome 2', and so on, along with the 'Addendum' that contains special features, and the DVD packaging was produced to look like a book. Prior to the series, Astier wrote a short film and ten pilot episodes; he has since written eight graphic novels that expand the adventures of the characters. He is also writing both a film trilogy that will continue their story and 'une série de nouvelles qui feront le "pont" entre le dernier épisode de la série et le premier film au ciné' (a series of short stories that will connect the last episode of the series and

---

[25] B. Olton, 'Was That in the Vulgate? Arthurian Legend in TV Film and Series Episodes', in *King Arthur in Popular Culture*, ed. Sklar and Hoffman, pp. 87–100 (p. 97).

[26] Chrétien de Troyes, *Le Chevalier de la Charrette*, ed. M. Roques, Classiques Français du Moyen Age 86 (Paris, 1983), 2.

[27] Pincas, 'Entretien'. Although Astier mentions the sixth century in this interview, the DVD covers and the official website of the series both clearly indicate that *Kaamelott* takes place in the fifth century.

[28] J. de Groot, *The Historical Novel* (London, 2010), p. 182.

the first feature film).[29] Clearly, the scope of Astier's corpus rivals that of any other Arthurian author, medieval or modern.

However, Astier does not claim to present us with the historical truth about Arthur, nor does his calling into question the veracity of the French Arthurian canon imply that the heroic legend of Arthur and his knights has no value for him. On the contrary, his Camelot is not simply 'a silly place', nor can we say that 'the series loses the epic struggle of good versus evil' as Elliott finds in the animated parody *King Arthur's Disasters*.[30] Rather, Astier's insistence on the fallibility of the literature encourages us to consider his contribution to the legend to be as valid as any that has preceded it. Astier says in a documentary about the sources of *Kaamelott* that he has read an academic book by a British scholar that gives equal weight to Geoffrey of Monmouth, Thomas Malory, John Boorman and Monty Python,[31] and he evidently embraces this approach. His view seems to be that we need not privilege the literary over the audiovisual nor the medieval over the modern accounts of Arthur, for in the absence of authoritative records, all versions of the tale are legitimate. Roberta Davidson states in an article about Arthurian filmmakers, 'The once and future king, today as in the Middle Ages, remains linked to a mixed identity: mythical, historical, political, and fictional, with the last of these qualities the most noticeable, and the least often acknowledged, by those who tell his story.'[32] Astier, on the other hand, eagerly acknowledges the king's fictional identity, reminding us over and over in the series that the vast majority of what we think we know about Arthur comes to us from fictional sources. When asked in the documentary what it means to her to have been cast in the role of an invented character, the actress who plays Guenièvre's mother Séli (and is Astier's real-life mother) says that she is proud of her part:

> Comme Alexandre l'explique souvent et comme on sait tous, la véritable histoire d'Arthur, il nous reste à peine dix pour cent sur le plan historique et archéologique. Il reste rien. Donc tout ce qu'on connaît d'Arthur et donc de Léodagan et de Guenièvre et de Lancelot et de tout le monde, c'est

---

[29] A. Astier, 'Kaamelott le film 2012: Kaamelott au cinéma', *LeMag-VIP* (3 April 2011), http://www.lemag-vip.com/stars_cinema/37907-kaamelott-le-film-2012-kaamelott-au-cinema-spoilers-a-astier.html. The collection of short stories will be entitled *Kaamelott: Résistance*, and Astier posted the logo, a modification of the logo used for the series, on his Twitter account (https://twitter.com/#!/sgtpembry/media/slideshow?url=http%3A%2F%2Finstagr.am%2Fp%2FMIfEuDQk_B%2F) on 21 June 2012.

[30] Elliott, 'The Charm of the (Re)making', p. 61.

[31] C. Chabert, *Aux sources de* Kaamelott, *Acte I: Les mœurs et les femmes* (Calt Production, 2006).

[32] R. Davidson, 'The "Reel" Arthur: Politics and Truth Claims in *Camelot*, *Excalibur*, and *King Arthur*', *Arthuriana* 17.2 (2007), 62–84 (p. 80).

quatre-vingt-dix pour cent quand même de littérature. Alors moi, je suis la dernière née de la littérature et maintenant Séli va rentrer, j'espère, dans la legend arthurienne pour les prochaines générations.

(As Alexander explains often and as we all know, the true story of Arthur, we have barely 10 per cent from a historical and archaeological standpoint. Nothing is left. So everything we know about Arthur and therefore about Leodagan and about Guenevere and about Lancelot and about everyone is really 90 per cent literature. So I am the last one to be born out of the literature and now Séli is, I hope, going to go back into the Arthurian legend for the next generations.)[33]

Behind the figure of Père Blaise crafting the legend of Camelot for the generations who will come after him, we can glimpse the creator of *Kaamelott* and those authors who have come before him. By reinventing Arthur and his entourage according to his own vision, Astier follows the tradition of his medieval predecessors, and his reinterpretation of the legend offers us a compelling new chapter in Arthur's ongoing story.

---

[33] Chabert, *Aux sources de* Kaamelott.

Details of earlier titles are available from the publishers

CONTENTS OF PREVIOUS VOLUMES